# Monuments of War

# Monuments of War

*How to read a war memorial*

Colin McIntyre

ROBERT HALE · LONDON

*Copyright © Colin McIntyre 1990*
*First published in Great Britain 1990*

ISBN 0 7090 4027 X

Robert Hale Limited
Clerkenwell House
Clerkenwell Green
London EC1R 0HT

Photoset in Goudy Old Style by
Derek Doyle & Associates, Mold, Clwyd.
Printed in Great Britain by
St Edmundsbury Press, Bury St Edmunds, Suffolk.
Bound by Woolnough

# Contents

# Illustrations

# Introduction: 'Lest We Forget'

I was named Colin after Flying Officer Colin Graham Sutherland Shields, Royal Air Force. Had he lived, he would have been my uncle. But he was posted 'Missing, presumed dead' on 10 May 1918. He was nineteen.

He had gone straight from school into the army, to an officer cadet unit to train for the Royal Flying Corps. His Record of Service is simplicity itself. Granted a commission as a temporary Second Lieutenant on probation on 26 September 1917, he served with No.39 Training Squadron at South Carlton in Nottinghamshire and then No.45 Training Squadron – learning to fly. He attended No.1 School of Aerial Fighting, and No.1 School of Air Gunnery in early 1918, and was deemed ready for active service.

The Royal Air Force came into being on 1 April 1918, and Second Lieutenant C.G.S. Shields was then formally transmuted into a Flying Officer (Aeroplanes and Seaplanes) in the RAF. Nine days later he joined No. 80 Squadron in France. The idea of the RAF was so new that he continued to give his address as 80 Squadron, Royal Flying Corps, British Expeditionary Force.

Four weeks later he was dead. His body was found eventually, and now lies buried in the official war cemetery at Cerisy-Gailly on the Somme: plot 2 – row A – grave 2. His family were told his death could be officially accepted a year later.

Colin Shields was an only son, with two younger sisters. As both of them lived abroad for a good deal of their lives, very few mementoes of his time on earth survive. There is a cup he won for the 100 yards at school in 1912, a framed picture of him as a cadet in London Scottish uniform, a dress version of his pilot's wings, and his last letter home – to his younger sister Barbara.

80 Squadron
R.F.C.
B.E.F.
France

2 May 1918
Dear Barbara,

Just time for a few lines. We are pretty busy again, and I did my first patrol for 10 days this evening.

Nine of us went and we had one casualty. As you'll observe it was not me!

I have a fine bus now, absolutely brand new and a fine engine.

Am very tired, so Goodbye.

Best love,

Colin

Not a great deal to show for a human life: a small cup, RAF wings, a photograph or two, a last letter and a single-sheet service record.

It led me to seek out his name on his local war memorial – at Beaconsfield in Buckinghamshire. And there was his name and initials – C.G.S. SHIELDS. One of exactly eighty names of those who died in the 1914–18 War, arranged neatly in groups of ten. An addition lists another sixty Beaconsfield names for 1939–45.

From then on I made a point of studying war memorials, principally the ordinary village memorials rather than the elaborate regimental monuments and statues. It became a lifelong hobby, and this book is an attempt to convey some of the fascination of what my family finally came to know as 'war-memorialing'.

In almost every village in Britain there is some form of tribute to the men (and women) who lost their lives serving their country. It often takes the form of that simple village cross on a green or in a market square. Where there is no cross, there is often a plaque or tablet in the parish church, or perhaps on the side of some public building. In garrison and cathedral towns there are more elaborate memorials and special chapels. At schools and universities there are often memorial libraries, pavilions and playing-fields.

What I realized, as I saw more and more war memorials – and I number them now in their thousands – was that each one was a primary source for Britain's history. They tell directly or indirectly about social habits and distinctions, population movements and local affiliations, about military matters and bravery, about attitudes prevailing in the society of the time – and attitudes to death. They range from the simple listing of names and initials, as at Beaconsfield, to a complete description of the military career of the person commemorated. Some carry the full name, rank and service number; the date of death, where it occurred, and the age of the deceased; they list the unit he belonged to, and in some rural areas the village, hamlet or farm from which the man came.

A key feature is that the shape and style of almost all the village memorials were decided at true grassroots level, by parish committees and local councils. Sometimes they were 'imposed' upon the village by the local squire or benefactor, but even then it was generally after consultation. There is a democracy of death in war.

That is not to say that the war memorials do not reveal hierarchical structures, with the squire's son in pride of place or the names ordered exactly by military rank. That is exactly one of the easiest things to notice: when ranks are listed, are the names recorded in order of seniority or simply alphabetically? Are the officers separated from the other ranks? Are the non-commissioned officers in correct order of seniority too? Are the naval dead listed first, corresponding to the Royal Navy's position as the Senior Service? Is there an awareness of the order of precedence of Regiments, so that the Household Cavalry and the regiments of cavalry of the line are followed in their correct order by artillery, engineers, guards and infantry of the line?

Almost every war memorial is different. Some will tell you almost nothing about the dead commemorated, others will offer insights into the British way of life (and death) that are worth thinking about.

There are clues on almost every war memorial to some sort of attitude or decision taken by the committee or the individual responsible for its design. Does the memorial, for example, carry the awards for bravery or is there an eschewing of every military indication – be it rank, unit or decorations?

Comparison of the stone war memorial with the plaque or framed roll of honour in the parish church is often very revealing, and in this study follow-up discoveries are sometimes included that do not necessarily stem immediately from the village cross and its inscriptions but from easily accessible other sources.

## BEACONSFIELD

Urban district, parish and market town, with railway station.
Twenty-eight miles north-west of London, five miles south of Amersham.
The war memorial is by the church of St Mary and All Saints.
At the Ends crossroads, Beaconsfield Old Town.

*1914–1918*

L. ALLOWAY
J. ARMES
W. BAILEY
J. BEEBEE
A.A. BERNARD
W. BRAY
R.S. BRITTEN
J. BUNKER
A.E. CHILD
R.J. CHILD

A.L. CHILD
E. CHILD
F.W. CHILD
W. CHILD
S.G. CHILTON
W.E. CLARKE
D. CORBETT
C. DALE
J.L. DALE
J. DALE

*'To the Glorious Memory of the Brave & True'*

J. DEALEY
W.A. DEALEY
W. DODS
C.E. FISHBOURNE
A.H.J. FLATT
H. GARTH
G.W. GILDER
A.W. GOFF
S. GOLDSTEIN
A. GREEN

F. GRENFELL
R. GRENFELL
S.I. GREY
A. HALLETT
F.W. HART
A. HEDGER
S. HEDGER
S.J. HOODLESS
G.T. HOPKINS
W. JAMES

*'Who Gave Their Lives in the Great War 1914–1918'*

W.J. KEDGE
J. LAKE
W. LAKE
W.B.W. LAWSON
J.R. LOVELOCK
K. MAPLES
F.G. MASON
H. NAISH
J. NICKLINSON
J.B. NORRIS

W.J. PARR
B. PELL
E. PRICE
A.T. ROLFE
G.T. ROLFE
J.W. ROLFE
L. ROLFE
K. ROY
C.G.S. SHIELDS
D. SNAPES

*'Eternal Rest Grant Unto Them O Lord'*

A.G. SHAW
B.H.G. SHAW
E.A. SHAW
S. SMITH
F. STEVENS
H. STONE
R. STONE
T. SWIFT
F.K.J. TABRUM
W. TILBURY

R. WALLER
E. WEBB
A. WESTON
H. WESTON
W. WESTON
C. WHITE
S.T. WILLIAMS
W. WINGROVE
G.A. WOODLEY
B. WRIGHT

*'And Let Light Perpetual Shine Upon Them'*

## 1939–1945

| | | | |
|---|---|---|---|
| S.J.D. | ACLAND | W.P. | GREEN |
| R. | ADAMS | H.M. | GRIMSDELL |
| S.G. | ADAMS | G.E. | GROVE |
| G. | BATTING | T.N. | HALFORD |
| D.B. | BEARDSALL | E.T. | HANCOCKS |
| A.H. | BERESFORD | D.A. | HARE |
| G.H. | BODDY | D.J.A. | HARRIS |
| J.R. | BUCKINGHAM | L.W. | HARVEY |
| T.B. | CHURN | N. | HAWKRIDGE |
| C.H. | CLARK | G.W. | HAYNES |
| H.A. | COSGRAVE | F.W.D. | HAYNES |
| W.J. | FROST | L.D. | HETHERINGTON-PALMER |
| R.L. | GOORD | B.K. | HEYWORTH |
| H.A. | GRAHAM | R.H. | HILLARY |
| | | | |
| J.C. | IVENS | J.P. | SAWYER |
| R.H. | JAGGER | R.W. | SAWYER |
| W.E. | KING | W. | SHANNON |
| J.B. | KING-CHURCH | R.J. | SMITH |
| M.G. | LAMB | A.W. | SNOWDEN |
| C.P. | St. LEGER | R. | SPONG |
| F.W. | LIDGLEY | A.T. | TAPPING |
| A.E.F. | LOVELL | A.W. | TAPPING |
| W.H. | MITCHELL | A. | TITCHENER |
| J. | MONTAGUE | T.B. | WARDLE |
| G.E. | NICHOLLS | J.H. | WHITE |
| R. | NICHILL-CADELL | F.W. | WINGROVE |
| E.J. | PALMER | V. | WINGROVE |
| C.H.S. | PRESTON | R.H. | WOLSKEL |
| D.G. | ROBERTSON | C.C. | WOOD |

D. YOUNG

The Beaconsfield war memorial provides an excellent example of where a nearby additional source tells us much more. On the memorial appear the names F. Grenfell and R. Grenfell, and one might be forgiven for thinking they were two ordinary villagers of no particular consequence, in this case not even distinguished there by a set of three initials, often a clue to social position – at least in the early 1900s. In fact, they were the twin sons of the owner of nearby Wilton Park, and one of them won one of the earliest Victoria Crosses of the war.

A memorial window in the parish church alongside tells the story:

To the Heroic Memory of
Captain Francis Octavius GRENFELL, VC, 9th Lancers
and
Riversdale Nonus GRENFELL, attached to 9th Lancers.

Twin sons of Pascoe du Pré GRENFELL, late of Wilton Park.
Born 4th September 1880.
Killed in Flanders 24th May 1915 and 14th September 1914.
They died for England.

'They were lovely and pleasant in their lives,
and in their death they were not divided.'

Captain Riversdale Nonus Grenfell, Buckinghamshire Yeomanry (Royal Bucks Hussars), attached 9th Lancers, was killed on 14 September 1914, aged thirty-four, at the beginning of the Battle of the Aisne, and Captain Francis Octavius Grenfell VC, 9th Lancers, six months later, at Ypres on 24 May 1915. Francis Grenfell won his VC in Belgium on 24 August 1914 during the retreat from Mons. Among other feats of gallantry for which it was given was helping save the guns of 119 Battery, Royal Field Artillery.

The twins were the eighth and ninth sons respectively of Pascoe du Pré Grenfell of Wilton Park, brother of Field Marshal Lord Grenfell. They were cousins of the better-known Grenfell brothers – Julian and Billy, sons of William Henry Grenfell, the first Baron Desborough. He had three sons (the two mentioned above both killed in the war, and one dying soon after) and there was no heir left. The two who were killed, Captain The Hon. Julian Henry Francis Grenfell DSO, 1st (Royal) Dragoons, died of wounds on 26 May 1915; his brother, Lieutenant The Hon. Gerald William Grenfell, 8th (Service) Battalion, Rifle Brigade was killed in action at Hooge, Flanders on 30 July 1915. Julian Grenfell wrote the best poem of the war by what might be called an unrecognized or amateur poet, the oft-quoted 'Into Battle'.

In less than a year four Grenfell cousins – all Old Etonians – died on the Western Front.

But this book is not about the Great and the Good, but the whole population of Britain. If the doings and lineage of the aristocracy are better chronicled, because of their literary connections or their landed interest, all the more reason for studying the war memorials where prince and pauper, peer and ploughman, publisher and publican, are forever united in the history of their land.

Nor is this book a *Good Memorial Guide*; it is not an architectural survey of the fascinating range of styles and even fantasies embodied in war memorials; it offers few judgements on them, or on war.

We must remember too that it has always been British policy to bury its fighting men where they fell. The memorials we will discuss are only those in Britain, and they are nearly all to men buried overseas or who have no known grave.

The book's one and only aim is to help people make up their own minds about war and society based on a neglected primary source – the village or parish war memorials of Britain. It concerns mainly the memorials to the dead of 1914–18, and the attitudes of the early 1920s, when nearly all of them were built.

The final view is that of the reader – in front of a war memorial.

# 1   Social History

The men were very good to us, they were a wall unto us both by
night and by day.

I Samuel 2

In the old burying-ground at Eyemouth, a Scottish fishing port a few
miles north of the border town of Berwick-upon-Tweed, there is an
interesting memorial – not a war memorial but one dated 14 October
1881. It was 'Erected by Public Subscription' to mark a nineteenth-
century disaster at sea. It is to the memory of 189 East Coast fishermen,
of whom 129 belonged to Eyemouth, who perished over a hundred years
ago.

'When Thou Passeth Through The Waters
I Will Be With Thee.'

129 men of Eyemouth, or who belonged to Eyemouth as the Scottish
phrasing has it, died in those east coast storms on a single day. The total
losses suffered by Eyemouth in the two world wars were ninety, so a figure
of 129 men drowned shows how nature on occasion can outdo even
man's barbarities to man.

I begin with a non-war memorial because it illustrates two of the main
themes of this book: the value of all such memorials as a primary source
for social or military history, and for the sense of place that the public
memorials put on record. Those lost in the Eyemouth storm disaster and
the names of the dead on the town's war memorial *belong* to Eyemouth –
for ever.

In the course of these chapters I shall examine some of the myths that
have accumulated and become embodied in our view of Britain's recent
social and military history. To a great extent these are my own personal
views, though I shall always try to give credit where I have appropriated
ideas or thoughts from others. Where any lack of knowledge or

information means I have perpetuated existing myths or brought new ones into being, I can only apologize.

For instance, some people think of Britain in 1914 as a green and pleasant land covered by a scattering of picture-postcard old-world villages. It was not.

Two centuries earlier, four out of every five people in Britain did live a rural country life. The population of Britain increased considerably in the eighteenth century, mainly because more children survived. By the 1830s most communities reached new record numbers. But a drift from the land had begun with the Industrial Revolution, and by the mid-1850s the rural picture had changed for ever. While the population of England and Wales generally had quadrupled, the numbers living in towns had increased nine times. By 1914, only twenty per cent of the population lived in a truly rural English countryside. Many more lived in town slums.

However, although urbanization had gone a long way, the character of many a village did still remain intact. The same families who had lived there for generations were still represented. Sons and younger brothers may have moved off to seek their fortune in towns or overseas, but other family members did stay on in the ancestral village. Churchyards provide magnificent evidence of the 'parish names', a pattern which was to repeat itself on the war memorials, particularly the roll-calls for 1914–18.

A book I have relied on extensively, because much of what it has to say is relevant to war memorials, is *The Churchyards Handbook*, published by the Council for the Care of Churches. In the introduction to its revised 1988 edition it says:

> Amongst the developments noticed since the previous edition of 1976 has been an increase of interest in headstone inscriptions by local and family historians. The form and decoration of memorials have been increasingly studied and valued by art historians and archaeologists. Nature conservators have seen the churchyard more and more as an ecological area of importance. But above all, perhaps, there has been a revival of a more open interest in the phenomenon of death, both in its macabre associations and in its psychology.

The war memorials of Britain are worth studying for this last reason alone. Not only those sited in churchyards, and thus already of interest to the categories of investigator mentioned above, but those found at road-junctions and in market-places, memorials in schools and colleges and banks, and rolls of honour everywhere. For anyone who has to come to terms with death, particularly sudden and violent death of an unnecessary kind, they have a lot to say. An understanding of the way in which their contemporaries commemorated, and sought to 'remember', the million killed in the First World War, together with those who died in World War II, might just help those living today to face that final reality themselves, by setting death in the context of a social history of their land.

Why have war memorials at all? By the time many of them were erected in the early 1920s, the war had already begun to be forgotten. Not by those who had been there – they would never forget – but by those who had stayed at home or were children at the time.

By the early 1920s the economic boom years of the war had receded. Those who had done well out of the war – both the genuine entrepreneurs and manufacturers, as well as the profiteers who had thrived on shortages – had to find new uses for their talents. The image of legless veterans selling matches in the streets and of unemployed ex-officers begging for jobs was certainly true. But many men did get their old jobs back, only to find they had grown out of them; many others, who had gone straight from school into the army, had to adapt to a wholly new and different way of life.

Most of those who returned felt guilty about the comrades they had left behind, buried in the mud of France and Flanders. They found that the communities to which they returned after the war had undergone considerable change. And always present as a reminder were the widows and orphans, and their permanently disabled colleagues. The guilt of the survivor is a well-recognized psychological fact, equally true of those who escape death in an accident, an aircraft bombing or a football disaster as for those who return from war.

Both Harold Macmillan and Enoch Powell have spoken and written about this feeling of guilt in relation to their own post-war lives. Harold Macmillan (later Lord Stockton) left Eton in 1909 and was in action as a captain with the Grenadier Guards in France by 1915. The *List of Etonians Who Fought in the Great War 1914–1919* has 5,650 names. 1,157 of them did not return. Allowing for 798 who only served at home, one out of every four from Macmillan's old school who went overseas died on active service in that war. One has only to look at the bronze frieze, carrying these names, which runs the entire length of the wall from the main entrance of Eton's Upper School to the entrance to Lower School. It is a monument to a generation of potential leaders dying in their prime, and a reminder that with privilege goes responsibility.

Many of the wounded were affected for life. Harold Macmillan was wounded three times: once at Loos, another time only slightly, and then more seriously on the Somme in September 1916. The last wounding probably saved his life, for it kept him out of action for the rest of the war. He was in and out of hospital for two years, with his wound only healing finally in 1920. It gave him pain for the rest of his life and accounted for his somewhat shuffling walk.

But, again, why have war memorials at all – be they simple village crosses or well-crafted rolls of honour in schools and colleges?

I suggest it is because they act as a catharsis, a means of purging that guilt of the survivor. They are a physical tribute, something designed to last longer than the flesh and blood of the living.

The war memorials of 1914–18 have mostly outlasted those who fought and survived. Even men who enlisted under-age in the First World War are now in their very late eighties or nineties. Indeed it comes as something of a shock to my own age-group to realize that most of those who served in *our* war, the Second World War – and whose dead comrades are so often honoured by an additional plaque or a later carving on the original World War I memorials – are now mainly Old Age Pensioners themselves and becoming a similarly dwindling band.

The war memorials, however, will survive several decades more. Unless there are radical changes in our society's view of them, they will remain 'protected' and readable for future generations. If this book achieves nothing else, it might perhaps encourage people to help preserve their local memorials: repair them where necessary, pick out the names again in time-resistant paint, and generally honour those who played a key role in Britain's twentieth-century social history. In studying war memorials, be they on a sunlit village green or in a quiet cathedral close, let us have no illusions about what they represent. The play and film *Oh What a Lovely War* made a particular point about the tens of thousands of men who died in France and Flanders and who have 'no known grave'. They are honoured in mass on such battlefield memorials as the archway British Memorial to the Missing at the Menin Gate, Ypres, and the Memorial to the Missing at Thiepval. These commemorate respectively 54,896 and 73,412 men. All with no known grave!

From a book by an Australian army chaplain, Dr Michael McKernan: 'After about three-quarters of a mile of this I came upon heaps of unburied bodies. They were Oxford & Bucks men and probably they had been there for 6 to 8 weeks. They were fairly dried but the horrible black-green metallic-looking flies covered them, and one did not go too close for fear of disturbing these flies.'

From the *War Diary* of the 1/5th Battalion King's Own Scottish Borderers (Dumfries and Galloway):

Helles, Gallipoli
12 December 1915 – Brought in bodies of Lieutenant Foster DLI and remains

of Captain Foster Jackson 5 Manchesters, sending belongings to the regiment through 155 Brigade.

14 December 1915 – Found 16 Manchester dead behind our Front Line trench, but had too heavy fatigues in hand to accomplish burial of all, six only being buried.

16 December 1915 – Completed burial of 2 officers and 6 men referred to on 12th and 14th; Chaplain Goldie officiating.

According to *Officers Died …* (a book examined at length in Chapter 2), Lieutenant Laurence Talbot Lisle Foster, 16 Durham Light Infantry (attached 5 Manchester Regiment), was killed on 5 August 1915; and Captain Stanley Foster Jackson (2/6 Manchesters) was killed on 4 June 1915; which meant the bodies had lain out in the open for four and six months respectively. One notes the distinction made in the *War Diary* between the body of Lieutenant Foster and the 'remains' of Captain Jackson.

In *Roll of Honour* (Volume I), Lieutenant L.T.L. Foster's biography describes him as the fourth son of the vicar of Wootton and rural dean of Haynes, and that he was born at Wootton Vicarage, Bedford, on 15 February 1885. He was educated at Eastbourne College (where he was a Scholar) and then became a forest manager in the Bombay and Burma Trading Company. He was commissioned a lieutenant in the 16th (Service) Battalion Durham Light Infantry on 21 November 1914, sailing to the Dardanelles as a reinforcement, where he was attached to the 1/5th Manchesters, in the Manchester Brigade of the 42nd (East Lancs) Division, which had been fighting at Gallipoli since May 1915.

Lieutenant Foster's name is one of 165 names of former Eastbourne College students who died in the First World War and who appear on two elaborate series of memorial tablets at the school.

Eastbourne College commemorated its dead well. It built a complete Memorial Building, with a Memorial Tower and wrought-iron gates leading to them inscribed 'In Memoriam 1914–1918'. The ground floor of the Memorial Building included a Memorial Hall, with the two floors above occupied by libraries and music-rooms. A south block housed an armoury and drill hall (no comment), five classrooms and a workshop; the north block would house laboratories, science rooms and more classrooms.

On the two outer panels of the tablets with the names of the dead are bronze replicas of the battle sword. The centre panel of the tablet on the north wall carries the words: 'My sword I give to him that shall succeed me in my pilgrimage, and my courage and skill to him that can get it. My marks and scars I carry with me, to be witness for me, that I have fought his battles who will now be my rewarder.' The words are spoken by Mr

Valiant-for-Truth in John Bunyan's *The Pilgrim's Progress*, right at the end of the book, when the pilgrims are being summoned one at a time to the Celestial Kingdom. The valiant pilgrim's story continues after the chosen quote: 'When the day that he must go hence was come, many accompanied him to the river side, into which as he went he said, "Death, where is thy sting?" And as he went down deeper, he said, "Grave, where is thy victory?" So he passed over, and all the trumpets sounded for him on the other side.'

Throughout this book, I have stuck to the old county boundaries, which is why you will find towns and villages placed in Huntingdon, Middlesex and Rutland, and mention of the three Ridings of Yorkshire and the division of Lincolnshire into Lindsey, Kesteven and Holland. And instead of the twelve new-fangled Regions of Scotland there are mentions of Caithness and Kincardine, Peebles and Ross & Cromarty. The old Welsh counties of Anglesey and Carmarthen, Montgomery and Radnor are there instead of Clwyd, Dyfed and Powys. And for World War I purposes Ireland is united, and Ulster has nine counties. This is because the British regimental system was very much based on county affiliations. Those who served as infantry were recruited on a territorial basis, the exceptions being the Foot Guards and two Rifle regiments (KRRC and Rifle Brigade), which recruited on a nationwide basis. Regular cavalry, artillery, engineers and the various corps were also recruited nationwide; but the Yeomanry and the rest of the Territorial Force were again passionately county in allegiances.

You will find many memorials reflecting these former divisions, as at Pennington near Ulverston (now in Cumbria), where the regimental allegiance is to the Royal Lancaster Regiment. Pennington, like Barrow-in-Furness, was then an integral part of Lancashire.

This matter of county, or even town, allegiance is a key to looking at war memorials. If the units to which the dead belonged are listed on the war memorial, in almost every case you can spot at once the infantry regiment in whose 'area' you are. This is particularly true when you are studying a memorial in a small town which supplied the men of a Territorial Force unit or one of the 'Pals' battalions of Kitchener's Army described in Chapter 2.

Recruiting for the Territorial units was in the hands of each county's Territorial Force County Association. Recruiting for the special Pals battalions of the New Armies was very much on a town and territorial basis, and even depended on the initiative and tribal loyalties great landowners could inspire.

I think of Lochiel's Camerons; of the men of the Earl of Lonsdale's battalion, the 11th (Service) Battalion of the Border Regiment; and the four 'City' battalions raised by Lord Derby for the King's (Liverpool) Regiment. With the names of many of their dead, appearing on war memorials across the country, are still given their detailed allegiances to these units, rather than to their parent regiment.

I illustrate this point about territorial and town allegiances by listing the war memorial of my own family home town (Auchterarder) as well as that of the fairly rank-conscious memorial at Eyemouth.


### AUCHTERARDER, Perthshire

Parish and market-town, in south-east Perthshire, by Gleneagles.

### THE GREAT WAR
### 1914–19

Erected in Grateful and Reverent Memory
of the Sons of AUCHTERARDER who Laid Down Their Lives
to Save Their Country in the Great War 1914–1919.

*1/6th Battalion BLACK WATCH*

| ARCHIBALD | James | Private |
|---|---|---|
| BAYNE | Alexander | L/Corporal |
| CAIRNS | Henry H. | Private |
| CAIRNS | William K. | C.S.M. |
| CAIRNS | William | Private |
| CLARK | Alexander | Private |
| DEWAR | John | Private |
| DOW | James | Corporal |
| EADIE | John | Private |
| GARDINER | James | Corporal |
| GIBBON | Allan | L/Corporal |
| HALDANE | R.P. | Lieutenant |
| HALLY | John | Captain |
| HUTCHISON | Andrew | L/Corporal |
| HUTCHISON | Dav. Alex. | Corporal |
| JAMIESON | John D. | Private |
| KAYE | John Brown. | Private |
| MASON | William | Private |
| MANNING | Michael | Private |
| MENZIES | Alexander | Private |
| McGLASHAN | John | Corporal |
| McINTOSH | Alexander | L/Corporal |
| McINTYRE | James | Private |
| McKENZIE | Charles | Private |

| | | |
|---|---|---|
| McLAREN | John S. | Private |
| NICOL | Robert | Private |
| RIDDOCH | Robert | Private |
| ROSS | Thomas R. | Private |
| SINCLAIR | Eben. Imrie | Private |
| STEWART | Malcolm | L/Corporal |
| WALKER | Henry | Corporal |
| WATSON | William | Private |
| WATTERS | Duncan DCM | Sergeant |
| WILKIE | Thomas | Private |
| WILSON | John | Private |

| | | | |
|---|---|---|---|
| LAING | George | Private | 8th Black Watch |
| SOMERVILLE | John | Private | 8th Black Watch |
| EADIE | Alexander | Private | 11th Black Watch |
| HERD | David | Private | 11th Black Watch |
| HEPBURN | William | Private | 1/7th Black Watch |
| PORTER | Robert | Private | 4/5th Black Watch |
| YOUNG | James R. | L/Corporal | 2nd Black Watch |
| DONALDSON | William | Bombardier | Royal Field Artillery |

[Obverse of memorial]

A City Set on a Hill Cannot be Hid
And They Shall Bring the Glory and Honour of the Nations Unto It.

| | | | |
|---|---|---|---|
| GIBSON | James | Gunner | Royal Field Artillery |
| MAILER | William | Driver | Royal Field Artillery |
| McLAREN | Peter | Sapper | Royal Engineers |
| | | | |
| CAW | James | Private | 4th Royal Scots |
| DRUMMOND | James | Private | 2nd Royal Scots |
| EADIE | Charles H. | Corporal | 11th Royal Scots |
| McINTYRE | William D. | Private | 15th Royal Scots |
| McLAREN | John | Private | 12th Royal Scots |
| WYLIE | Andrew | Private | 12th Royal Scots |
| | | | |
| DRUMMOND | Malcolm | Private | 2nd London Scottish |
| LEONARD | Harry | Private | Liverpool Scottish |
| McINTYRE | Colin | Private | 6/7th R.S.F. |
| GORDON | Geo.Andrew | Piper | 2/4th K.O.S.B. |
| McCULLOCH | Isaac | Private | 8th K.O.Y.L.I. |
| MAILER | Robert | Private | 1st H.L.I. |
| SINCLAIR | Hope | Private | 15th H.L.I. |
| DONALDSON | Joseph | Private | 2nd Seaforths |
| SALMOND | George | L/Corporal | 7th Seaforths |

| | | | |
|---|---|---|---|
| SCOTT | James | L/Corporal | 1st Seaforths |
| BROWN | John | Private | 2nd Gordons |
| MAXTONE | James F. | L/Corporal | 2nd Gordons |
| McKAY | Alexander | Private | 8th Gordons |
| ALEXANDER | James | Private | 7th Camerons |
| GRAEME | L.O. CMG | Lt-Colonel | 1st Camerons |
| MOORE | Joseph B. | Private | 6th Camerons |
| ARCHIBALD | Donald | Private | 11th A. & S.H. |
| KAY | John | Private | 8th A. & S.H. |
| WALKER | John | Private | Bucks Hussars |
| HAXTON | John | Private | Army Service Corps |
| INNES | Alexander | Private | 10th M.G.C. |
| NICOL | William | Corporal | 1st A/M Royal Air Force |
| | | | |
| SHARP | George | Sergeant | 16th Australians |
| SHARP | Duncan | 2/Lieutenant | 11th Australians |
| WYLIE | James | Private | 3rd Australians |
| STEWART | Hugh John | S.Q.M.S. | 2nd Australian L.H. |
| | | | |
| BURGH-SMEATON | Jack | Cadet | 27th Canadians |
| DOIG | David John | Corporal | 79th Canadians |
| DOIG | James | Private | 107th Canadians |
| NEWLANDS | Peter | Corporal | 13th Canadians |
| SALMOND | W.M. McIntosh | Private | For. Corps Canadians |
| STEEL | John T. | Sergeant | A. & S.H. Canadians |
| RAMSAY | D.B. | Leading Seaman | Royal Naval Reserve |

## EYEMOUTH, Berwickshire

Coast town and parish. At mouth of Eye Water.
A modern-looking war memorial, within a precinct.

## SACRED TO THE MEMORY OF THE OFFICERS, NCOs AND MEN OF EYEMOUTH WHO FELL IN THE GREAT WAR
### 1914–1919

*Lest We Forget*
*Those Who Laid*
*Down Their Lives*
*That We Might Live*

### [Officers]

| | | | |
|---|---|---|---|
| Lieutenant | Linn D. | ROBERSON MC | KOSB |
| Lieutenant | John | WOOD | KOSB |
| Lieutenant | F.W.H. | LINTON | Border |
| 2/Lieutenant | Eric W. Wright | SANDISON | Royal Scots |
| 2/Lieutenant | Thomas Murray | MILLER | KOSB |

### [NCOs]

| | | | |
|---|---|---|---|
| Corporal | George | CRAIG | KOSB |
| Corporal | George Leith | DOUGALL | KOSB |
| Corporal | John | WINDRAN | Canadians |
| L/Corporal | Robert | CRAIG | KOSB |
| L/Corporal | William | LOUGH | KOSB |
| L/Corporal | Robert | THOMPSON MM | Scottish Rifles |

### [Men]

| | | | |
|---|---|---|---|
| Private | Peter | GOWE | Royal Scots |
| Private | Thomas Arthur | DOUGALL | Royal Scots |
| Private | John | BLACKIE | KOSB |
| Private | Thomas | BOLTON | KOSB |
| Private | James | BURGON | KOSB |
| Private | William | EMSLIE | KOSB |
| Private | Alexander | FAIRBAIRN | KOSB |
| Private | Joseph | GIBSON | KOSB |
| Private | George | JOHNSTON | KOSB |
| Private | Thomas F. | LOUGH | KOSB |
| Private | Robert Rae | LOUGH | KOSB |
| Private | George | PATERSON | KOSB |
| Private | James Ewart | PATERSON | KOSB |
| Private | David | RITCHIE | KOSB |
| Private | John S. | WAIT | KOSB |
| Private | Richard | ARMSTRONG | N.F. |
| Private | John | ARMSTRONG | R.H. |
| Private | William | CROMBIE | Seaforths |
| Private | Robert | GILLIE | Seaforths |
| Private | Robert | WADDELL | A & S.H. |
| Private | Alexander | PATERSON | Scottish Rifles |
| Private | Robert | COLLIN | East Kents |
| Private | John | BURGON | Scots Guards |
| Private | James | BORTHWICK | AIF |
| Private | Adam | MILLER | AIF |
| Private | William | COOPER | Canadians |
| Private | Alexander | WINDRAN | Canadians |
| Private | Farquhar M. | MACRAE | London Rifles |

## ROYAL NAVAL RESERVE – TS

[Skipper]
William COLLIN

[Mates]
James Robert COLLIN
James COLLIN
George CRAIG
Robert COWE
John DOUGAL
Daniel STOTT

[Seamen]

| | |
|---|---|
| Robert ANGUS | Alexander PATERSON |
| George CORMACK | John SWANSTON |
| James COLLIN | James SWINEY |
| Peter COLLIN | John WADDELL |
| Robert CROMLIE | James WINDRAM |
| Alexander LOUGH | Andrew C. YOUNG |
| William MALTMAN | Alexander YOUNG |
| John PATTERSON | William YOUNG |

Walter R. DAVIDSON Royal Naval Division

[Obverse of memorial]

## SACRED TO THE MEMORY OF THE OFFICERS, NCOs AND MEN WHO GAVE THEIR LIVES IN THE GREAT WAR II
### 1939–1945
*They Died That We Might Live*

[Officers]

| | | |
|---|---|---|
| Commissioned Skipper | James JAMIESON | RNVR |
| Flight-Lieutenant/Pilot | William S. LOUGH | RAFVR |
| Flying Officer/Pilot | Alexander S. AITCHISON | RAFVR |
| Flying Officer/Pilot | George LOUGH | RAFVR |
| Pilot Officer | William W. BURGON | RAFVR |

[NCOs]

| | | |
|---|---|---|
| L/Corporal | Archibald STEBBING | KOSB |
| Flight-Sergeant | Robert D. FISHBOURNE | RAFVR |
| Flight-Sergeant | George F. WISHART | RAVFR |
| Sergeant/Observer | James AITCHISON | RAF |
| Sergeant/Pilot | James F. HUGHES | RAFVR |

[Men]

| | | | |
|---|---|---|---|
| Able Seaman | Christopher | BORTHWICK | R.N. |
| Able Seaman | Peter | CRAIG | R.N. |
| Able Seaman | David | DOUGALL | R.N. |
| Writer | Henry N. | LOUGH | R.N. |
| Guardsman | Robert | COLLIN | Scots Guards |
| Driver | Robert | GILLESPIE | RASC |
| Private | Thomas J. | HENDERSON | KOSB |
| Leading Aircraftsman | James O. | RAMSAY | RAFVR |
| Gunner | John Maltman | FOXTON | Royal Artillery |

| *Fishermen* | *Merchant Navy* | | |
|---|---|---|---|
| James R. CHAPMAN | Cadet | Joseph | PURVES |
| Richard COLLIN | A.B. | William | ANDERSON |
| William JACKSON | A.B. | George | CRAIG |
| Robert THOMPSON | A.B. | William A. | MEEK |

*Egypt – 1952* Leading Aircraftsman James CRAIG RAF

# 2   Military History

Seventy years after the peace treaty which ended World War I, it is easier
to look at this war in a dispassionate way. The once-popular view of the
war – as consisting entirely of mass slaughter in No Man's Land and in
the trenches, the result of a hidebound military caste of generals on both
sides indulging in a war of attrition because they could think of no other
way out of an impasse, and of gallant failures by a few men such as
Churchill to break the deadlock by sideshows at Antwerp and Gallipoli –
has given way to calmer and more intellectual appraisals.

However, television, with its simplicities and its military type-casting
of officers and men of the time, has had an overweening and often
pernicious influence on the views of recent generations. The generals
wrote their memoirs, later generations of historians interpreted these
according to the fashion of their times, and TV producers then adapted
these findings to fit their own preconceived view of what the public
expected and their film-budgets allowed. Myths were created and allowed
to pass unchallenged into folklore. Earl Haig – who did not write his
memoirs – has of late deservedly been reassessed by historians such as
John Terraine, who has done so much to put events into perspective. It is
too easy to forget that Haig made victory possible by beating the
Germans in the West in 1918.

War memorials record the facts and some of the views which obtained
in the 1920s. *That is their value as a primary source.*

A first detail worth noting on war memorials is what each community
considered were the years of war: 1914–18 or 1914–19. We should
remember that, although the Armistice took place on 11 November
1918, the Peace Treaties were not signed till June 1919 and were not
officially ratified by the respective governments until 31 August 1921.
The war with Turkey, in fact, was not officially declared at an end until 6
August 1924. Some War Office documents talk of 'The War of

1914–1920', but I have found this combination of dates only very occasionally on war memorials, one such example being a marble plaque in the parish church to the men of Blyth and Hodsock, in north Nottinghamshire, who died 'in the Great War AD 1914–1920'.

War memorials which give the dates of death of soldiers help provide a picture of the military forces involved. It is possible to distinguish in the dates of death a likely pattern of service. Similar clues are given when the war memorial lists the battalions or units to which a soldier belonged. Most infantry regiments had two regular battalions, the 1st and 2nd battalions, the 'line' battalions. Their 3rd battalion was generally a reserve battalion in Britain.

Most of those dying in 1914 were regular soldiers or reservists; by 1915 many Territorials and the first men of the New Armies were in action, particularly at Loos; and then in 1916 came the Somme, in which Kitchener's volunteer army was the main force.

Sir Arthur Bryant, in his history of the Rifle Brigade, *Jackets of Green* says (p.272): 'For the first nine months of the war it had been the Regular Army – long-service, professional, officered by the gentry and recruited from the poor – which had borne the heat and the dust of the day while an unprepared Britain made ready. For the remaining three and a half years the burden passed to the New Army which was the nation itself or, rather, that part of it which was of military age and had voluntarily offered itself for service.' Arthur Bryant goes on to quote the military correspondent of *The Times*, Colonel Repington: 'The old Army died a glorious death, but its spirit survived in the first hundred thousand, and in the second, and in the third. Not once, but many times, were some of its units completely renewed.'

The value of war memorials to military historians lies in their recording of army units and recruiting patterns which have passed into history. Time and again one is reminded on 1914–18 memorials of customs that belonged to an epoch seemingly as remote to 1939–45 soldiers as those red-coated skirmishes on the veldt at the turn of the century.

Britain began the Great War with seven separate types of soldier:

Serving Regulars
Regular Army Reserve
Regular Army Reserve of Officers
Special Reserve
Territorial Force
Territorial Force Reserve
The 1910 Register (of men who had served in any British or Imperial Force)

Where a war memorial gives a soldier's army number and the battalion in which the man was serving, we can often decide to which of the seven categories he belonged, at least in the early days of the war. Though many Special Reserve officers were commissioned to the regiments' 3rd battalions, they generally died while serving with regular or service battalions overseas.

Just to confuse things, in addition to the Cavalry and the Guards, which had their own patterns, in 1914 five infantry regiments of the British Army had four regular battalions instead of two. They were the Royal Fusiliers (City of London Regiment), the Worcestershire Regiment, the Middlesex Regiment, the King's Royal Rifle Corps and the Rifle Brigade. In the case of these regiments their 5th or 6th battalions would be the reserve ones.

The Territorial Force battalions (the title Territorial Army did not come in until after the war) generally followed on in the numbering, after the reserve battalion. Thus in most regiments the 4th or 5th – and in some cases the 6th, 7th, 8th, 9th or even the 10th – battalion could be Territorial Force units. These are generally shown as 1/4th or 1/5th for the first TF battalion raised, and 2/4th or 3/5th where later battalions were raised and went overseas.

Next in the order of battalion numbering came the service battalions of the New Armies, Kitchener's men. Sometimes these battalions are shown on war memorials or on rolls of honour simply as the 8th, or 11th, or 16th battalion of a regiment; sometimes they are designated 11 (Service) or 14 (S) Battalion. The style is seldom the same.

Kitchener's service battalions of 1914–18 volunteers were not only a unique manifestation in the history of the British Army but had one particular feature never likely to be repeated: the so-called 'Pals battalions', units of about a thousand men coming from a particular town or city or from specialist classes, such as sportsmen, city workers, railwaymen or public schoolboys.

One of the best-documented of these special battalions is the 11th (Service) Battalion (Accrington), of the East Lancashire Regiment, 'the Accrington Pals'. It was one of many battalions that was to be virtually destroyed on the Somme on that fateful 1 July 1916.

In 1914 Accrington was a mainly textile town, twenty miles north of Manchester, with some 45,000 people. Poverty is always a great spur to recruitment, and there was both industrial unrest and heavy unemployment in Accrington at the time. (Another aid to recruiting came with the reduction of physical requirements for the Army – from 5 feet 6 inches and a 35-inch chest to 5 feet 3 inches and a 34-inch chest.) The town raised in effect an Accrington & District battalion, with A Company entirely Accrington; B Company from Clayton-le-Moors, Church, Oswaldtwistle, Rishton and Great Harwood (The District); C was from Chorley and Blackburn, and D Company from Burnley.

In 1914 Lancashire was the home of seven infantry regiments – 7½ if you include the York & Lancaster Regiment, though this regiment was mainly Yorkshire-based. The seven Lancashire regiments – each with two regular battalions – were the King's Own (Royal Lancaster Regiment), the Loyal North Lancashire Regiment, the King's (Liverpool) Regiment, the Manchester Regiment, the Lancashire Fusiliers, the South Lancashire Regiment and the East Lancashire Regiment.

Kitchener's call for 100,000 volunteers to form service battalions of infantry for his New Armies was followed shortly afterwards by the idea of allowing large groups joining together to serve together. Eventually there would be some 145 Pals battalions.

'The Accrington Pals' soon had a strength of thirty officers and 1,350 men. After training in Britain, the battalion went to Egypt, but by the winter of 1916 it was in France. They went over the top on the Somme in four waves: 234 were killed, (131 have no known grave); 360 or so were wounded, fourteen of these dying within the month. Of the thirty or so officers, seven were killed, twelve wounded, one missing. The battalion was brought up to strength again by some 700 reinforcements from home and returned wounded, and fought on.

The Accrington War Memorial, in Oak Hill Park, stands as eloquent testimony to just one battalion of a unique World War I 'experiment'.

War memorials give clues to the likely military status and service of the man involved. There are thousands upon thousands of exceptions, and patterns are much harder to discern when it comes to the supporting arms and services: artillerymen, the men of the transport columns, flyers, Machine-Gun Corps volunteers and labour and garrison battalions – but patterns can be found there too.

At the risk of perpetuating a myth, it is fair to say that the Battle of the Somme – largely fought by Kitchener's volunteers – saw an army which took two years in the making destroyed in ten minutes. One only has to look at that ghastly league table of casualties appearing as Appendix 5 in Martin Middlebrook's excellent book *The First Day On The Somme* to see the truth of this generalization. The 10th West Yorks had twenty-two officers and 688 men as casualties, the 1st Newfoundland Regiment twenty-six officers and 658 men killed and wounded. And so it goes on, with well over 500 casualties in the 4th Tyneside Scottish, 1st Tyneside Irish, 8th York & Lancs, the County Down Volunteers, the Donegal and Fermanagh Volunteers, and a territorial unit, the 1/8th Royal Warwicks, before we reach a regular line battalion (1st Battalion Hampshires) with its twenty-six officers and 559 men as casualties.

The Somme stands as a landmark, a dividing line and a symbol of all that was terrible about World War I. G.Y. Cheyne, who in his book about the fighting at Beaumont Hamel, *The Last Great Battle of the Somme*, successfully challenges many of the Somme myths, says:

> Today, seventy years after the event, a calmer, more objective assessment is possible. It remains beyond dispute that the Somme was a tragedy and its casualties appalling. No-one who reads the balanced, dispassionate account in the *Official History* can escape being sickened by the waste of whole battalions in repeated, futile attacks on near-impregnable positions. There was muddle, incompetence, and dangerous self-deception, especially at the higher levels of command; and the victims, always, were the ordinary fighting soldiers.

Cheyne goes on to say that there were, however, exceptions: cases of careful planning, clever tactics and brilliant improvisation, which seem to be ignored in more partisan accounts of the fighting. He also pleads for not giving undue prominence to the first day of the Somme. The huge loss of life on that day has understandably haunted later generations, but it should be remembered that the battle lasted another five months, and, as he puts it, '...in that space of time the fate of the German army was virtually sealed and the outcome of the war decided. For the Somme was a major turning-point. Until then the issue had hung in the balance; but by the end of November the ordinary German soldier realised that victory had slipped from his grasp, and the ordinary British soldier was convinced that he could now win.' This all gives greater poignance to that ever-recurring date of 1 July 1916 which appears on so many war memorials: the British suffered 57,470 casualties on that one day, including 19,240 dead.

After the Somme, it is much harder to decide from a simple memorial inscription what kind of soldier is involved, and recourse will almost certainly have to be made to other sources: service records, the eighty volumes of *Soldiers Died in the Great War* (described later in this chapter), local newspapers or more detailed rolls of honour in regimental histories.

Soldiers were transferred to regiments other than their own; whole battalions were amalgamated; and the promises made to Territorials and men of the Pals battalions that they would always serve together crumbled in the face of military necessity. In some cases, breaking this promise to Pals battalions was academic – they had nearly all died together on the Somme already.

The best explanation of the complete re-organization of the British Army that occurred following the decision to recruit the thirty divisions of the New Army is found in Brigadier E.A. James's *British Regiments,*

*1914–1918* (introduction to Part II). He notes that formation of the first
six of these divisions was authorized by Army Order 324 of 21 August
1914, headed 'Augmentation of the Army', paragraph 3, ruling: 'The
new battalions will be raised as additional battalions of the regiments of
Infantry of the Line and will be given numbers following consecutively
on the existing battalions of their regiments. They will be further
distinguished by the word "Service" after the number ....' Brigadier
James says the title 'Service' seems to date from the Boer War, when
companies raised by the Volunteers for attachment to their regular
battalions in South Africa were called 'Service Companies'.

The names of men who died in the war on Home Service, or from
wounds in hospitals in Britain, are often to be found on memorials in
cemeteries situated near military hospitals. It is here we will find mention
of men of the 112 battalions of the Training Reserve, constituted in 1916
from a general pool of infantry reserves, and all the Second Reserve and
Local Reserve battalions of all but the Irish regiments.

In October 1917 46 Graduated and 23 Young Soldier battalions of this
Training Reserve were affiliated to twenty-three infantry regiments. The
Graduated battalions were numbered 51st and 52nd and the Young
Soldier battalions 53rd in their regiments. Any of these numberings and
affiliations might appear on your local war memorial. There were also
Garrison battalions, many of which were sent overseas, plus other Home
Service Garrison battalions, which did not go abroad. None of these
units forms part of the structure of the British Army today, and they
simply belong to military history.

Men who were wounded overseas were, wherever possible, sent to
military or specialist hospitals near their homes, to make it easier for
relatives to visit. Names recorded in the big town cemeteries often
provide insights into some of these seemingly complex regimental and
territorial patterns discussed here.

Almost every big cemetery in London, such as Battersea, Brompton,
Edmonton, Lambeth, Nunhead, Paddington, Streatham, Tottenham
and Wandsworth, has a Cross of Sacrifice and a wall or plaque listing
those buried there. They all make interesting reading, as do the
individual military headstones provided by the Imperial War Graves
Commission (now the Commonwealth War Graves Commission). These
headstones – the same kind provided for the vast military cemeteries in
France and Flanders and elsewhere – are also found in small village
churchyards where individual servicemen who died in Britain are buried.

For 1939–45, those marking the burial grounds of whole bomber crews
whose planes crashed on landing, or pilots killed in training (as at Byley,
Ches.,) are somehow among the saddest of them all.

In some cases hundreds of men – and a few women (nurses, airwomen,

Solid cement war-memorial cross, with plaques on low wall behind

*'Their Name Liveth for Evermore'*

## THESE MEMBERS OF HIS MAJESTY'S FORCES DIED IN THE SERVICE OF THEIR COUNTRY AND LIE BURIED ELSEWHERE IN THIS CEMETERY.

### 1914–1918

|  |  |  |  |
|---|---|---|---|
| CQMS | G. BELL | Royal Scots | 26 February 1919 |
| CSM | W. BOXHALL | Royal West Surreys | 9 March 1915 |
| Private | G. BREWER | Duke of Wellingtons | 17 November 1918 |
| Gunner | L. DUGGAN | Royal Field Artillery | 7 December 1917 |
| Private | T. DUNN | Yorkshire Regiment | 16 April 1917 |
| Private | H.E. ELLIOTT | Duke of Wellingtons | 8 October 1916 |
| Corporal | A. ELLIS | King's Own Yorkshire Light Infantry | 5 October 1916 |
| Private | E.H. GILDERDALE | Labour Corps | 31 May 1918 |
| Driver | A.G. HUBBARD | Royal Field Artillery | 29 September 1914 |
| Private | M. KIRWAN | Royal Army Service Corps | 1 June 1915 |
| Private | F. QUIGLEY | West Yorkshire Regiment | 7 August 1917 |
| Private | G.H. ROBINSON | Duke of Wellingtons | 7 January 1917 |
| Private | H. SEYMOUR | Durham Light Infantry | 21 September 1916 |
| Private | J.H. SUGDEN | Duke of Wellingtons | 3 March 1919 |
| Private | C. WILKINSON | West Yorkshire Regiment | 31 December 1918 |

### 1939–1945

|  |  |  |  |
|---|---|---|---|
| Gunner | G. DOWNEY | Royal Artillery | 2 November 1942 |
| Private | J.W. FINCH | West Yorkshire Regiment | 28 February 1940 |
| Private | J. KILKENNY | Manchester Regiment | 17 January 1944 |
| Private | M. McGOWAN | Royal Army Medical Corps | 18 October 1945 |
| Corporal | G.R. OLIVER | Pioneer Corps | 13 August 1945 |

auxiliary workers) – are listed on the big town memorials. It is seldom that one finds officers on these lists, as they tended to be cared for in officers' hospitals or nursing-homes, separate from those catering for wounded other ranks. Officers dying in hospital were often buried in family plots in churchyards near their homes.

A list more manageable than those of the large London cemeteries is that at Undercliffe Cemetery, Bradford, Yorks. This is a fine Victorian cemetery in the north-eastern suburb of Undercliffe, which lies south of Peel Park (where many troops trained). It is half a mile from Calverley Hospital, between Fagley and Thornbury.

There is information to be found on service headstones everywhere. Typical are those at St Katharine's Church, Merstham, Surrey:

| | |
|---|---|
| 20136 Private W.A. BROWN | R.C. STANBURY |
| South Lancashire Regiment | Cook's Mate RN M/10961 |
| 2nd June 1916 | HM Torpedo Boat No.5 |
| | 1st September 1916 – aged 24 |

and at Watlington, Oxford:

| | |
|---|---|
| 21068 Private A.E. PAGET | 2587 Private H.J. YOUNG |
| Wiltshire Regiment | Queen's Own Oxfordshire Hussars |
| 6 May 1917, aged 20 | 14 February 1921, aged 33 |

The key research tool for trying to trace names appearing on war memorials is a publication in eighty volumes issued by His Majesty's Stationery Office in 1921, colloquially referred to as *Soldiers Died* ....

*Soldiers Died in the Great War 1914-19* is today available as a facsimile reprint from J.B. Hayward & Son, Polstead, Suffolk. The (1989) price of each volume in hardback varies from about £7 for the thinner ones of some sixty pages up to around £30 for those with 296 pages, such as Part 2 containing all the Royal Horse and Field Artillery, and the 312-page part containing the men of the London Regiment and the officers' training units.

The books can be bought from specialist military publishers, such as the London Stamp Exchange, Buckingham Gate, WC2. The pages have also been recorded on 35 mm roll film by the City of Manchester Central Library. Six reels at £30 each, or £140 for the complete set (1989), works out a good deal cheaper, but only if you have the necessary display equipment to be able to read the pages shown.

It must be accepted that *Soldiers Died* ... and its one-volume counterpart for those holding commissions, *Officers Died* ..., are not wholly accurate. They were compiled by a great variety of clerical effort of very varying quality. The records are only as good as the information supplied to the compilers. A statement at the beginning of each part makes this clear:

These rolls have been compiled from information furnished to Officers-in-Charge through the Official Casualty Lists.

They are published to enable information, which has from time to time been circulated during the war, to be available in volume form.

Attention is invited to the explanations of abbreviations which are printed at the commencement of each part.

Nothing whatever contained in these rolls is to be quoted or made use of in any representation which it may be desired to make on the subject of rank, decoration, nature or date of casualty, or anything consequent upon any casualty.

The War Office,
September 1921.

Considering the circumstances under which these documents were compiled, it is unfair to poke fun at them, but as one finds one's way around in the eighty volumes of *Soldiers Died ...*, it is possible to begin spotting obvious errors of dictation and comprehension. Towns and places that are familiar to every newspaper reader today were clearly not known to the clerks (or the person supplying the information), and the phonetic interpretations are often amusing. This is mentioned only as a reminder of the imperfection of many primary sources, including even those carved in stone by men who knew the dead commemorated. Every primary source should be subject to careful scrutiny.

# 3   The Ideal War Memorial

And By The Long Road They Trod
With So Much Faith And With Such
Devoted Self-Sacrificing Bravery
    We Have Arrived At Victory
And Today They Have Their Reward.

Earl Haig
Alveston, Warwickshire

The ideal or complete war memorial from the social and military historian's point of view will give as much information as possible about those commemorated there.

Beginning with the correct identifying service number, rank, full Christian name(s) and surname, award(s) and decoration(s), it will go on to identify the exact unit with which the deceased was serving at the time of his death, the place and date and manner in which the soldier, sailor or airman died, and the age at death. In the case of rural or district memorials, it is even more useful when the locality from which each individual came is also given. (This is discussed in Chapter 11, Local Affiliations.)

But such detailed war memorials are very much the exception. Only a handful will be found, scattered throughout the country, and to no particular pattern. Again they emphasize how local a decision it was as to which facts are recorded on each memorial.

Even if an ideal pattern of recording all available information were to have been followed, and done in a consistent fashion throughout the whole country, it would surely still leave many questions unanswered. A last-minute transfer from one regiment to another would probably go unmarked. There would probably be no indication as to how long that individual had served with his unit, or in the forces generally. Was the dead serviceman indeed a regular soldier or a reservist recalled to the colours, a Territorial or a New Army volunteer or, later on in the war, an unwilling conscript?

Cross-checking with other references, in particular the eighty volumes of *Soldiers Died in the Great War*, should provide other details, in particular where an individual came from and where he enlisted. In order to use *Soldiers Died ...*, one really needs to know the exact unit to which an individual belonged or, if only the corps or regiment is known, face a lengthy search through long lists of dead to find the sought-after name.

A good example of what I would define as 'the ideal war memorial' is at Bradfield, Berks., three miles south-west of Pangbourne. This war memorial gives us almost a mini-history of the First World War and illustrates many of the themes studied in this book.

The Royal Navy – 'the Senior Service' – takes precedence in the list but is represented here only by two boy-seamen who died at the Battle of Jutland in 1916. This raises the question of how many Royal Navy men lost their lives in the war, compared with those in the Army. The answer is that roughly 2,000 Royal Navy officers and 21,000 men were killed or died of wounds received in action during 1914–18.

Most of the naval men died aboard the thirteen battleships, three battle cruisers, twenty-five cruisers, sixty-four destroyers, fifty-nine submarines and some forty other naval vessels which were sunk during the First World War. In addition another 550 officers and 9,500 men died serving with the Royal Naval Division, but as these men died fighting as infantry at Gallipoli or in France and Belgium, they are perhaps more appropriately considered along with the Army casualties.

The 23,000 Royal Navy men lost at sea should therefore be compared with the 677,515 men from the British armies who were killed or died of wounds on the Western Front alone. Even allowing for the much smaller numbers in the Navy, it was clearly much safer to be part of the war at sea than serving in the trenches.

The next interesting point is that the men of Bradfield's county regiment, Princess Charlotte of Wales's (Royal Berkshire Regiment), are listed next, in order of rank, and with their Army numbers. The place and date of death are given, though not the age at death.

It does not take much detective-work to see that most of the fighting done by the Royal Berkshires was in France, though in fact two battalions served on other fronts: the 1/4th (TF) Battalion in Italy for a year, and the 8th (Service) Battalion in Salonica/Macedonia.

Whereas most war memorials do not distinguish between those who were killed in action or died of wounds, Bradfield is very specific. Private Hurst died at No. 32 Casualty Clearing Station in France, and Private Braybrooke at the 1st General Hospital in France. Two others died in military hospitals in Britain – in the case of Sergeant Rumble MM, a year after the war ended. And at the end we see Private William Small who died three years after the war was over, from poison gas.

Poison gas was one of the nastiest innovations of what was actually a very innovatory war, but the casualties from gassing were proportionately not very heavy. As G.Y. Cheyne says (p.91), 'Contrary to popular belief, poison gas as a weapon was less lethal than bullets or shells. Of the 181,000 British gas casualties, 6,000 died – about 3.3%. The mortality rate for all other battle injuries was 25%. Reliable figures are not available for German casualties, but it is unlikely that their percentage mortality was very different.'

The historian Major-General J.F.C. Fuller makes the same point in *The Conduct of War 1789–1961* (p.174): 'Contrary to common belief, gas was the most humane weapon used in the war, and one of the most effective; even when the respirator gave 100 per cent immunity, when worn it reduced the soldier to half a fighting man, and it gave little protection against mustard gas.' General Fuller quotes American statistics for gas poisoning, saying that, whereas some 27.4 per cent of the 250,000 United States casualties in World War I were from gas, only 1,400 of these resulted in death. That is two per cent compared with the 25 per cent ratio of dead to wounded for other battle casualties.

One doubts if Private William Small of the Royal Berkshires, or his relatives, would have derived much comfort from these statistics.

Men of Bradfield who died with other regiments or other arms are listed by order of rank, though in several cases names have been added or inserted in the columns on the memorial. Here we do find men dying far from home: in Mesopotamia, Baghdad and South Africa. Again the number who actually died in hospital is interesting, including Driver Scudamore who died in 1920 and Lieutenant W.T. Stevens of the Leicester Regiment, dying in July 1922.

In contrast with the eighty volumes of other ranks names, the single volume of *Officers Died in the Great War* merely lists, in order of regiments and arms of service, the Christian names, rank, decorations and manner and date of death. It generally gives the number of the battalion to which the officer was commissioned and, if he was on attachment at the time of death, the unit he was with.

Officers serving as volunteers with other arms – such as the Royal Flying Corps, the Machine Gun Corps or the Tanks – will generally appear twice in *Officers Died* ...: once in their new arm of service, again in their original regiment.

Officers of the regular battalions and those commissioned to the Service battalions of the New Army are listed together in Part I (Old and New Armies) at the front of the book, in alphabetical order. Officers commissioned in the Yeomanry, Territorial battalions and other

Territorial Force units appear in Part II, alphabetically, but by ranks. This second form of listing often makes it hard to find subalterns, separated into Lieutenants and Second Lieutenants, and spread over several Territorial Force units.

An 'acting' rank embossed with great permanency on a war memorial may not necessarily be credited in *Officers Died* .... Sometimes a fond parent would list a higher rank obtained by the deceased during his service, even if at the time of death, as far as the Army was concerned, that individual had reverted to a substantive or lower rank. This also often affects other ranks who died of wounds in hospital and who forfeited their acting regimental rank as soon as they left their own unit.

Although there is no indication in *Officers Died* ... of the home-town of the officer concerned, or when he joined, further official information is generally available about an officer in the appropriate *Army List*, published several times a year, or found by searching through the *London Gazette* if an award or decoration is listed on the memorial.

Senior officers, lieutenant-colonels and above, often achieve a mention in the many volumes of the *Official History*, as will majors and even captains who were temporarily in command of their battalions in action. Commanding officers will almost certainly appear in regimental histories, possibly with further details of their home-towns, background and previous service.

Another 'good' war memorial from perhaps both the social and military historian's point of view is that at Sandon, Staffs. A small parish and village north-east of Stafford, it embraces Sandon Hall, seat of the earls of Harrowby (family name Ryder).

The war memorial is a fine statue of a soldier in full kit, wearing his tin helmet and holding his rifle, as on parade. It is a very typical estate memorial, valuable for the picture it gives of an agricultural society that is no longer with us.

Perhaps the most interesting feature of the Sandon memorial is the detailed list of the numbers of men who went forth from Sandon, Gayton and Marston. Eighty men joined the forces, and twenty were killed or died of wounds – that is, one in four. Another three died in the service, and eighteen were wounded. In other words, almost exactly a half of those who went to war from Sandon and environs became casualties.

Nearly all those who joined up served in France and Flanders, some of them serving in other places abroad as well, which accounts for the greater total of places than men. Judging by those who died, they included a high proportion of leaders and technically minded men who could ill be spared from a rural community.

## THE SANDON ESTATE MEMORIAL

(Sandon – Gayton – Marston)

### The Great War 1914–1918

### LEST WE FORGET

**Killed in Action**

| | | |
|---|---|---|
| Major | RYDER, HON. R.N.D. | 8th Hussars<br>Gauche Wood<br>30 November 1917 |
| 2/Lieutenant | BENTLEY, H.L. | 2nd Royal Fusiliers<br>Sailly-Saillisel<br>28 February 1916 |
| Bombardier | CLAYTON, W.H. | Royal Field Artillery<br>near Ypres<br>21 August 1917 |
| Bombardier | TAVERNAR, E.H. | Royal Garrison Artillery<br>Epehy<br>26 September 1918 |
| L/Corporal | HAYWOOD, J.G. | 1/5th South Staffords<br>Vermelles<br>17 August 1917 |
| L/Corporal | KILBOURNE, F. | 7th North Staffords<br>Baghdad<br>11 March 1917 |
| Private | ASKEY, J. | 2nd North Riding<br>near Arras<br>30 August 1918 |
| Private | BARNES, C.W. | 18th Welch<br>near Bethune<br>17 April 1918 |
| Private | DAVENPORT, F. | 8th KSLI<br>near Salonica<br>18 September 1918 |
| Private | DAVENPORT, T. | 1st KSLI<br>Morval<br>26 September 1916 |
| Private | HEDGES, W.C. | 10th Glosters<br>Hulluch<br>25 September 1915 |
| Private | HODSON, J. | 13th King's (Liverpool)<br>Mailly Maillet<br>15 October 1916 |

| Private | JAMES, J.M. | 16th Royal Warwicks<br>Fricourt<br>26 January 1916 |
| Private | KIRK, J. | 25th Northd. Fusiliers<br>near Croisilles<br>28 March 1918 |
| Private | WARD, J.H. | 1st Coldstream Guards<br>Vermelles<br>17 October 1915 |
| Private | WARD, J.T. | 8th East Yorks.<br>Trones Wood<br>24 July 1916 |

### Died of Wounds

| 2/Lieutenant | BENTLEY, G.W. | Royal Flying Corps<br>Geneva<br>13 January 1917 |
| Bombardier | MEWENDON, J. | Royal Field Artillery<br>near Ypres<br>22 September 1917 |
| Private | CHEADLE, R.H. | 7th Buffs<br>Valenciennes<br>12 April 1918 |
| Private | CHEADLE, W. | 8th KSLI<br>near Salonica<br>13 January 1918 |

### Died

| L/Corporal | CHEADLE, E. | Royal Air Force<br>14 March 1919 |
| Private | DAINTY, S. | 1/5th North Staffs<br>2 March 1919 |
| Sapper | SNAPE, F. | Royal Engineers<br>9 October 1917 |

| *Joined the Forces* | 80 | | *Service Areas* | |
|---|---|---|---|---|
| Killed in Action | 16 | | Served on High Seas | 2 |
| Died of Wounds | 4 | | Fought in France & Flanders | 71 |
| Died | 3 | | Fought at Gallipoli | 1 |
| Wounded | 18 | | Fought in Salonica | 8 |
| | | | Fought in Mesopotamia | 6 |
| *Honours* | | | Fought in South Russia | 3 |
| Distinguished Conduct | | | Fought in Egypt | 2 |
| Medal | 1 | | Fought in Palestine | 1 |
| Military Medal | 1 | | Fought in Italy | 1 |
| | | | Fought in East Africa | 1 |
| | | | Fought in India | 1 |

The Sandon dead also include Major The Honourable Robert Nathaniel Dudley Ryder, 8th Hussars, a younger son of the fourth Earl of Harrowby and a brother to the fifth Earl, who inherited the estate in 1900.

World War I officers on the whole tend to be much better documented than other ranks. This is particularly so if they hold a title or are landowners, when they can be traced in *Who's Who, Burke's Peerage* or *Debrett, Kelly's Handbook* or other works of reference. If one knows where an officer was educated, there are almost certain to be published works or bound copies of school magazines available. The published *Roll of Honour* books, a form of war memorial in themselves, are discussed in Chapter 17.

Officers are also often listed on several separate memorials or rolls of honour. As well as appearing on the war memorial of their town, or village, their names may be seen on school and university memorials, or those of their professional organizations. Many were honoured by their parents with tablets or windows in a parish church, or by gifts or scholarships or presentations to their old school or university.

In some cases, names appear on one memorial based on a parish register, and then again on another memorial based on a district affiliation. Duplications are often found where local boundaries are undefined, or disputed.

But non-public school or university soldiers do often get additional mentions too: in school or club memorials and at their places of work. If they were decorated, they too can be traced through the *London Gazette* or in their local newspapers, with Victoria Cross winners being particularly well-documented.

Almost qualifying as another 'good' war memorial is that at Harrod's, the famous London department store. Although it does not give the Army number or place and date of death, it records the department in which the soldier worked. In doing so, it helps give a fuller picture of those listed, particularly where a job specialization is obviously carried over into the army.

Thus Privates Hawthorn and Jolliffe from Motor Hire died with the Army Service Corps, as did Lieutenant Kauffman from Electrical. George Spice from Harrod's Motor Cars was with the 2nd Battalion Tank Regiment when he met his death. Private Cyril Hardouin from the building department became a Royal Engineer; while the 8th Royal Sussex (a Pioneer battalion) had recruited Privates Merryweather from Rail Despatch, Gabell from Packing-Cases, and Hurn from Export Casemakers. The 5th Connaught Rangers were no doubt glad to have the services of Corporal John Patrick Walsh from house catering, and the 4th Middlesex those of Private Lewin Hugh Thomas from Harrod's bakery.

## HARRODIANS WHO DIED FOR THEIR COUNTRY (Panel 1)
### 1914–1918

| Rank | Name | | Regiment | Department |
|---|---|---|---|---|
| Rifleman | Harold | MYDDLETON | 9th London Regiment | Hire |
| Private | W. | CARTER | Royal Fusiliers | Restaurant |
| | J. | BENNETT | Norfolk Regiment | Printing |
| Captain | James | CARR | Royal Fusiliers | Sports |
| Private | H. | WHITELOCK | Royal Irish Rifles | Shipping |
| Private | Stanley | PALMER | London Scottish | Photographic |
| Lieutenant | Arthur | KAUFFMAN | Royal Army Service Corps | Electrical |
| Private | Frank | LITTLE | East Surrey Regiment | Linen |
| | Cyril | MACDONALD | | Linen Warehouse |
| Sergeant | | HARDOUIN | Royal Engineers | Building |
| Private | | HAWTHORN | Army Service Corps | Motor Hire |
| Private | | JOLLIFFE | Army Service Corps | Motor Hire |
| Sergeant | Edgar A. | SMITH | 7th London Regiment | Motor Accessories |
| | Albert R. | GODWIN | 23rd Rifle Brigade | Motor Accessories |
| | Joseph H. | BURTON | 145th Labour Corps | Removals |
| Sergeant | A. | SMART | Royal Field Artillery | Removals |
| | Harry W. | PAGE | 13th East Surrey Regiment | Removals |
| | Albert E. | DEAR | 23rd Lancashire Fusiliers | Removals |
| Corporal | Edward | EXTON | 2nd Wiltshire | Counting House |
| | G. | REEVES | | House Catering |
| | Frederick | MUNNS | Rifle Brigade | Jewellery |
| | Frederick | BIBLEY | Cameron Highlanders | Country Despatch |
| | Thomas | PARISH | | Motor Cars |
| | George | SPICE | 2nd Battalion Tank Corps | Cabinet Factory |
| | F.C. | MOODY | London Regiment | Optical |
| | P. | HILLMAN | 12th London Regiment | Drapery Country Orders |
| | H.A. | MEADE | 2/18 Londons | Meat Department |
| | Henry | HARVEY | 13th East Surrey Regiment | Provisions |
| | Edward | GOVE | Wiltshire Regiment | Grocery |
| | John Ralph | GOLDSBROUGH | 13th East Surrey Regiment | Motor Hire |
| | Hubert | CAMPBELL | Royal Field Artillery | |

## HARRODIANS WHO DIED FOR THEIR COUNTRY (Panel 2)

### 1914–1918

| Rank | Name | Regiment | Department |
| --- | --- | --- | --- |
| Private | J. PEEK | Devons | China |
| Sergeant | JOLLY | 9th County of London (QVR) | China |
|  | FRICKER | 17th Royal Fusiliers | Cooked Meats |
|  | L. SMITH |  | Building |
| Private | Frank SHEER | Royal Marines | House Engineers |
| Wireman | H.A. HARROP | King's Royal Rifles | Carpets |
| Private | Edgar PAYNE | Royal Army Medical Corps | Perfumery |
| Private | Francis G.A. WARD | 22nd Royal Fusiliers |  |
| Private | Harold E. RIPLEY | Machine Gun Corps |  |
| Sergeant | Philip MAGUIRE | Royal West Kents |  |
| Private | FROST | 23rd London Regiment |  |
| Sergeant | J.A. WRIGHT | Grenadier Guards | Juv. Tailoring |
| Private | Herbert SHRIMPTON | King's Royal Rifles | Manchester |
| Private | Frederick SMITH | City of London (TF) Cyclists | G.M.O. |
| Private | William S. READ | 22nd Royal Fusiliers | Rec. Bank |
| Private | Ernest R. CLARK | 17th Royal Welsh Fusiliers | Tailoring |
| Private | Stanley CHATER | East Surrey Regiment | Tailoring |
| Sergeant | Bertram GILL | Royal Field Artillery | Counting House |
| Private | Andrew S. OUGH | Lancashire Fusiliers | Audits |
| Sergeant | Frederick W.G. FELTHAM | 12th Rifle Brigade | Sanction Office |
| Private | Henry PETTY | 9th London Regiment | Drugs |
|  | A. BOWER | 13th Royal Fusiliers | House Catering |
| Rifleman | W. JUDD | 1st Rifle Brigade |  |
| Lance Corporal | G. BURTENSHAW | King's Royal Rifles |  |
| Private | C.G. STANIFORD |  | Grocery |
|  | George SPICER | 9th Norfolks | Grocery |
| Rifleman | Stanley A. MORRELL | Queen's Westminsters | Town Despatch |
|  | Francis F. MARSHALL |  | Gents Boots |
|  | HILL |  | B.A. |
|  | W.G. VARLOW | Royal Marine Artillery | Bedding Factory |
|  | Arthur MILES | Grenadier Guards | Saddlery & Trunks |
|  | Arthur P. BROCKS | 3rd London Regiment (RF) | Antiques |
|  | W.J. BEAK | Royal Garrison Artillery | Bedding |
|  | Patrick F. DONOGHUE | Irish Guards | Hudson Bay |
|  | Frank Henry DOE | King's Royal Rifles | Removals |
|  | Leopold R. GREGORY | 12th Middlesex | Town Despatch |

## HARRODIANS WHO DIED FOR THEIR COUNTRY (Panel 3)
### 1914–1918

| Rank | Name | | Regiment | Department |
|---|---|---|---|---|
| Sergeant | George F. | HAWKINS | 2nd Royal Fusiliers | Building |
| Private | Robert H. | BARTLETT | 13th London Regiment (Kensington) | Country Despatch |
| Sergeant | William | SOUTAR | Royal Field Artillery | Town Despatch |
| Rifleman | Percy | POYNTON | 13th Rifle Brigade | Box Factory |
| Private | Walter A. | KEAREY | 3rd City of London (RF) | Furnishing |
| Lance Corporal | Percy A. | SWISS | 2nd City of London (RF) | Sanction Office |
| Private | Alfred E. | HOELLEN | 9th County of London | General Drapery |
| Corporal | George J. | BUTLER | King's Own Yorkshire L.I. | Minerals |
| Private | Lewis C. | JOHNSTON | 22nd London Regiment | Tailoring |
| Private | John P. | WALSH | 5th Connaught Rangers | House Catering |
| Private | A. | WEIGHT | 11th Essex Regiment | China |
| Bombardier | Ernest J. | MERRYWEATHER | Royal Sussex Pioneers | Rail Despatch |
| Private | William | WARNEFORD | 7th Bedfordshire | Country Orders |
| Corporal | Lewin H. | THOMAS | 4th Middlesex | Bakery |
| Private | Charles H. | JARVIS | 28th Brigade R.F.A. | China |
| Gunner | Leonard | GABELL | 8th Royal Sussex Pioneers | Packing Cases |
| Private | Henry G. | STRATTON | 11th Royal Fusiliers | Jewellery |
| Private | Harry M. | WILLIAMS | 19th County of London | Grocery Warehouse |
| Sergeant | Herbert T. | GEATER | 177th Brigade R.F.A. | Meat |
| Lance Corporal | Percival | HURN | Royal Sussex Pioneers | Export Casemakers |
| Rifleman | Charles | PARSLOW | 2nd Royal Fusiliers | Mail Orders |
| Sergeant | Albert S. | CASTLE | 12th King's Royal Rifles | Export Shipping |
| Rifleman | Thomas W. | BALL | 4th Royal Fusiliers | Library |
| Sergeant | Herbert C. | PAWSEY | 17th County of London | Tailoring |
| Private | Cyril W. | DICKENSON | 12th King's Royal Rifles | Photographic |
| Lance Corporal | Augustine J. | CRITCHEN | London Irish Rifles | Pianos |
| Private | Eli J. | MONTGOMERY | 9th County of London (QVR) | Turnery |
| Private | Charles H. | EGGS | 23rd London Regiment | House Catering |
| Corporal | Eric S. | SHINKFIELD | City of London Regiment (RF) | Ironmongery |
| Pioneer | Henry R. | HAYWARD | London Rifle Brigade | Optical |
| Private | Thomas G. | FIELDER | 12th West Yorkshire | Bakery Despatch |
| Private | Albert J. | HEALY | 18th Queen Mary's Own Hussars | Works |
| Sergeant | Thomas H. | SHAW | Royal Engineers | Manchester |
| Private | William A. | LAWRENCE | 2nd London Regiment (RF) | Country Orders |
| Private | Harold R. | CREWELL | 22nd East Surreys | Sports |
| Sergeant | John R. | COOLEY | 4th Cameron Highlanders | Furnishing Drapery |

## HARRODIANS WHO DIED FOR THEIR COUNTRY (Panel 4)
### 1914–1918

| Rank | Name | Regiment | Department |
|---|---|---|---|
| Lance Corporal | Frederick H. DORÉ | 9th County of London (QVR) | China |
| Private | Arthur ALLISON | 6th Queen's Royal West Surrey | Country Despatch |
| Private | Albert E. BRAUND | 19th King's Royal Rifles | House Catering |
| Rifleman | Frederick H. WITTINGTON | 1st Rifle Brigade | Packing Case Makers |
| Private | Oscar E. PERRY | 23rd County of London | Gents Shirts |
| Private | Albert F. JOHNS | 2nd City of London (RF) | Counting House |
| Lance Corporal | Robert J. HOBBS | 9th Royal Sussex | Mail Orders |
| Private | William COOMBS | 13th County of London | General Drapery |
| Private | Albert E. WHEATLEY | Queen's Westminster Rifles | Postal |
| Private | Albert B. CRANE | East Surrey | Fruit |
| Private | Thomas GREENWOOD | 4th Royal Fusiliers | Hans Mansions |
| Private | William SUTCLIFFE | 5th Lancashire | General Staff |
| Seaman | John R. RAVEN | RN (went down on HMS HAWKE) | General Drapery |
| Lance Corporal | Francis P. SARSFIELD | 22nd Royal Fusiliers | Town Returns |
| Sergeant | Arthur C. POOLEY | Royal Engineers | Buildings |
| Private | Gerald P. HOULIHAN | 12th County of London | Audit Office |
| Private | Thomas V. MOOR | 1st City of London (RF) | Furniture (Cabinets) |
| Private | Charles DAY | King's Royal Rifles | Restaurant |
| Lance Corporal | James H. SANDFORD | East Surrey | Hire |
| Rifleman | Frederick T. RANCE | 11th County of London | Stationery |
| Private | Harry TOPLIFFE | 10th Middlesex | Barnes Removal |
| Lance Corporal | Reginald BLEWITT | Royal Berkshire | Building |
| Corporal | Jeremiah J. STEVENSON | Royal Berkshire | Building |
| Private | Henry DEAN | 17th Middlesex | Cooked Meats |
| Private | Harry W. COOK | 22nd Royal Fusiliers | Sanction Office |
| Corporal | John H. MURRAY | Machine Gun Corps | Mail Orders |
| Private | Sydney E. HARRIS | 3rd City of London (RF) | Upholstery |
| Sergeant | Thomas F. COOTE | 4th Royal Fusiliers | Motor Garage |
| Rifleman | Albert E. LONG | Queen's Westminster Rifles | Shipping |
| Lance Corporal | Frederick W. BRUMAGE | Queen's Westminster Rifles | Linens |
| Sub-Lieutenant | Douglas Robert G. P. ALLDRIDGE | Royal Naval Division (RNVR) | House Engineer |
| Lance Corporal | Percy W. BAKER | 12th Middlesex | Town Despatch |
| Rifleman | Edwin HUDSON | 18th County of London (LIR) | House Catering |
| Rifleman | James W. WRIGHT | 10th King's Royal Rifles | Wines |
| Private | George W. CLARK | 3rd Royal Fusiliers | Meat |
| Private | Daniel H. REYNISH | 23rd County of London | Tailoring |
| Private | Henry G. GILLETT | Wiltshire | House Engineer |
| Private | Herbert C. HALL | 6th City of London (Rifles) | Grocery |
| Lance Corporal | Albert J. FREEMAN | 12th Middlesex | Watch & Clock |
| Private | Thomas W. WHEATLEY | 10th Durham Light Infantry | Town Despatch |
| Private | Herbert H. CLEMENTS | 9th East Surrey | Printing |
| Private | Oswald BURRELL | 21st County of London | Staff Office |
| Lance Corporal | John WALSH | Royal Fusiliers | Building |
| Rifleman | William R. J. PRICE | 11th County of London | China |

A Victorian clock tower, built in 1891 to mark the longest reign in British history (VR 1837–87), and to which war memorial panels have been added. At Atworth, Wilts.

The Cenotaph in Whitehall, London. Designed by Sir Edwin Lutyens, it carries no cross and a single dedication to 'The Glorious Dead'.

A Celtic cross on the parish war memorial of Cranston in Scotland, on the A68 between Coldstream and Edinburgh.

A very early version: an obelisk in the Royal Hospital Gardens at Chelsea dedicated to 255 officers, NCOs and men of the 24th Regiment who fell at Chilianwalla in 1849 in the second British–Sikh War.

A typical village war memorial – at Abbots Bromley, Staffs. This one is floodlit by night.

The Cenotaph theme repeated in the London Borough of Edmonton's memorial, but with the inscription changed to read 'To Our Glorious Dead'.

A cross and military headstones in a small burial-ground near Clandon in Surrey. Most of the men died of wounds at Clandon Park, which was used as a Great War hospital.

A cross in gardens near Putney, overlooking the forty-two acres of war memorial playing-fields by the A3 near Richmond Park.

A Boer War battle scene on the memorial on the Thames Embankment to the men of the VI Dragoon Guards (The Carabiniers) who died in the South African War 1899–1902, mainly of wounds or disease.

An ornate war memorial in the market square at Uttoxeter, Staffs.

Standing amidst the graves of their ancestors, a memorial to the men of Stadhampton, Oxon.

The 'Boy David' Machine Gun Corps memorial at Hyde Park Corner in London, with its challenging inscription: 'Saul hath slain his thousands/but David his tens of thousands.'

The tall obelisk on Oliver's Mount at Scarborough, North Yorks., which carries the names of the Service dead and also those of civilians killed in naval bombardments and air raids.

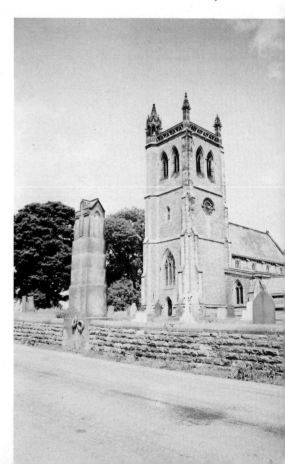

A square red sandstone war memorial in front of St Martin's Church, Osmanton, near Ashbourne, Derby.

Even if, from the social and military historian's point of view, the ideal or complete war memorial is the one that carries the *most* information about the men commemorated that it is possible to include, there is no way one can decide on what is a *typical* war memorial.

Just about every possibility seems to have been used somewhere. A check-list might provide fun for children playing 'I Spy' on a car-journey, but even after viewing some ten per cent of the 40,000 possibilities (or five per cent if one accepts that counting those inside churches and buildings could easily take the total to 100,000), I would still hesitate to decide what are the essential elements which constitute a war memorial.

There are crosses of just about every kind; there are obelisks and cenotaphs, catafalques and commemorative walls, cairns and columns, archways and lich-gates. Some consist of Calvary scenes or angels descending, there are statues of Winged Victory and weeping widows and orphans, there are classical and heroic figures, there are panels with battle scenes and historical allegories.

The crosses alone are multi-categoried. There are short, fat crosses, long, thin, elegant ones, Celtic crosses and crosses worked around with fleur-de-lys decorations; there are crosses with St George slaying a dragon in their centre, and crosses with wreaths in or around them.

And above all, there are the soldiers: soldiers with bayonet thrusting forward, soldiers on parade and standing at attention or at ease. There are soldiers who have just come through a battle; wounded and dying soldiers; soldiers mourning with reversed rifles. Each individual soldier-statue tells some sort of story and represents some sort of attitude. A few of the soldiers are mature men, with moustaches; many are bare-headed and physically powerful; some are portrayed as devastatingly and heart-breakingly young.

Only occasionally is an officer seen, and then generally only when there are at least two men on the monument – as in the regimental memorial to the York and Lancaster Regiment, Weston Park, Sheffield, Yorks. Exceptions to this rule occur generally at those schools and universities which provided the officer corps.

At Sheffield there is a Winged Victory on top, bearing a wreath, and around a cenotaph-type memorial there are two bronze figures: a captain, with drawn revolver, wearing helmet and service-dress jacket; a private soldier in cloth cap, with rifle slung, and full equipment, helmet on shoulder, bayonet, entrenching tools. The inscription is one of those regimental ones that tell you how many men from the regiment died in each war, a better way of comparing the ratio perhaps than by comparing the numbers on war memorials.

TO THE EVERLASTING HONOUR
AND GLORY OF THE 8814 OFFICERS
NON-COMMISSIONED OFFICERS AND
MEN OF THE YORK AND LANCASTER
REGIMENT WHO FELL
IN THE GREAT WAR 1914–1919

ALSO OF THE 1222 MEMBERS
OF THE REGIMENT WHO FELL IN THE WAR 1939–1945.

# 4  Names

Their Name Liveth For Evermore.

The 40,000 or so parish war memorials of Britain are magnificent primary sources for studying British Christian names and surnames.

Each memorial is a kind of parish record listing a representative selection of those who belonged to that village or town at certain set periods in recent history: during the Boer War (1899-1902), the First World War (1914-18) and the Second World War (1939-45).

Surname research is on the whole a remarkably neglected field of study, and it is fair to say that a scientific approach to mastering the social history provided by surnames is still in its infancy. Modern scholarship, with its greater understanding of linguistics, of population movements and economic and social history generally, will provide us with an increasing fund of knowledge in this area. Computerized analysis of records such as title deeds, electoral rolls and telephone directories will soon become the norm. Meanwhile, surname researchers, genealogists and social and family historians will do well to remember all these war memorials and parish rolls of honour – and the names which appear upon them.

Tracing the origins of surnames is a fascinating hobby in itself, as any reading of the Oxford *Dictionary of Surnames* will reveal. Thus, Garnon or Garnons stems from the nickname given to a man wearing a moustache, which was very much an exception among the clean-shaven Normans in whose era it is first found. Hence Algernon = 'with a moustache'.

Or Orme, from either the Old Norse personal name Ormr (snake, dragon) or perhaps from the Old French *orme*, used to describe someone who lived near a landmark elm tree.

And Yerburgh, a habitation name in Lincolnshire, probably from the land measure 'yard' plus 'burh' for fortress or town.

Some seventy-five names account for about 15 million people – in other words, one in four Britons have a fairly common name. It takes

51

another thousand names to cover half of the population. After these there is an infinite variety of surnames in the British Isles.

The most common names are Smith, Jones, Williams, Brown and Edwards.

Names generally derive from four sources, which Basil Cottle in his straightforward layman's guide *The Penguin Dictionary of Surnames* divides into four groups – with the acronym FLON:

(a) First names or patronymics;
(b) Local names deriving from landmarks or places;
(c) Occupational names stemming from jobs, products or calls;
(d) Nicknames describing appearance or character traits.

Surnames only really came into being from the twelfth century onwards. There were almost none in the eleventh century; by the fourteenth or fifteenth century nearly everyone had one, for they became necessary as the population became more mobile, and better documented. The two most numerous categories are those deriving from *First* names, the personal or given names of the head of the household; and secondly those for *Location*, which describe where a man lived or came from.

Britain was/is a patriarchal society, and wives and children took the man's name almost without exception. The few exceptions might include an heiress and landowner in her own right or, at a lower level, a prominent widow of long standing.

What can war memorials tell us about our history both before and after 'the time of surnaming', when surnames became established on a hereditary basis as opposed to being a local identifying description of a particular individual at a certain moment in time?

We must remember the way in which the earliest inhabitants of Britain (Celts, Cornish, Britons, Picts) were joined by Romans and Gaelic-speaking Scots from Ireland, plus all those waves of northern invaders (Jutes, Saxons, Angles, Danes, Norwegians and Normans – the latter originally 'northmen' too). The Normans, appearing and covering the country just when surnames became necessary, were also responsible for many of the local names. Distinguishing one Guillaume from another often needed reference to the knight's Norman estates or his English ones.

It is not always easy to pinpoint the names deriving from Christian or given names. Some remain unchanged, with only a possessive 's' or a 'son' (Mac, O, Ap) added: from Andrews, Bartholomew and Charles to McRobert, Sampson and ApSimon. Others derive from diminutive or familiar versions of the full name: Kittow, Peet, Robb, Simnell, Tandy, Tomkin and Wilmot. Some are much harder to identify, such as Dybell, Kopps, McCure, Mewis, Rensen and Yeoward, stemming respectively from Theobald, Jacob, Ivor, Bartholomew, Lawrence and Ewart.

The names coming from a locality are generally self-explanatory and refer to the habitation of a holder, or the village, town or county from which he came. The complications arise from the use of dialect, misspellings and misunderstandings by bureaucrats, and by generations of mispronunciation and the use of local accents.

Occupational names are often a very reflection of history, in the way in which they record trades and customs long since gone. Similarly names derived from nicknames tell us a great deal about the communities in which these became fixed surnames for families, after one individual villager had been thus 'christened' by his peers.

## SWANLEY, Kent

Two ecclesiastical districts and village, in north-west Kent.
In front of parish church of St Mary the Virgin.
War memorial of Angel of Victory, flourishing sword and wreath.

### TO THE GLORY OF GOD AND IN GRATEFUL MEMORY OF THE MEN OF SWANLEY WHO LAID DOWN THEIR LIVES IN THE GREAT WAR 1914–1918

| | | | |
|---|---|---|---|
| F. | ALEXANDER | R.C. | DARLEY |
| E.W. | AUSTIN | E. | DAVITT |
| T.H. | AUSTIN | H. | DRURY |
| J.W. | BARRELL | H. | EDGINTON |
| F.W. | BASCOMBE | H. | FITZ |
| J.A. | BATES | G. | GAMMON |
| W.C.A. | BATES | B. | GEDGE |
| A.W. | BENNETT | J. | GEDGE |
| E. | BOOKER | P. | GEDGE |
| A. | BOWLES | H.H. | GRAHAM |
| C.P. | BRAUND | W. | GREEN |
| E. | BRIDGES | W.D. | GRIGGS |
| E.W. | BRIGDEN | S. | GROOMBRIDGE |
| A. | BROAD | J.C. | HAMMOND |
| W. | BROOK | T. | HILLS |
| A.H. | BROOKS | W.I. | HOGBEN |
| H. | BRYANT | F.T. | HOLMES |
| W.J. | BUTLER | W. | JACKSON |
| R. | CARCARY | E. | JEFFREY |
| J.K. | CHITTY | J.F.C. | JESSUP |
| L.W. | CHITTY | G.W. | JOHNSON |
| H.T. | COLLINS | E.W. | KEMSLEY |
| J.H. | COOPER | H. | KILLICK |

| | |
|---|---|
| A. COUSINS | W.G. LAMBKIN |
| A.L. DAFFERN | J.T. LAWSON |
| R.L. DALLEN | J.R. LAWSON |
| S. DALTON | L.R. MACE |
| | |
| H. MARTIN | F.C. SELVAGE |
| F. MASTERS | A.W. SHAW |
| H. MASTERS | H.J. SHAXTED |
| R.C. MILES | C. SMYTHE |
| R.C. MILLS | W. SPOONER |
| R.H. MILLS | E. STEVENS |
| W.H. MILLS | J. STYLES |
| W.L. MILLS | C. SUTTON |
| J.C. MOFFATT | W. SUTTON |
| A.E. MOODY | R. SYKES |
| T.W. MOORE | C.W. TALLETT |
| J.R. MURLESS | C. TAYLOR |
| W. NICKELLS | G. TUCKER |
| H.W. OSBORNE | F. TURNER |
| W. OSBORNE | F.T. TURNER |
| F.E. PALMER | A.W. TYLER |
| H.T. PERRIN | H.V. VERRELL |
| W.C.J. PLUMB | H. VINALL |
| A.S. PRALL | E. WELLARD |
| H.E. RANDALL | E. WELLER |
| F. ROBERTS | E.G. WHARTON |
| T. ROBINSON | E.E. WHITE |
| R. ROCHESTER | H. WHITE |
| F.J. ROGERS | R. WHITEHEAD |
| H. ROOTS | T.W. WHITEHEAD |
| R.C.B. RUDD | T.H. WICKENDEN |
| F.A. SAKER | J. WILLIAMS |
| W. SEARLES | C.J. WOODGATE |

On the war memorial in front of the parish church of St Mary in Swanley, Cottle's four categories of names account for over ninety per cent of those listed. Some fall into two or more categories, with those deriving from a nickname the most interesting – and revealing.

In terms of *first, personal or given names* the Swanley list has: Alexander, Austin, Bates, Bennett, Braund, Bryant, Collins, Davitt, Griggs, Hammond, Jackson, Jeffrey, Jessup, Johnson, Lawson, Mace, Martin, Miles, Moore, Nickells, Osborne, Perrin, Randall, Roberts, Robinson, Rogers, Searles, Stevens and Williams (29).

Names which stem from a *locality or habitation* are equally numerous: Bascombe, Bridges, Brigden, Brook, Carcary, Chitty, Dallen, Dalton,

Darley, Edginton, Graham, Green, Groombridge, Hills, Holmes, Kemsley, Mills, Moffatt, (Moore), Prall, Rochester, Shaw, Styles, Sutton, Sykes, Wellard, Weller, Wharton, Wickenden and Woodgate (29). (Chitty, which also qualifies as one of the nickname category, is a locality in Kent, as are Kemsley and, of course, Rochester.)

As always, there are a fair number of *occupational* names: Barrell, Booker, Bowles, Butler, Cooper, Masters, (Miles, Palmer), Plumb, Saker, Smythe, Spooner, Taylor, Tucker, Turner and Tyler (14).

Barrell could come from the trade of cooper or barrel-maker but also originates as a nickname for a fat man shaped like a barrel or a sozzled one who has over-indulged in its contents. Miles might be from the Latin for soldier but more probably belongs among the personal names, coming from the Germanic Milo or even the French Mihel.

A spooner was a man who covered a roof in wooden shingles; a saker a maker of sacks or bags; a tucker was a fuller; and a turner (the twenty-third most common name in England and the thirtieth in the USA) one who made small items out of wood, bone or metal turned on a lathe.

Names deriving from *nicknames* or descriptions are much more fun: (Barrell), Broad, (Chitty), Cousins, Drury, Fitz, Gammon, Gedge, Hogben, Lambkin, Moody, Palmer, Roots, Rudd, Selvage, White and Whitehead (15).

'Cousin' in Shakespeare's time had a general meaning of kinsman or relative, often used when claiming a relationship with someone higher up the social scale than oneself. Hence puns on 'cozening' (cheating) for the confidence trickster who often used the term cousin, as the Oxford *Dictionary of Surnames* puts it, to invoke a spurious familiarity.

Hogben is apparently a peculiarly Kentish nickname for someone with a crippled or deformed hip, from the Middle English huckbone, hip bone.

Gedge is an East Anglian nickname for a loose or flighty girl, or for an awkward or boorish man; while Roots describes a cheerful person, from the Middle English 'rote' (glad), or alternatively a player on the rote, a medieval stringed instrument.

Without labouring the point, every single town or village war memorial constitutes a lead into a study of British social history.

Studying the Swanley war memorial, using only the few books of reference mentioned in the bibliography for this chapter, accounts for almost all the ninety-four different names appearing. The few exceptions, probably obvious to a trained surname-researcher, but which I miss, include Daffern, Murless (Muro = wall), Tallett, Verrell (Barrell again ?) and Vinall (possibly 'of the vine').

From my own service days I traced Killick, described by the Oxford

*Dictionary of Surnames* as 'a south-east English name of unknown origin, apparently not a habitation name'. It comes from a nautical term for a heavy stone used on small vessels as an anchor. Which in its turn became a word for the anchor itself, and hence the naval slang for a leading seaman, who wears an anchor on his sleeve.

The Christian, first or personal names appearing on war memorials are often worth studying for the clues they give about those commemorated. In some cases, these provide evidence of the religious affiliation of a village or district, or an individual.

A Jewish first name, coupled with a Jewish surname, should confirm an ethnic affiliation, where surnames alone are not as conclusive. Biblical names often testify to strong evangelical or denominational commitment in a parish or district. Thus the appearance of, say, Elijah, Elisha, Enoch and similar on a memorial will almost certainly testify to Puritan or Dissenting opinion in the district.

Of course, a great proportion of war memorials carry only initials; others may register only a single first name for each individual, irrespective of how many he may have been given at birth. Sometimes, in a long list of Christian names, one individual will appear with only his initials. Unless one delves deeper, one will never know if this was because he was known only by his initials, as 'J.B.' or 'H', or because he was merely a name on a casualty list to those organizing the inscriptions, with no Christian name available.

On some memorials where initials only are used, Christian names are given only when there is a need to distinguish between say, Ralph and Robert Gilbertson, both private soldiers in the King's Own Scottish Borderers (Dumfries) or between Alfred, Arthur and Augustus Smith, all three Private A. Smiths of the 1/5 Gloucester Regiment (Gloucester). The case of a father and son with the same names is often resolved by adding 'Senior' and 'Junior' to the names.

*The Guinness Book of Names* by Leslie Dunkling carries a selection of lists of the 'Top 50 First Names for Boys' in England and Wales over the last century and a half.

The list for boys born in 1900, which I worked with, as being the nearest date of birth in the Guinness book for many of those appearing on 1914–18 war memorials, shows little variation at the top between the preceding lists for 1838, 1850 and 1875. William heads all four lists, with John in second place each time. With very minor variations in order, after William and John the Top Ten generally include George, Thomas, James and Charles. Four names which appear in the 1900 Top Ten are Frederick, Arthur, Albert and Ernest. These had occupied lower placings in 1850 and, except for Frederick (relegated to a lowly no.47), had disappeared completely from even the Top 50 by 1950.

Biblical names suffer fairly strong variations in popularity. Included in the 1900 Top 50 are Joseph, Samuel and Benjamin; by 1950 only Joseph scrapes in, at an equal fiftieth.

The British have of late regarded using family names as a Christian or first name as a rather quaint transatlantic custom, but we should not forget just how many English Christian names also derive directly from aristocratic surnames. In our 1900 list are Sidney, Percy, Stanley, Cecil and Clifford. This is true too of Scotland, with such family names as Blair, Bruce, Cameron, Campbell, Douglas, Forbes, Farquhar, Gillespie and Gordon, and on to Scott, Sinclair and Stuart or Stewart, all appearing as first names as well as surnames.

1914–18 was, of course, too early for any names popularized by films to be in use, but by 1939–45 there are several such names. Nowadays we too accept the American practice of using surnames as first names – in cases such as Darren, Dean, Gary, Lee and Wayne, as well as names of literary and show-business personalities: Ellery, Elroy, Elton, Elvis.

The only two hero-worship names in 1900 just scrape into the Top 50: Baden as an equal no.48, and Redvers equal last at no.50. Baden recognizes the heroism of the then Colonel Baden-Powell who had defended Mafeking in the Boer War; while Redvers was a tribute to Sir Redvers Buller, who commanded the British forces in the war in South Africa. Whereas Baden retained some popularity after 1900, as a result of Baden-Powell's founding of the Boy Scout movement in 1908, Redvers hardly survived the decease of General Buller in that same year. The exception was its continuing use as a traditional family first name.

One can sometimes trace apparent local preferences in the spelling of Christian names: Sidney or Sydney, Wilfred or Wilfrid, Frederic or Frederick, and so on. Sometimes the choice seems to be at the arbitrary whim of the war memorial committee. There are often conflicts with the spelling appearing in *Soldiers Died* ..., though whether the book is correct, as a result of being based on official Army records, or is wrong, as a result of poor handwriting by an Army clerk or misheard dictation, will probably never be known.

Another point about Christian names on war memorials is whether they record nicknames or shortened versions, such as Tom, Dick and Harry, or Bill and Ben. In many cases we see 'Alex.' or 'Doug.' appearing. Has the name been shortened because this particular Alexander or Douglas was actually always known as Alex or Doug or because the abbreviation fits better into the typographical layout of letters? Can 'Don' be always taken as a simple abbreviation of Donald, or were the six Dons appearing on the war memorial at Dunnet, Caithness, all known by the shortened version locally?

When we see Bert, is it short for Albert or was he actually christened thus? Is Bertie a family pet name for an Albert or derived from Herbert or even Bertram? Some memorials, especially pre-1914 ones, favour 'Jno' as an abbreviation for John, which hardly seems worth doing to save one letter, though it serves to bring the Johns into line with all the other names on a memorial which are abbreviated: Chas., Edw., Geo., Hy., Jas. and Wm.

Why do some memorials choose to put the Christian name or names *after* the surname? Sometimes the officers are given their ranks and Christian names first, while this is reversed for other ranks. As in almost everything else about our war memorials, there is no obvious pattern or reason for it.

In most cases, although the 'style' of presentation of the 1914–18 names is followed by a similar style for 1939–45, there are many exceptions even to this rule. Not only are some of the additions for the Second World War more democratic, being ordered alphabetically by name and not decided by rank, but you will also find cases where instead of Christian names only initials are given, and vice-versa.

The Top Fifty First Names for Boys (**1900**)

| | | | |
|---|---|---|---|
| 1. | William | 26. | Stanley |
| 2. | John | 27. | Reginald |
| 3. | George | 28. | Francis |
| 4. | Thomas | 29. | Fred |
| 5. | Charles | 30. | Cecil |
| 6. | Frederick | 31. | Wilfred |
| 7. | Arthur | 32. | Horace |
| 8. | James | 33. | Cyril |
| 9. | Albert | 34. | David |
| 10. | Ernest | | Norman |
| 11. | Robert | 36. | Eric |
| 12. | Henry | 37. | Victor |
| 13. | Alfred | 38. | Edgar |
| 14. | Sidney | 39. | Leslie |
| 15. | Joseph | 40. | Bertie |
| 16. | Harold | | Edwin |
| | Harry | 42. | Donald |
| 18. | Frank | 43. | Benjamin |
| 19. | Walter | | Hector |
| 20. | Herbert | | Jack |
| 21. | Edward | | Percival |
| 22. | Percy | 47. | Clifford |
| 23. | Richard | 48. | Alexander |
| 24. | Samuel | | Baden |
| 25. | Leonard | 50. | Bernard |
| | | | Redvers |

How well does the Guinness list for the popularity of Christian names in England compare with those on some war memorials? Sampling just three, it proves very accurate.

At Guiseley, in the West Riding of Yorkshire, there are eleven Williams and eight Johns. Except for a singleton Charles and three Fredericks, all the Guinness Top Ten number five or more. The Guinness pattern holds good in Guiseley down to about position no. 30 (though there is no Harold, Walter, Stanley or Francis). Thereafter, as one might expect, the remaining twenty places are more haphazard, and there are a couple of dozen names outside the Top 50. These include some more names of biblical origin (Caleb, Ebenezer, Enos, Jesse, Jonathan and Joshua) and some Scottish ones (Hugh, Graham, Malcolm, Ninian, Stewart).

At Chalfont St Giles, Bucks., William again heads the list, with all but Thomas from the Top Ten represented among a much smaller total than at Guiseley. An Archibald, a Ronald and a Vincent appear, who are not in the Top 50 for 1900.

At Uttoxeter, Staffs., the 1900 list quoted in the Guinness book is again very accurate. This time there are twenty-four Williams and ten Johns, and with the exception of only two Walters at no. 19, there are at least three of every single name down to Edward at no. 21. No particularly rare first names at Uttoxeter, except for Nelson, Sampson – and a Christine.

It is perhaps interesting to note that there is not a Donald on any of these three memorials, though Donald is at no. 42 in terms of popularity. This is, of course, different north of the border.

But where indeed *are* the Donalds? The Guinness list is for England and Wales, so that to appear even at no. 42 would suggest some usage in the south. Yet, looking at 1914–18 memorials on which Christian names are given, we find none at Benson, Brize Norton, Burford, Chalgrove, Clifton Hampden, Dorchester, Duns Tew or Eynsham (Oxon), and not a Donald at Hazlemere, Holmer Green, Horton, The Lee, Little Brickhill and so on (Bucks.).

Moving up through Britain, no 1914–18 Donalds at Colsterworth, Kirton-in-Lindsey, Rippingale (Lincs.); none at Abbots Bromley, Alrewas, Audley, Brereton (Staffs.); nor at Breedon-on-the-Hill, Great Dalby, (Leics.); or Crick, Gretton, Yelvertoft (Northants); nor again at Elvaston, Grindleford, Matlock Bath (Derbys.)

Obviously there might be Donalds hidden in those war memorials that give only initials, but we still find none at Samlesbury (Lancs.), nor at Boroughbridge, Gargrave, Greengates or Guiseley (Yorks.). The great long list at Berwick-on-Tweed has a scattering of the initial D among them, but there are no Donalds spelled out at Muncaster, Newton

Arlosh or Plumpton (Cumbria), nor at Birtley, Corsenside, (Northumb.), nor again Grasmere, Kirkby Lonsdale (Westmorland).

But what surprised me even more, once I began my search for Donalds, was how equally rare the name is in the Borders of Scotland. Among the 212 men of the King's Own Scottish Borderers listed at Dumfries is a lone Private Donald McNaught. None at Annan, Canonbie, Dornoch, Dunscore, Ecclefechan, Gretna or Lockerbie. There is a Lance-Corporal Donald McNaughton of the Black Watch at Tinwald, but in neighbouring Kirkcudbrightshire not a Donald at Castle Douglas, Corsock, Dalry; and the name seems equally rare in Peeblesshire, Roxburgh, North Berwickshire and so on.

It is only when we begin to get up into Campbell and McDonald country in Argyllshire, or deep into the Highlands and Islands proper, that Donald comes into its own as a first name. Donald is very much a Sutherland name, used by Sutherlands and Mackays; and also in Caithness among Dunnets, Gunns and Oags. It appears regularly in Ross & Cromarty, and in Inverness-shire.

One should not make heavy weather of such findings, except as an illustration of how war memorials can serve as a primary source for research and examination of theories about names, population movements and other genealogical and sociological matters.

It has been suggested, as no more than a rough rule-of-thumb, that the more aristocratic a soldier was, the more Christian names he was likely to have. Detailed examination of the officer casualty lists of the more exclusive cavalry regiments or of the Eton roll of honour only partially bears this theory out. Certainly very few of those appearing in the above categories had a *single* Christian name, but most seem to have had two rather than three. In many cases, the second or third name was a family name, rather than the kind of royal sequence borne by the late Duke of Windsor: Edward Albert Christian George Andrew Patrick David.

Looking at those killed in the First World War while with the Royal Horse Guards (The Blues) we find the following Christian names:

| | |
|---|---|
| George | Francis |
| Geoffrey Vaux Salvin | Angus Alexander |
| Harold Ernest | George Vyvyan |
| W. Laurence | Colwyn Erasmus Arnold |
| Spencer Douglas | Guy Harper |
| Henry William | Richard Lander |
| Thomas Gordon | Leonard Arthur |
| Algernon Henry Charles | Albert Edward Charles Robert |
| Percy Voltelin | Gordon Chesney |
| Guy Ferguson | Herbert Hayden |
| Charles John Alton Chetwynd | Charles Sackville |

Thus in a total of twenty-two names we find two with four Christian names, three with three each, the great bulk of the Royal Horse Guard officers with two names and (according to *Officers Died ...*) only two blessed with but a single Christian name. One must sound the usual note of caution here, for this single source may not be accurate. Brigadier-General Lord George Binning and Second Lieutenant The Hon. Francis Lambton may have had other names not recorded here.)

Choosing a random page from *List of Etonians Who Fought in the Great War 1914–1919*, and not counting members of the peerage (whom this list allows no Christian names), of the twenty-two names on that page, five have three Christian names, sixteen have two, and one has only one.

Plus three or more initials on a World War I memorial often indicates an officer or a member of the richer classes, but not necessarily so.

The origin of the Christian names of England, and those of Ireland, Scotland and Wales, deserves far greater study than is given here.

I mentioned earlier the use of names from the Bible, which might testify to a Jewish soldier or perhaps more often to a Puritan or Dissenting tradition in the district where the memorial is situated. But why not test out some of these theories on a few war memorials of your choice? Compare the popularity of names; look for biblical or other names with clear linguistic origins; and check on the use of surnames as first names. Another comparison might be between the Christian names of the Great War dead and those for 1939–45.

*The Oxford Dictionary of English Christian Names* by E.G. Withycombe (who does not declare his or her Christian names) provides a good introduction to the subject.

We see just how great our debt to the Bible is, both from the original Hebrew and its later translations and modifications into Greek and Latin. From Bartholomew and Benjamin through Ebenezer and Ezekiel – and all the Js such as Jacob, James, Jeremy, Jonathan, Joseph, Josiah and Jude – we carry on to Zachary and Zedekiah.

But our 'Christian' names derive from many other traditions: early Celtic, Old English, Old German, Norse and Norman. From the Celtic we get Aidan, Barry, Brian, Colin and so on; from Old English the many stemming from the roots 'ed' (rich, happy) and 'os' (god) such as Edgar, Edmond, Edward, Edwin and Osbert, Osborn, Oscar, Oswald, Oswin, as well as the more recognizable Ethelbert and Etheldred. The Oxford *Dictionary* traces those coming from Old German (Baldwin, Bernard, Bertram, Ernest, Everard); from the Norse (Eric, Olaf) and Norman (Jocelyn); from the Latin (Julian, Julius, Justin), the Greek (Basil, Eugene) and the French (Oliver). To these we must add saints' names (Quentin) and Christian names deriving from places (Beverley, Rodney) and people (Winston).

War memorials also highlight the fact that some Christian names are used for both men and women, with fashions which change over the years. Among them are Evelyn, Jocelyn, Noel, Robin and Shirley.

The introduction to *The Oxford Dictionary of English Christian Names* is also valuable for its comments on the use of two or more Christian names, the revival of obsolete names, practices in other countries where the naming of children is prescribed by law, and our own modern eclecticism where Christian names are concerned. Future social historians will have to cope with children given the eleven names of a football team or the four names of a pop group.

We ascribe some of the changes seen today to the Americans, but it is perhaps interesting to note that the Christian names on the Eagle Squadron memorial in Grosvenor Square, opposite the American Embassy in London, are heavily traditional: William, John, George, Thomas, James. Only a few (Fuller, Hillard, Hiram, Newton, Virgil) sound transatlantic. Perhaps these American volunteers who flew with the RAF in advance of their country's entering the last war were, as their Christian names on the memorial suggest, more discernibly anglophile?

Finally, a reminder about the importance of Christian names. The Established Church recognizes only the names given in baptism; the law accepts that the Christian name as well as the surname is part of an individual's legal description. Royalty signs its decrees with a 'George Rex' or 'Elizabeth Regina', and a bishop uses his Christian name and the name of his diocese to identify himself and sign as Hugh Birmingham or John Bath and Wells.

Christian names on war memorials help identify the origin of individuals:

| | |
|---|---|
| Daffyd | JONES |
| Donald | McDONALD |
| Seamus | O'DONOGHUE |
| Bertie | SMITH |

# 5 Age

They shall grow not old, as we that are left grow old;
Age shall not weary them, nor the years condemn.
'For The Fallen', September 1915 Laurence Binyon

Recording the age of the deceased has been traditional for many centuries. Look at the tombstones in any churchyard, and the ages of those buried there are generally spelled out, though sometimes the tombstones simply carry the dates of birth and death.

It is a strong human instinct to want to know the age at which someone died, as any reader of newspaper obituaries will confirm. One relates it automatically to oneself, feeling that the person in question has died needlessly young (if younger than oneself) or in the fullness of years (if comfortably older than oneself). The age of death is seen as significant when it is shockingly early, as in the deaths of children or those 'cut off in their prime', or alternatively when it greatly exceeds the traditional biblical life expectancy – 'three score years and ten'.

This concern with age is strongly reflected in almost all the memorial plaques found in churches, and in their rolls of honour. It is rarer to find on the outdoor war memorials in villages and towns, though when the ages of those commemorated *are* there, they are almost always of interest. After all, one of the first facts that journalists are taught to include in their stories is the subject's age. It provides an extra identifying handle for describing somebody, particularly when the age of the subject is relevant to the story being told. When ages are recorded on war memorials or on the rolls of honour in churches, or published in print, they are included to stress the sacrifice of youth. The age says that those honoured gave their lives when young, making the sacrifice that much greater.

A good example is that from the roll of honour in the parish church at Braughing, near Buntingford in Hertfordshire.

## BRAUGHING, East Hertfordshire
### 'As Gold in the Furnace Has He Tried Them and Received Them as a Burnt Offering'

Names of the Men from Braughing Parish who Died for their King and Country
**1914–1919**

Lieutenant Frederick LONGMAN
*Fell at Herlies, Northern France*
4th Royal Fusiliers
18 October 1914 (aged 24)

Private Frederick FURNEAUX
*Fell in Battle of Ypres*
4th Bedfordshire Regiment
19 April 1915 (aged 24)

Bombardier Thomas WRIGHT
*Died in England from an accident*
Royal Field Artillery
6 August 1915 (aged 26)

Lance Corporal John DICKERSON
*Fell at Loos, Northern France*
2nd Bedfordshire Regiment
25 September 1915 (aged 24)

Trooper Jack BALDWIN
*Died in England from an accident*
9th Lancers
28 September 1915 (aged 24)

Private Robert Arthur Cyril NASH
*Fell in Battle of the Somme*
8th Bedfordshire Regiment
15 September 1916 (aged 19)

Private Ramah DEVILLE
*Fell in France*
2nd Royal Berkshire Regiment
12 November 1916 (aged 32)

Private William HAMILTON
*Reported missing in France*
Gloucestershire Regiment
18 November 1916 (aged 39)

Private Frederick George BUNCE
*Fell in action in France*
13th Cheshire Regiment
10th June 1917 (aged 19)

Private Frederick WHYMAN
*Fell in action in France*
Royal Berkshire Regiment
31 July 1917 (aged 21)

Private Charles LEWIS
*Fell in action in France*
Royal Berkshire Regiment
11 August 1917 (21 that day)

Private William John SKIPP
*Fell in action in France*
Northumberland Fusiliers
16 August 1917 (aged 39)

Major Cecil Herbert SHEPHERD-CROSS
*Died of wounds received near Passchendaele Ridge*
Duke of Lancs. Own Yeomanry

15 October 1917 (aged 39)

Private Arthur SMITH
*Reported missing in France*
Royal West Kents
7 March 1917 (aged 29)

Private William Herbert COOK
*Reported missing in France*
West Yorks Regt.
9 October 1917 (aged 29)

Sergeant John William BALL
*Fell at Passchendaele*
6th Somersets
16 December 1917 (aged 31)

Private George Victor TAYLOR
*Died in hospital at Bradford*
1st Hertfordshire Regiment
4 January 1918 (aged 26)

Driver Robert ROGERS
4th Bedfordshire Regiment

| | |
|---|---|
| *Fell near Ypres* | 23 March 1918 (aged 24) |
| Trooper Alderman CLARK | 4th Dragoon Guards |
| *Died from wounds in France* | 28 March 1918 (aged 22) |
| Private Herbert Reginald PARKER | 2nd Middlesex Regiment |
| *Killed in France* | 24 April 1918 (aged 18) |
| Sapper Arthur John CANNON | Inland Water Transport RE |
| *Accidentally drowned* | 9 June 1918 (aged 24) |
| Private Charles COLLINS | 1st Herts |
| *Fell near Cambrai* | 4 September 1918 (aged 29) |

The Braughing list provides the social or military historian with useful evidence about the servicemen whose deaths are recorded. It is a fair guess that a 24-year-old full lieutenant killed in October 1914 would be a regular, especially if serving with a regular battalion. (The Royal Fusiliers was one of those five infantry regiments to have four regular line battalions, rather than the customary two.)

In fact, the military career of Lieutenant Frederick Longman is interestingly atypical. The second son of a publisher, C.J. Longman of Upp Hall, Braughing, he was born in 1890 and educated at Harrow and Pembroke College, Cambridge. He played football for Harrow and became a featherweight boxing champion in the army. Lieutenant Longman had been an enthusiastic member of his school corps and of the OTC at Cambridge, before being commissioned in the Hertfordshire Territorial Regiment. He recruited forty-one men in Braughing and taught them shooting at his local rifle club. In February 1912 he was gazetted a regular Second Lieutenant in the Royal Fusiliers, becoming a full lieutenant shortly after the declaration of war. Wounded in the arm at the Battle of the Marne, he spent a short time at a base hospital before rejoining his battalion, only to be killed in action on 18 October 1914.

Similarly, Private Nash, killed with the 8th Bedfords on the Somme in 1916, would almost certainly be a Kitchener volunteer, serving in a K3 battalion. Note the comment on Private Charles Lewis of the Royal Berks who fell in action on 31 July 1917 – '21 that day'.

One would expect the greatest proportion of all deaths to be in the age-range nineteen to thirty-nine, and so it is at Braughing. The only 18-year-old was killed late in the war, by which time the ban on sending men abroad before they were nineteen had ended.

One of the three 39-year-olds commemorated, Major Cecil Herbert Shepherd-Cross, of the Duke of Lancaster's Own Yeomanry, was a pre-war Territorial Force volunteer, with seniority as an Honorary Lieutenant in the Army dating back to August 1901. He also served on attachment with the Westmorland & Cumberland Yeomanry.

The Braughing roll of honour was presumably compiled very soon after the end of hostilities, all the deaths recorded having occurred before the

Armistice. This presumably accounts for the fact that three of the men (including one of the other 39-year-olds, Private Hamilton of the Gloucesters) are still described as 'Reported Missing in France'.

A village war memorial, as opposed to a church roll, which puts a strong emphasis on age is at Grindleford in North Derbyshire. Here the names of the dead are given, as at Braughing, in the order of date of death (except for two brothers listed together) but are prominently spelled out as part of the public memorial – so much so, that it almost constitutes a 'theme' on this particular war memorial, a theme possibly set by the first death in the village, that of 18-year-old Lieutenant John Wilmot Maynard.

Lieutenant Maynard was the younger son of Edmund Maynard JP of Hoon Ridge, Hilton, Derby, and of Margaret Blanche, daughter of Robert Sacheverell Wilmot-Sitwell of Stainsby House, Derbys. Born in 1896 and educated, like his father before him, at Harrow, he had been commissioned into the regular 3rd Battalion King's Royal Rifle Corps six months after his eighteenth birthday, and he was killed in action four months later, in Second Ypres on 24 April 1915.

Looking at the war memorial at Grindleford, in which the age figures so prominently, we see that this 1914–18 emphasis recurs for the Second World War additions underneath. However, the listing in order by date of death which applied in 1914–18 becomes straightforwardly alphabetical for 1939–45.

**GRINDLEFORD, North Derbyshire**
Two miles south-east of Hathersage.
Celtic cross in enclosure, on roadside green by B6001

**THEIR NAME LIVETH FOR EVERMORE**
Erected by Public Subscription
*To the Memory of Grindleford Men*
*Who Fell in the Great Wars*

**1914–1918   1939–1945**

| Lieutenant | John Wilmot MAYNARD | 24 April 1915 | aged 18 years |
|---|---|---|---|
| Sergeant | Randall COOPER | 1 July 1916 | aged 20 years |
| Private | Fred UTTLEY | 1 July 1916 | aged 22 years |
| Private | Joe HODGKINSON | 4 September 1916 | aged 21 years |
| Private | George HODGKINSON | 21 March 1918 | aged 20 years |
| Private | William Arthur KENYON | 31 July 1917 | aged 30 years |
| Private | Harry WHITE | 28 September 1917 | aged 19 years |
| Private | Frank PENNOCK | 11 November 1917 | aged 30 years |
| Captain | Frank Sydney HOLLAND | 27 November 1917 | aged 22 years |

| Signalman | John Clifford | PRIESTLEY | 29 November 1917 | aged 29 years |
| Private | William | PAGE | 19 March 1918 | aged 24 years |
| Gunner | Frederick Moor | BROCKSOPP | 21 March 1918 | aged 21 years |
| L/Corporal | William | TENNISWOOD | 17 May 1918 | aged 43 years |
| Private | John | DRONFIELD | 27 May 1918 | aged 18 years |
| Private | Luther | PRIESTLEY | 10 July 1918 | aged 20 years |
| Private | Frank | WESTBY | 11 August 1918 | aged 20 years |

### 1939–1945

| Corporal | Ernest Cecil | BARLEY | 11 October 1941 | aged 19 years |
| Midshipman | Robert Gordon | BOWER | 25 November 1943 | aged 18 years |
| Pilot Officer | Charles Trevor | DAVIS DFC | 26 March 1941 | aged 20 years |
| Lieutenant | Michael Harburn | DAVIS | October 1940 | aged 26 years |
| Gunner | Kenneth | FRENCH | 5 March 1943 | aged 20 years |
| Private | Peter Robert | KENYON | 31 August 1940 | aged 25 years |
| Staff Sgt | Charles Eggington | PENNOCK | 3 September 1942 | aged 26 years |
| Corporal | Frank Leslie | PENNOCK | 8 May 1941 | aged 28 years |
| Lieutenant | Henry Bonnington | RIDGEWAY | 3 August 1944 | aged 21 years |
| Sergeant | Leslie Leonard John | SMITH | 8 May 1944 | aged 20 years |
| Private | Walter | SMITH | 15 May 1945 | aged 19 years |
| A/Flt-Lieutenant | Ronald Victor | TRUEMAN | 24 July 1941 | aged 22 years |

Note the exception to the date-of-death order for the Hodgkinsons, presumably brothers, with the second moved up from 1918 to accompany Joe Hodgkinson killed in 1916. George Hodgkinson would have been a mere eighteen when his older brother was killed at twenty-one in 1916.

There is also an interesting contrast between the dead of the two wars in terms of rank. The great bulk of 1914-18 names – twelve out of sixteen – are private soldiers, whereas all but three of the twelve 1939–45 dead held higher ranks, five of them being commissioned.

The rules which stopped young soldiers being sent to France early in the First World War seemed not to apply to officers. Many managed to get commissioned at eighteen, or even earlier, and found themselves in France a few months later.

When war broke out, 17-year-old Ulric Nisbet decided not to go back to Marlborough but join up. He was turned down by his local Territorial battalion, already at full strength with 19-year-olds who could be sent overseas. But having been in his school OTC, he pulled strings and got a commission as a Special Reserve officer. He was commissioned on 15 August 1914 – one of the first new officers appointed after the start of the war, and at seventeen one of the youngest lieutenants in the Army. He would go into action two years later on the Somme and be wounded – still not yet nineteen. After recovering from his wound he was back in France in February 1917 and was shot in the shoulder by a sniper. This would prove a life-saving wound, for he did survive the war.

Obviously the major exceptions to any pattern of age at death are the most interesting. Many under-age youths did enlist in the forces, their true age often emerging only when they were killed. At the other end of the scale, many over-age veterans concealed their years in order to serve as front-line soldiers.

Proportional to the numbers involved, there were more under-eighteens killed in the Royal Navy and Merchant Marine than in the Army. Midshipmen and ratings in Boys' Service in the Royal Navy often died at fifteen or sixteen, cabin-boys and apprentices in the merchant service equally young.

At the start of the war, the regular army did not plan to send soldiers to France before they were twenty, and though the official starting-age was soon lowered, it was not till well on in the war, in the face of a shortage of manpower, that it was accepted that 18-year-olds could serve at the front.

The merchant service, incidentally, because it accepted under-aged and over-aged men who could not gain entry to the forces, often put its own experienced sailors under additional strain as a result.

The youngest Victoria Cross of the Great War was Boy (First Class) John Travers Cornwell, who was awarded the VC for bravery when HMS *Chester* was hit at Jutland on 31 May 1916 and who died of his wounds two days later. He was 16½.

A plaque in Ferring parish church, near Worthing, Sussex, records the death of Midshipman Philip Sadler Candy, lost with all those aboard HMS *Monmouth* at the Battle of Coronel off Chile on 1 November 1914. He was 15½.

When the battleship HMS *Goliath* was sunk by a torpedo from a Turkish destroyer in the Dardanelles on 12 May 1915, among those who died was Midshipman Torquil Harry Lionel Macleod, son of Roderick Willoughby Macleod of Invergordon Castle on the Cromarty Firth, who had joined HMS *Goliath* as a naval cadet on 1 August 1914. He too was 15½ when he died.

Returning to the Army and studying the *Craven Roll of Honour* of the men from Skipton and District (Yorks.), the youngest name appearing is that of 16-year-old Private W. Brayshay of Bradley in the West Yorks Regiment; the oldest there is of 55-year-old Sergeant James Preston, originally of Gargrave but losing his life with the New Zealand Forces.

The differing call-up and volunteering systems which applied in the Regular Army, the Territorial Force and Kitchener's Army, did result in strange anomalies. The recall of all registered reservists when war was first declared had its drawback in terms of age. Some of those called to rejoin the 1st Gordon Highlanders on mobilization had served with the regiment in Egypt as far back as the Battle of Tel-el-Kebir in 1882, which meant they were probably well into their fifties by 1914.

As the war went on, the Army found ways of using its older men: in Garrison Battalions, which could be sent abroad to India and elsewhere, to relieve other units for active service; in Labour Battalions for use on lines-of-communication work behind the front; and in Home Service and Royal Defence Force battalions in Britain – for until the very end of the war it was thought Germany might invade to break the stalemate on the Western Front or at least stage large-scale raids to lower morale.

Some of these patterns can be seen by studying the names and details of those buried in British cemeteries. Those buried at home include not only front-line soldiers who died of wounds in nearby hospitals but also many others killed in accidents while training or while ferrying supplies to the docks, and inevitably a proportion of servicemen who died of natural causes while in uniform. Many others died during the great influenza epidemic which hit Britain and much of the rest of the world in 1918 and 1919.

The standard home cemetery war memorial – with the Cross of Sacrifice and its sword – is common to most home cemeteries as well as the War Graves Commission ones overseas. On a panel or wall behind the cross are listed the names and initials, rank and number, date of death and, where known, the age of the deceased. A typical 1914–18 list is that at Willesden in North London.

### WILLESDEN CEMETERY
Traditional war memorial Cross of Sacrifice
A wall with seven plaques, the central one being 1939–45.

#### 'Their Name Liveth For Evermore'

| Rifleman | W. ADAMS | London Rifle Brigade |
|---|---|---|
| 1684 | | 16 August 1916 (33) |
| Gunner | W.A. ALDEN | Royal Field Artillery |
| 17657 | | 1 December 1915 |
| Driver | A. ATKINSON | Royal Field Artillery |
| 120628 | | 6 March 1918 |
| Private | B.C. BALL | Royal Defence Corps |
| 28455 | | 26 February 1919 |
| Private | W.E. BARDELL | Royal Fusiliers |
| G/68101 | | 12 November 1918 (32) |
| Private | S.W. BARKER | Royal Marine Light Infantry |
| CH/11035 | | 28 October 1914 (36) |
| Private | C.J. BARRITT | Middlesex Regiment |
| G/34485 | | 12 May 1918 (27) |

|  |  |  |  |  |
|---|---|---|---|---|
| Private | L/9607 | A. | BICKERSTAFF | Royal Fusiliers 11 July 1916 |
| Private | 11926 | A.H.A. | BILLINGS | Middlesex Regiment 27 November 1916 |
| Private | 494712 | W.A. | BULPIT | 13th Kensington Bn Londons 28 February 1920 |
| Private | 046166 | H. | BUTLER | Royal Army Service Corps 20 April 1920 (40) |
| 1st Air Mechanic | 48783 | H.S. | CHARLTON | Royal Air Force 8 November 1918 (42) |
| Private | T/1027 | A.R. | CLARK | Middlesex Regiment 8 October 1914 |
| Private | M/395578 | H. | COLE | Royal Army Service Corps 15 December 1918 (24) |
| Private | G/27416 | D.J. | COLLIS | Middlesex Regiment 16 February 1917 |
| Private | 82902 | H.P. | COOPER | The Queen's 14 October 1920 (20) |
| Corporal | 243108 | C.E. | COPE MM | Norfolk Regiment 22 October 1918 (19) |
| Corporal | 0229 | C.N. | DE FRAINE | East Yorks 22 August 1916 (26) |
| Private | 742387 | W. | ESTAFFE | 15th Bn Canadian Infantry 31 January 1919 (33) |
| Corporal | S/5097 | A.E. | FARRANT | Rifle Brigade 7 January 1918 |
| Sapper | 159602 | J.C. | FRYATT | Royal Engineers 16 February 1919 |
| Private | T4/083766 | J. | GILLING | Royal Army Service Corps 5 December 1916 |
| Private | 39144 | W. | GOSSOP | Northumberland Fusiliers 27 December 1916 |
| Serjeant | 204437 | C. | HEARSEY | Royal Air Force 10 August 1919 (38) |
| Gunner | 30888 | R.A. | HILL | Royal Field Artillery 12 December 1918 (33) |
| Driver | T2/11341 | H.E. | HOUGHTON | Royal Army Service Corps 21 February 1918 (38) |
| Pioneer | 604886 | C. | JACKSON | Royal Engineers 1 January 1921 |
| Sapper | 32821 | T. | JEFFRIES | Royal Engineers 22 April 1918 (28) |
| Private | 7714 | A.E. | JONES | Norfolk Regiment 3 November 1918 |

|  | |  |  |
|---|---|---|---|
| Private | G/11251 | G.W. KEMP | Royal Sussex<br>8 April 1917 (21) |
| Private | 309984 | J.L. KING | Tank Corps<br>5 October 1918 |
| Private | 781490 | M. LAWRENCE | 29th Bn City of London<br>2 October 1918 (25) |
| Rifleman | 325388 | W.A. MIDSON | City of London Rifles<br>30 November 1918 (18) |
| 2nd Private | 1850552 | J. MILEHAM | Royal Air Force<br>22 December 1918 |
| Lance-Corporal | 215657 | F.W. OVEN | Royal Engineers<br>16 March 1917 |
| Private | 3284 | W. PEART | Middlesex Regiment<br>30 December 1915 |
| Sailmaker RN | 172065 | H.W. PHILLIPS | HMS Pembroke<br>11 October 1916 |
| Private | 13689 | E. PRESTON | Middlesex Regiment<br>8 June 1916 (23) |
| Private | 3048 | J.E. ROBINSON | Royal Fusiliers<br>29 August 1916 |
| Private | PO/8968 | H.J. SMITH | Royal Marine Light<br>Infantry<br>12 January 1916 |
| Gunner | 6035 | W.E. STEVENS | Royal Garrison Artillery<br>21 May 1917 |
| Private | L/12330 | J. STILES | Middlesex Regiment<br>16 March 1919 |
| Lance-Serjeant | 9495 | J. TEMPLETON | Northumberland<br>Fusiliers<br>30 April 1915 |
| Driver | 84476 | W.J. THOMPSON | Royal Field Artillery<br>5 December 1918 (35) |
| Able Seaman RN | J/76350 | F. WELLER | HMS Cinceria<br>19 February 1919 |
| Gunner | 82204 | H.J. WEST | Royal Field Artillery<br>17 October 1916 (28) |
| Lance-Corporal | 579729 | J. WESTHALL | Labour Corps (& Q.V.R.)<br>12 March 1919 (32) |
| Private | G/8624 | E.E. WHITE | East Kents (The Buffs)<br>7 August 1916 |
| Private | 205052 | W. WHYATT | Seaforth Highlanders<br>21 November 1919 (28) |
| Air Mechanic | 159859 | E. WOODBRIDGE | Royal Air Force<br>14 September 1918 (17) |
| Engineman RNR | 1045/ES | W.J. WOODLEY | HMS Pekin<br>13 January 1918 |

[added in cement]

| Private | B. BUSH | Middlesex 3 November 191 |
| Private | G. TAYLOR | Middlesex 18 November 19 |
| Serjeant | T.M. JENKINS | Royal Welch Fusiliers |

Volume I of *The All Ranks Roll of Honour* is an expensively bound book, containing, as its frontispiece tells us, 'A Biographical Record of All Members of His Majesty's Naval and Military Forces Who have Fallen in the War'. Edited by the Marquis of Ruvigny, this first volume was published in December 1916 and contains 8,000 names and 2,500 portraits. They are mainly of those killed in the first year of the war, though some are added from the volumes planned for later years, in order to place them with relatives. It makes fascinating reading, particularly on the subject of age.

We find here, for instance, the story of Frederick John Sheppee, born in London and educated at Emanuel School, Wandsworth Common, who was killed in action with the Australian forces at Gallipoli in August 1915. Sheppee was in New Zealand when war broke out but when he tried to enlist there was refused as over-age, having been born on 25 April 1873 and thus being forty-one. Nothing daunted, Fred Sheppee took himself to Australia and under the alias Frederick Johnson joined the 2nd (New South Wales) Battalion of Australian Infantry. Wounded in the landing at Gallipoli on 25 April 1915 (his forty-second birthday), he spent some time in hospital in Egypt, before returning to die at Gallipoli during the second week of August. In his same Australian battalion was 2251 Lance-Corporal John Auguste Emile Harris, also killed in action at Gallipoli. He was aged fifteen and ten months.

The two lines of poetry quoted at the beginning of this chapter, from Laurence Binyon's poem 'For the Fallen' – or the full four-line verse from which they come – appear on many war memorials throughout the country. The final line, 'We will remember them', is also used frequently and generally refers back to this poem, which was extremely well known at the time.

Laurence Binyon (1869–1943) served in the Red Cross in the 1914–18 war and went to the front with his unit. His wartime experiences are reflected in his better poetry. Most of his post-war work was at the British Museum, where he was the Keeper of Prints and Drawings, though he was also Professor of Poetry at Harvard for 1933–4.

'For The Fallen' consists of seven verses, and the poem as a whole – dare one say it? – is fairly pedestrian and very much in the Georgian tradition. One should note that it was written quite early on in the war

(September 1915). The fourth verse in particular caught the public imagination and is still read at many commemorative services, generally by the visiting dignitary, a service veteran or a young Territorial Army officer. At the end of the reading, the audience is expected to repeat the final words 'We will remember them', though as time goes on, fewer people witnessing the ceremony seem aware of this expected response.

> They shall grow not old, as we that are left grow old:
> Age shall not weary them, nor the years condemn.
> At the going down of the sun and in the morning
> We will remember them.

# 6  Rank and Number

Their Sun Went Down
While It Was Yet Day.

Talgarth, Brecon

If captured by the enemy, a soldier was instructed to give only his name, rank and number. This was thought sufficient to identify a prisoner without betraying any military information of use to the enemy, such as the unit or formation to which a man belonged.

It was never suggested during my own service that soldiers should disguise their rank when this did convey at least a clue to their unit. Private soldiers come in a multitude of species – rifleman, fusilier, guardsman, sapper, driver, gunner, trooper, marine, mountaineer – all of which point to a regiment or arm of service. The non-commissioned ranks of corporal and sergeant tend to be slightly more non-denominational, but it is obvious that bombardier, corporal-of-the-horse or pipe major still hint closely at particular regimental affiliations.

Many war memorials carry the army or service ranks of all those commemorated, instead of simply listing names and initials, and thus add a further distinguishing piece of information.

In terms of social history, when the ranks are given, we often find the names listed in an order of service seniority. This table of precedence is far less common for 1939–45, even where it may already have been used on that same memorial for 1914–18.

The separation of officers from the other ranks, and indeed in some cases the warrant officers and NCOs from the private soldiers, is an interesting social comment. Are those we mourn to be frozen forever into a military hierarchy, or should they all have been presented, in alphabetical order, equal in the eyes of God?

This is perhaps illustrated in cases where a village war memorial cross or cenotaph carries the names in order of rank, whereas the same names appear in a roll of honour inside the parish church simply in alphabetical order.

An example of this occurs at Penn, in Buckinghamshire, where, on a small green opposite the Crown public house, the war memorial lists the dead in strict seniority of rank, starting with Lieutenant-Colonel Hugh Hill MVO DSO, followed by Majors Spencer Britten and Arthur Henderson, then by a captain and three lieutenants. The remaining fifteen names on the war memorial at Penn are all private soldiers. In the adjoining Holy Trinity Church there is a roll of honour which lists the same twenty-two names alphabetically, with no ranks given. There Lt-Colonel Hugh Hill is listed alongside Private Harry Hill.

In passing, two points of interest about the Penn memorial. The proportion of seven officers to fifteen other ranks is high, though not exceptional in a rich rural area. It is interesting that not a single Penn soldier died holding any non-commissioned rank and that the three Privates Busby turn out to be brothers. A plaque inside the church tells us that the three Busbys were the sons of the Parish Clerk and were all killed within six months of each other.

The plaque reads:

> In Honoured Memory of
> Frederick, William and George,
> sons of Alfred BUSBY, Clerk of this Parish,
> and of Emma his wife.
>
> They voluntarily gave their services to their country in 1914
> and died for her in 1917
> Frederick
> In Salonica 24 April aged 24
> William
> In France 26 September aged 21
> George
> In France 19 August aged 19

On the memorial the three Busbys appear as Fred, Willie and George.

Some rolls of honour (generally in church, though occasionally on a war memorial) actually list all those who served, as well as noting the dead. In the parish church of St Mary Magdalene at Duns Tew, Oxon., in terms of rank we find a proportion of four officers and two NCOs out of the total of twenty-two who served. All four officers are Dashwoods, two second lieutenants being killed. Two of the Dashwoods, both the NCOs and four of the privates served in the county regiment, the Oxford & Bucks Light Infantry. Of the twenty-two men from Duns Tew, six were killed, three wounded and two more invalided out. Three of the privates are Gillams, two of whom died. (Gillam presumably comes from the French Guillaume – William.)

In the church at Horley, the first Oxfordshire village across the border from Warwickshire, in the north-west corner of the county, a plaque lists twelve dead. Second Lieutenant Richard Selby Lowndes Maul is the only officer, and he and four others are 'Oxford & Bucks'. There is only one name for 1939–45: Captain Richard Henry Lee Maul, Royal Marines, killed aboard HMS *Dunedin*.

Each community, or parish, or in some cases the major landowner decided on the 'style' of the war memorial, and very few regional patterns are discernible. In Oxfordshire and Buckinghamshire, the majority of the war memorials examined stick to names and initials, or full Christian names spelled out. Some add units, other ranks and units. A few give not only the rank and unit but the date and place of death overseas, as at Tadmarton, Oxon.

It is certainly impossible to discern any really consistent pattern across Britain for the use of ranks on war memorials, nor is there generally any common practice on a countywide or area basis.

The memorial books lodged in chapels of remembrance in garrison or depot towns are generally consistent in following hierarchical military patterns. War memorial crosses presented to the community by the squirearchy almost always list the names by order of rank. Exceptions must exist where the squire's son was not an officer when killed. Many who might have been expected to earn a commission because of education and training died in the early days of the war serving in the ranks of their Territorial Force units or with their friends in the Pals battalions. Sometimes one finds indications of status on private memorial panels inside the church, where a private soldier is commemorated and it is clear from the wording that his parents belonged to the landowning or professional classes.

If one is researching into the personal histories of the fallen, things are much easier if the individual is an officer, simply because of numbers. If officers died in a very rough ratio of 1:20 other ranks, they are obviously much easier to trace. Similarly the more senior an officer, the more likely he is to be mentioned in the *Official History*, which generally stops short of mentioning individuals below the rank of lieutenant-colonel, unless that person is commanding a battalion or winning a VC. In the *Official History*, majors who are acting as CO are given a name, while others of the same rank, almost irrespective of the part they play in the narrative, generally remain anonymous.

If one knows the regiment or corps involved, easily found in the wartime *Army Lists*, reading the HMSO publication *Officers Died ...* becomes immediately productive. You learn the full Christian names, rank held at the time of death (and its status: Temporary, Acting or Brevet) and the date and manner of death (killed in action or killed accidentally, died or died of wounds, or drowned). Thereafter, research becomes easier.

Thus at Appleby, Westmorland, the first name on the memorial is that of Lt-Colonel P.W. Machell CMG, DSO. No further details are given on the cross concerning regiment, date of death or exact manner of dying. In *The Official History of the Great War – Military Operations: France and Belgium 1916* (Volume I, p.401) we find that Lt-Colonel P.W. Machell died on the first day of the battle of the Somme, while commanding the 11th Battalion of the Border Regiment. This, we know from other sources, was a service battalion raised by the Earl of Lonsdale from the areas around Carlisle, Kendal and Workington, based on Penrith and known as the Lonsdale Battalion.

In *Kelly's Handbook* for 1929, we find full details of Colonel Machell's widow, Lady Valda, second daughter of the late Admiral HSH Prince Victor of Hohenlohe-Langenburg (Count Gleichen) RN, a nephew of Queen Victoria. Kelly's also tells us that in 1905 Lady Valda married Lt-Colonel Percy Wilfrid Machell CMG, DSO JP, of Crakenthorpe Hall, Westmorland (killed in action 1916). They had one son. Her address in 1929 was St James's Palace.

A whole family history emerges, if one then traces the record of Lady Valda's brother, Count Gleichen, a regular officer in the Grenadier Guards. He would end the war as Major-General Lord Edward Gleichen, having commanded 37 Division in 1915–16 before becoming the Director of the Intelligence Bureau, Department of Information, for the remaining two years of the war. He retired in 1919, aged fifty-six. An extra clue leading to a whole field of follow-up research emerges from that simple inclusion of the rank (and awards) on the Appleby memorial. We might ask ourselves more about Colonel Machell's home at Crakenthorpe Hall, or about the whole history of the family he married into. His wife's father, as mentioned, was a nephew of Queen Victoria, and her mother a sister of the fifth Marquess of Hertford. His brother-in-law had served as an equerry to the Prince of Wales (Edward VII) and later as an extra equerry to Queen Victoria, in the course of which service (1892–1901) he married one of Queen Victoria's maids of honour, the Hon. Sylvia G. Edwardes. Lt-Colonel Machell's death would have made an impact on royal circles, as well as on the squirearchy of what is now Cumbria.

'P.W. Machell' on the memorial would not have been as revealing.

For those who are well-informed about ranks, it is interesting to see on war memorials, particularly for the 1914–18 war, ranks and appointments that no longer exist. Many of these are, of course, connected with horses – such as Farrier, Shoeing-Smith and Saddler. Soon after the 1914–18 war, Brigadier-Generals would be replaced by the appointment of Brigadier, and Privates in the Guards Regiment became Guardsmen.

Brevet rank for officers is an interesting feature of these times and is sometimes noted on a war memorial. Brevet rank – one rank above that for which the officer was being paid – was given to officers as a reward for distinguished service and generally meant that the officer in question had been earmarked or was thought worthy of immediate promotion but that there was no vacancy for him at the time. Although it conferred seniority in that rank on the officer within the Army, it did not do so within his regiment. This sometimes led to a Brevet Lt-Colonel's having to serve as a company commander under a Lt-Colonel to whom he was senior in the army as a whole, but junior in regimental terms. After the war, when all officers reverted to their substantive rank and a strict *Army List* order of seniority, you might even have two Brevet Lt-Colonels, covered in decorations after four years in action, serving under a Major who had been captured in the first days of the retreat from Mons in 1914, who had spent the rest of the war as a prisoner but who emerged to take command as CO in 1919.

The film *Tunes of Glory*, starring Alec Guinness and John Mills, deals with a similar problem of regimental seniority and command, occurring in a Highland regiment after World War II.

### LAUDER, West Berwickshire
Solid war memorial, at road junction.

## ERECTED TO THE MEMORY OF THOSE
## FROM THE PARISH AND BURGH
## OF LAUDER
## WHO LAID DOWN THEIR LIVES FOR
## THEIR COUNTRY IN THE WAR OF 1914–1918.
*'Their names live for ever'*

| The Hon. A. | MAITLAND | Major | Camerons |
|---|---|---|---|
| Robert | LOGAN | 2/Lieutenant | KOSB |
| | | | |
| John | JOYCE | Lance-Sergeant | Royal Scots |
| William | ALLAN | Corporal | Gordons |
| James D. | BRUCE | Corporal | Army Service Corps |
| Alexander P. | KELLY | Corporal | Royal Socts |
| Robert | OLIVER | Corporal | Scottish Rifles |
| William | HALLIDAY | Lance-Corporal | HLI |
| William | LOCKIE | Lance-Corporal | Camerons |
| William | TODD | Lance-Corporal | KOSB |
| | | | |
| George | ANDERSON | Private | Gordons |
| Andrew | ANDERSON | Private | KOSB |

| | | | |
|---|---|---|---|
| Robert F. | ANDERSON | Private | Dragoon Guards |
| James | ANDERSON | Private | KOSB |
| William | BELL | Private | KOSB |
| John | BRODIE | Private | Australians |
| William | BROWN | Private | KOSB |
| Andrew | BRUCE | Sapper | Royal Engineers |
| George | BRUCE | Private | Scots Guards |
| Thomas | BRUCE | Private | Scots Guards |
| John | COLTHERD | Private | Camerons |
| Thomas R. | DICKSON | Private | Scots Guards |
| Adam | FLEMING | Private | KOSB |
| Andrew | GUTHRIE | Private | KOSB |
| John | GALBRAITH | Private | KOSB |
| George | HALLIDAY | Sapper | Royal Engineers |
| David | HARDIE | Private | A & SH |
| John | HOPKIRK | Private | KOSB |
| Alexander | HUNTER | Private | Canadians |
| William | HUNTER | Private | KOSB |
| Andrew | KELLY | Private | RSF |
| John | KINNON | Private | KOSB |
| James | LAIDLAW | Private | HLI |
| William | MAUCHLINE | Private | KOSB |
| William | MIDDLEMISS | Private | Royal Scots |
| Thomas | MOORE | Private | Canadians |
| Thomas | NISBET | Private | RAMC |
| William | NOBLE | Private | Rifle Brigade |
| Thomas | PATERSON | Private | Lancs Fusiliers |
| William | PATERSON | Private | KOSB |
| Robert H. | ROBERTSON | Private | KOSB |
| Alexander | RUTHERFORD | Private | KOSB |
| Adam Gunn | SCOTT | Private | KOSB |
| Armour | SCOTT | Sapper | Royal Engineers |
| Adam | SKELDON | Private | A & SH |
| James | STEVENSON | Private | KOSB |
| John | STUART | Private | Seaforths |
| John James | TODD | Private | Canadians |
| William | TORRIE | Private | Australians |
| George | WHITE | Private | KOSB |
| John | WHITE | Private | KOSB |
| James | WELSH | Private | KOSB |

## 1939–1945

| | | | |
|---|---|---|---|
| Donald A. | BAIRD | Lieutenant | RAMC |
| David | COLVILLE | Captain | KOSB |
| John | ELLIOT MC | Major | KOSB |
| Thomas Norman | ELLIOT | Able Seaman | RN |
| Gordon | HODGE | Sergeant | RAF |

| Viscount Oliver C. | MAITLAND | Lieutenant | Lothian & Border Horse |
|---|---|---|---|
| James | MERCER | Flight-Sergeant | RAF |
| Ian | MONRO | Private | Cameronians |
| George | McDOUGALL MC | Captain | Royal Engineers |
| Hector | McDONALD | CPO | Royal Navy |
| Thomas | REDPATH | Lance-Corporal | Royal Scots |
| George B. | REDPATH | Lance-Corporal | Royal Scots |
| Leslie | ROSS | Piper | KOSB |
| Robert | WATSON | Pilot Officer | RAF |

## ST BOSWELLS, Roxburghshire

Parish and village, on River Tweed.

### *'In Memory of the Men of St. Boswells Parish Who Fell in the Great War 1914–1918'*

| George | BALLOCH | Royal Field Artillery |
|---|---|---|
| Alexander | BELL | Lancers |
| John | BLAIN | KOSB |
| John | BROWN | KOSB |
| Andrew | CHARTERS MM | KOSB |
| William | GOW | HLI |
| Joseph D. | GRAHAM | Army Veterinary Corps |
| James | GRAY | Gordon Highlanders |
| James | GURNEY | Scots Guards |
| John L. | KELSALL, Lieut. | Royal Field Artillery |
| Andrew | LINDORES | KOSB |
| John | McVITIE | KOSB |
| David | MARSHALL | KOSB |
| Walter | MELROSE | KOSB |
| John | MUNRO | Royal Scots |
| Walter S. | PATON, Lieut. | Border Regiment |
| William | PRESTON | Manchesters |
| John McD. | RAE, L/Cpl | Royal Scots |
| George | ROBERTSON | KOSB |
| David W. | SCOTT | RGA |
| Henry | SCOTT MM, Sgt | KOSB |
| Robert | SCOTT | KOSB |
| John | SOMERVAILLE | London Rifle Brigade |
| George | SWINTON, Piper | KOSB |
| Robert | TAIT | KOSB |
| A.F. | WATSON, 2/Lieut. | Royal Highlanders |
| William | WALTER | Royal Field Artillery |

Adam WEATHERSTONE Argyll & Sutherland Hdrs
George B. WILSON Post Office Rifles
John WILSON KOSB
John YOUNGSON Seaforths

*'Also in Memory of Those Who Fell
in the World War 1939–1945'*

Corporal James RUTHERFORD KOSB
Private W. SCOTT RASC
Guardsman George BRACK Scots Guards
Sergeant D.W. McMILLAN DFM RAF
Private James LAIDLER KOSB

Some war memorials carry the full Army numbers of all those listed, and this is generally done with a mention of the man's unit. Without the unit, the number is fairly meaningless, for in the 1914–18 war numbers were issued on a unit basis, unlike the Second World War, where numbers were generally on an all-Army basis.

One of the war memorials to carry the Army numbers of all those killed is at Alness, Ross & Cromarty, ten miles north of Dingwall.

Officers were not given numbers in the First World War; they *were* in the Second World War. However, few memorials other than official Army headstones list the six-, seven- or eight-figure numbers generally used for soldiers by the Second World War, nor the up-to-six-figure-numbers issued to officers.

Numbers on war memorials help us in two ways: they help us to judge the 'seniority' of that soldier in the unit, and they confirm the identity of the man concerned when checked against other records and his entry in *Soldiers Died* …. Low numbers generally indicate that the soldier was an 'original' member of that unit; a high number suggests a later recruit or even a cross-posting draftee or transfer from another unit. Knowing a serviceman's number is really essential for more detailed research, as when consulting a unit's muster-roll, a war diary or Army records. With only seventy-five names covering a full quarter of the British population, there will be many a Lance-Corporal John Smith or privates called Thomas Atkins.

On the whole not much has been published on the subject of Army numbers, despite their value to researchers.

Until 1921, the Australian military forces followed the British Army system of allotting numbers to servicemen. This made each unit responsible for issuing numbers (which were known as regimental numbers) to its members. Numbering started at 1, and this was invariably given to the Regimental Sergeant-Major. When RSMs changed, the incoming man was given 1, followed by a suffix A, B etc. Otherwise numbers were issued only once and not used again when a soldier left a unit or was killed. If a number was re-issued in error, it was given a suffix, as for the RSMs, of A, B etc. As mentioned, in the First World War officers did not have numbers. An officer promoted from the ranks would retain his number for record purposes, but it would not be referred to in connection with his commissioned service.

Needless to say, this World War I system of numbering led to a great deal of confusion, with men being issued a new number to remember each time they were transferred to another unit.

One problem that war memorials solve in different ways is that of two men with the same name. Some simply ignore it and exactly the same name and initials are printed twice, with no distinction. Some insert the Christian names when these are different, even though all the others on the war memorial are given only initials. In other cases, when the initials and even the Christian names are the same, the regiment is given in brackets. This is done at Alnwick, North. though here the system falls short of complete identification as two similarly named men served in the same regiment, so that we have:

BELL W. (NF)
BELL W. (NF)
BELL W. (Yorks Regt)

In other cases, the dates of death of a soldier are added to distinguish between the similarly named.

Skipton in the West Riding of Yorkshire has several sets of identical names and initials and distinguishes between them in three different ways:

G. HIGGINS
Harold HILLARY
Horace HILLARY
J. HILLARY

N. SMITH
P.E. SMITH
W. SMITH (10 June 1917)
W. SMITH (11 Oct. 1918)
J.R. SPENCER

Frederick THORNTON
J.H.B. THORNTON
Fred THORNTON

Incidentally, one mistake it is easy to make, particularly on a small memorial, is to read the names downwards when in fact they will be found to go round the memorial in alphabetical order.

Once again, war memorials illustrate over and over again that the decisions were made at local level, without reference to other villages or parishes or towns a few miles away. Thus in Leicestershire we find that the war memorial at Great Glen lists those killed in action by rank, only to break step on this when it comes to those who died of wounds later. For 1939–45 the list is strictly alphabetical, with no mention of rank at all.

At Great Dalby, Leics., the list for both wars is strictly alphabetical, whereas those who died from Kibworth Beauchamp and Kibworth Harcourt, on the other side of Market Harborough, are in order of rank, except for two late additions, for 1914–18, and then alphabetical, with no ranks given at all, for 1939–45.

At Royston, Herts., where the dead are in strict order of rank (again except for late additions), the first name is that of Captain Harold Ackroyd VC MC, an RAMC doctor attached to the 6th Battalion Royal Berks., who was killed a few days after winning his VC. (With his name beginning with the letters Ac, Ackroyd would also have headed the list if this had been alphabetical.) In addition to appearing on the town war memorial, Captain Ackroyd had a road named after him in Royston.

Nor does Scotland give us any discernible pattern on this question of listing names by order of rank or alphabetically. Alness, which assiduously lists all the Army numbers, is strictly hierarchical for 1914–18, while up the coast in Sutherland, both Brora and Golspie are alphabetical. In Caithness, Dunbeath, Dunnet and Halkirk list their dead in order of rank, but Castletown and Thurso are alphabetical, Castletown including ranks but Thurso making no mention of ranks at all.

Further south, in Peeblesshire, we find that Innerleithen lists officers, warrant officers and non-commissioned officers in order, and even its trooper, gunners and sappers in correct order of arm of service precedence for 1914–18, but goes alphabetical for 1939–45. Broughton in the same county has no discernible pattern of rank, alphabet or regimental and service precedence, so that one can only presume it is listed on some other principle, such as the exact date of death. This is true of Peebles itself, which is alphabetical by year of death in 1914–19 but presumably non-alphabetical by exact date of death for 1939–45.

In the Borders, Annan in Dumfriesshire gives no ranks, and the names and initials are simply divided by regiments. Dumfries itself, Langholm and Lochmaben all divide by regiments but are strictly alphabetical thereafter. Lockerbie divides by regiments but keeps to an order of rank, as does Moffatt.

In neighbouring Kirkcudbright, Castle Douglas divides by regiments, then follows the order of rank. Balmaclellan lists the dead in the order of their exact date of death. Carsphairn in the same part of the world – a stronghold of Clan Kennedy – is strictly alphabetical. It lists two Captains Clark-Kennedy (hyphenated) with the Ks, with a Captain and a Lieutenant Kennedy.

It is quite interesting to see, too, how each parish tackles the question of the double-barrelled or hyphenated name. Sometimes they appear alphabetically, based on the first of the two names; sometimes, as at Carsphairn, with the second name giving the alphabetical placing. In fact, many surnames were used together as a pair, without necessarily taking a hyphen. It is a custom often dependent on usage, seldom clearly defined or understood.

A final glance at two war memorials where rank and awards, while mentioned, give way to that proper democracy of death. The 155 names for 1914–19 at Jedburgh, Roxburghshire, are strictly alphabetical, with the much-decorated Captain George Stuart Henderson VC, DSO & Bar, MC, of the 2nd Battalion Manchester Regiment, taking his place between Private Archibald Henderson of the Machine Gun Corps and Private William Henderson of the Gordons.

At Tow Law, Durham, things are fully alphabetical, and Lt. Colonel Charlton, D.H., takes his place after Private Cave, T.W., and before Private Charlton, S., all of the Yorkshire Regiment.

# 7  Awards and Medals

HONOR ET GLORIA
Berriedale, Caithness


The individual character of British war memorials and – if one may be excused the pun – their unregimented nature are nowhere better illustrated than in their recording of awards and decorations.

Many of the more local memorials simply record a name and initials or a single identifying Christian name. The passer-by is left to wonder not only about each man's rank and regiment but whether any of those listed were decorated for heroism or other services. Some memorials, while still eschewing mention of rank or unit, do add decorations to the name. Sometimes the 'policy' on whether to include decorations on a memorial changes from one war to another.

Thus at Southam, Warwicks, no decorations are recorded for 1914–18, even though we know from the evidence of an Army headstone in the same churchyard that at least one of those commemorated, 9011 Private J. Duckett of the Royal Welch Fusiliers, was awarded the Military Medal. On the same Southam war memorial, for 1939–45, the DSM won by T.H. Porteous *is* inscribed.

The study of British awards and decorations, and particularly the collecting of medals, is a science and hobby in itself. It would take too long to explain here. The bibliography for this chapter suggests some further reading on the subject. There are also a number of medal-collector societies and specialist magazines, such as *Medal News*.

From a war-memorial point of view, the decorations that *are* recorded do tell us more about the individuals listed. In ninety per cent of cases, the decorations show whether the dead soldier is an officer or an 'other rank' and in many cases help us identify the armed service to which a man belonged.

The obvious exceptions are the Victoria Cross and George Cross, awarded regardless of rank and arm of service, and a few 'officer medals' for which senior warrant officers were also eligible. There are a goodly number of cases, too, of men who were decorated while in the ranks and later commissioned. Although uncommon, it is not unusual to find men holding various combinations of officer and other-rank decorations on a war memorial.

Some decorations were originally unique to a single armed service, but distinctions became very blurred as sailors fought on land as infantry or artillerymen with the Royal Naval Division, and soldiers were transferred from the Royal Flying Corps to join the Royal Air Force when it was formed on 1 April 1918. Thus the Distinguished Flying Cross was introduced in June 1918 after the formation of the RAF, for gallantry while flying in active operations against the enemy. Before that, Army officers in the Royal Flying Corps were given the Military Cross. From mid-1918, the DFC was awarded not only to RAF officers but also to naval airmen of the Fleet Air Arm, and in World War II to Army personnel such as glider pilots and the pilots of Army observer aircraft.

Here one should mention two air awards for bravery not necessarily required to have been performed 'in the face of an enemy': the Air Force Cross and the Air Force Medal. These were also introduced with the start of the RAF but cover peacetime feats by test-pilots and a dozen awards made during the Berlin Airlift in 1948. Fewer than 5,000 Air Force Crosses have been awarded (2,000 of them since World War II), as against nearly 25,000 Distinguished Flying Crosses. In the case of Air Force Medals, fewer than a thousand have been awarded, as against some 7,000 Distinguished Flying Medals. The higher proportion of 'officer medals' (DFC/AFC compared with DFM/AFM) reflects the fact that most pilots held commissioned rank.

It is also rare to find the orders of knighthood – in particular the Garter, Thistle and St Patrick – recorded on ordinary village or town war memorials, as their possession generally implied a seniority removed from the dangers of front-line death. Nonetheless, we do find an occasional brigadier-general on a World War I war memorial who held a CB at the time of his death.

The 1939–45 names on the war memorial at Seale, Surrey, include Admiral Sir Tom S.V. Phillips KCB, RN, who went down with HMS *Prince of Wales* off Malaya in December 1941. The same memorial records the death of Captain S.H.M. Russell MP of the Coldstream Guards (Conservative member for Darwen, Lancs.).

The Order of the Bath is an award which was made to distinguished officers of the Army and Navy from 1815 onwards, after the Napoleonic Wars. It has three military divisions, the GCB (Knight Grand Cross), KCB (Knight Commander) and CB (Companion).

The Order of the British Empire, the most junior of the British Orders was founded only in 1917, very much for the same reasons as the Order of the Bath in 1815 – to reward both soldiers and civilians for their services to a country at war. The Order of the British Empire also has civil and military divisions.

The Distinguished Service Order was instituted on 6 September 1886; the award of a bar (that is, a second award of the same order) to the DSO became possible after 23 August 1916. The fact that an officer also held a bar to his DSO is sometimes indicated on a war memorial by the word 'Bar', or a rosette, and sometimes it is not shown at all.

An article in the *RMC Record* in 1917 appealed for funds to extend the chapel at Sandhurst as a memorial to former cadets at the Royal Military College who had lost their lives in the war. It said 2,357 had died in the first three years of the Great War – from 4 August 1914 to 4 August 1917. During that same period former gentlemen cadets were awarded twenty-one Victoria Crosses, 734 Distinguished Service Orders and 804 Military Crosses.

Although front-line soldiers sometimes modestly pretended that awards 'came up with the rations', on the whole decorations were taken seriously. A few line battalions stubbornly refused to recommend officers for awards for bravery, implying that courage was expected of all professional soldiers anyway. However, the right sort of medal ribbons were important indications of a man's 'quality' and were visible evidence of his standing in his profession. By the end of the war, most units were abiding by the same rules. But there were still variations in battalion attitudes, and in those of individual commanding officers. It is therefore always invidious to draw up comparative league tables for bravery based on awards.

The Scots Guards, for example, with two battalions serving in France throughout the war, and over 400 officers and 12,000 men on active service during the 1914–18, earned five Victoria Crosses and over 600 other British decorations. In addition to some two dozen officers awarded knighthoods or membership of various orders, Scots Guards officers or warrant officers earned twenty-six DSOs and eighty-five Military Crosses (MC). Other ranks in the Scots Guards received ninety-five Distinguished Conduct Medals (DCM), 338 Military Medals (MM) and thirty-nine Meritorious Service Medals (MSM). In very rough terms, and if one includes some eighty foreign decorations also awarded to Scots Guards, as well as allowing for duplication, this means that about one in twenty of those serving overseas received an award or decoration of some kind. In the case of those who were also killed, their award or decoration might appear on the war memorial carrying their name – or, again, it might not.

It is clear that the Victoria Cross occupies a special place in British consciousness. It is also probably the world's best-known medal for bravery. Inscribed simply 'For Valour', it has been awarded to fewer than 1,350 men since it was instituted by Queen Victoria in 1856. The crimson ribbon of the VC takes precedence over all other medal ribbons worn in the British armed services. The Victoria Cross is now given for acts of conspicuous bravery in the face of the enemy, without regard to rank, long service, wounds or any other consideration. Where a number of equally brave acts take place together, those involved can elect from their number the man or men they consider the most worthy to receive it.

Although women are eligible for the VC, none has been awarded it so far. Four civilians have won the VC – three in the Indian Mutiny and one in 1879 in Afghanistan.

Most Victoria Crosses were awarded during four major wars: the Crimean War, the Boer War and the First and Second World Wars. But awards were also made for actions outside these major wars. Victoria Crosses were awarded for bravery during the Indian Mutiny (1857), during fighting on the North-West Frontier of India and more recently in Korea, Vietnam and the Falklands. In the case of Vietnam, the VCs were won by Australians, as the British Army was not engaged there.

Because so many Victoria Cross winners died in gaining the award or were killed in other front-line actions soon afterwards, mention of the Victoria Cross is to be found on war memorials all over the country – sometimes as an inconspicuous addition to a man's name and initials in those war memorials that do not give many further details; sometimes a VC-holder is given pride of place in the listings.

It can be a moving moment to find, on a simple list of the village or parish dead on a war memorial, one of the names with the letters VC after it. I think of those of Geoffrey Cather VC (Limpsfield, Surrey), Neville Marshall VC (Potter Street, Harlow, Herts.) and Lance-Corporal E. Seaman VC (Scole-near-Diss, Norfolk).

A unique distinction belongs to St Peter's, Eaton Square, London, whose parish roll of honour plaque outside the church lists two VCs simply as Charles FitzClarence VC and John Milbanke VC. Both won their awards in the Boer War but died in the Great War. By then they were Brigadier-General Charles FitzClarence commanding 1st (Guards) Brigade and Lt-Colonel Sir John Milbanke Bart, commanding the Sherwood Rangers. They were killed respectively at Polygon Wood in November 1914 and at Gallipoli in August 1915.

In the Crypt of St Paul's Cathedral, the list of officers of the 1st County of London Yeomanry killed in the 1914–18 war is headed by two who won the VC in that conflict: Lt-Colonel Oliver Cyril Spencer Watson VC, DSO and Major Alexander Malins Lafone VC.

War memorials reveal that the VC was often not an award for an isolated act of bravery but for a whole continuum of courage. An example of repeated bravery is the listing of W.N. Stone VC, DSO, MC at Shrewsbury. As one would deduce from his other awards, W.N. Stone was an officer, a captain in the Royal Fusiliers. He died, winning his posthumous VC, on 30 November 1917, near Cambrai.

On the memorial at Jedburgh in the Scottish Borders we find: 'HENDERSON G.S. VC DSO MC Captain Manchester Regiment'. Captain Henderson also had a bar to his DSO (in other words, that second DSO) and was killed after the war in Iraq. He died on 24 July 1920, near Hillah in Mesopotamia, but his name appears among the First World War dead on the memorial at Jedburgh. As *The Register of the Victoria Cross* tells us, Captain Henderson's name was also to be found on the Basra Memorial, Iraq, on his regimental memorial in the chapel at Sandhurst and on a plaque at his old school at Gordon, Berwickshire.

For World War II we find village or parish listings for such as John Grayburn VC (Chalfont St Giles, Bucks) and in neighbouring Chalfont St Peter for Geoffrey Heneage Drummond VC. Although Drummond's name appears among the 1939–45 dead, he won his Victoria Cross in the 1914–18 war. Serving as Lieutenant G.H. Drummond RNVR, he won it aboard HM *Motor Launch 254* off Ostend on 9/10 May 1918. He died twenty-two years later, during the Second World War, at Rotherhithe in the London docks, while serving as a seaman in the River Thames Patrol Service.

In a few cases, not even the Victoria Cross is listed on the war memorial, as in the case of the VC mentioned in the introduction – Captain Francis Octavius Grenfell, 9th Lancers. He appears on the memorial at Beaconsfield simply as 'F. Grenfell'.

The burial places of VCs, in the case of those who died in Britain, either of wounds or from natural causes, are all well documented.

The youngest VC of the First World War, Boy (First Class) John Travers Cornwell (1900–16) who died of wounds received at Jutland aboard HMS *Chester* is buried at Manor Park Cemetery in London. He is also commemorated in the churchyard of St Botolph-Without-Bishopsgate and in Chester Cathedral.

Midshipman George Leslie Drewry, who won his VC on the collier *River Clyde* at Gallipoli in April 1915, died at Scapa Flow in Orkney in August 1918. He too lies buried in the City of London Cemetery, Manor Park. He is also commemorated by a window in All Saints' Church, Forest Gate, where he was born, and by a scholarship fund for the sons of Merchant Navy officers killed in action. This scholarship recognizes the fact that Midshipman Drewry began at sea in the merchant service, and was the first Royal Naval Reserve officer to win the VC.

Gunner Peter James Collis, who won a VC in Afghanistan in 1880 and who died in Battersea in 1918, aged sixty-two, is buried with the First World War dead in London's Wandsworth Cemetery and appears on the memorial.

Captain George Henry Tatham Paton MC, 4th Battalion Grenadier Guards, killed in action winning the VC at Gonnelieu in 1917, is buried in the British Extension of the Metz-en-Couture Communal Cemetery in France but is also commemorated at Putney Vale Cemetery, Surrey.

Flight Sub-Lieutenant Reginald Alexander John (Rex) Warneford, the first British airman to shoot down a German Zeppelin, in June 1915 over Belgium (he was killed ten days later), has an elaborate memorial tombstone in Brompton Cemetery, London, put up by the *Daily Express*. It is a belligerent tombstone, which bears a naval officer's face and wings peering over a scene of a large Zeppelin bursting apart in two places as a result of a dive-attack by a small British aircraft, pictured upper right. An inscription explains: 'Erected by readers of the *Daily Express* to commemorate the heroic exploit in destroying a Zeppelin airship near Ghent on 7 June 1915.'

Some forty VCs were awarded for bravery during the Gallipoli Campaign. They included six VCs (three posthumous) awarded to officers and men of a single battalion, the 1st Lancashire Fusiliers, for their bravery on 25 April 1915. Nine other Gallipoli VCs were awarded for the V Beach landing (six to the Navy, three to the Army), when the *River Clyde*, carrying the 1st Battalion Royal Dublin Fusiliers, 1st Battalion Royal Munster Fusiliers, 2nd Battalion Hampshires, West Riding Field Company (Royal Engineers) and Anson Battalion Royal Naval Division, was beached under intense fire.

There have been ten Royal Marine Victoria Crosses, commemorated in a booklet published by the Royal Marines Museum at Eastney, Hants.

Among Victoria Cross winners who occupy pride of place on their monument are the two at Blackpool, Lancs. The list of the dead, on the cenotaph on the esplanade by North Pier, begins with the names of:

Lieutenant A.V. SMITH VC
    East Lancashire Regiment

2/Lieutenant S.H.T. BOUGHEY VC
    Royal Scots Fusiliers

The Blackpool memorial has a frieze of war scenes, with soldiers and civilians, and four main figures at each corner: two soldiers, an armed sailor, an aviator. The names of the 1914–18 war dead are on two catafalques at the foot of the obelisk cenotaph. Except for the VCs, all names are listed alphabetically under their regiments or corps by name and initials. Again except for the VCs, no ranks are given at Blackpool, and no other awards are mentioned.

The Victoria Cross is extremely well documented, and a tremendous amount has been written about it and the award-winners. These range from *Boy's Own Paper*-type accounts of the exploits in which they were won to serious analyses of what it is that constitutes courage. *The Register of the Victoria Cross* is a must for anyone interested in the award. It lists 1,348 winners of the Victoria Cross (three men won it twice) and has photographs or illustrations of all but a few of them.

Much of our latter-day awareness of the Victoria Cross is due to the work of the late Brigadier Sir John Smyth VC MC Bart, who died in 1983 at the age of sixty-seven. He was the founder-chairman of the VC and GC Association 1956–71, and latterly its life president.

Because patterns of making awards varied from unit to unit, from campaign area to campaign area, comparisons are not easy to make. We have already looked at the over 600 awards made to two battalions of Scots Guards, who fought for four years in France and Flanders, and had some 400 officers and 12,000 men on active service in that time.

The Royal Army Medical Corps, serving in every theatre of the First World War, won numerous awards, including seven Victoria Crosses. Captain Chavasse, serving with the Liverpool Scottish, won a bar to his VC and died a day or so later; Lieutenant (as he then was) Martin-Leake won a bar to the VC he earned in the Boer War. Thus the only two double VCs in the Great War were both RAMC doctors. Additionally the RAMC won:

499 Distinguished Service Orders
1,484 Military Crosses
395 Distinguished Conduct Medals
3,002 Military Medals

The main value of this list is to show the proportion of awards between the Army's four principal decorations (the top two for officers, the other two for other ranks) and to give some idea of the likely rarity of an award found on a war memorial. For we must remember that these totals are for all awards – made to both those who survived and those who died. We should also remember that the Military Cross was introduced only at the end of 1914 and that before that the usual officer medal, even for subalterns, was the DSO.

All RAMC men who lost their lives in the Great War are commemorated in Westminster Abbey. In the Chapter House, along the East Cloister, is a Golden Book listing the names of 6,873 men of the Royal Army Medical Corps who died. They are also honoured in a section of the stained-glass window in the abbey's north wall.

Based on the total RAMC awards, we would expect and do find that the Military Cross and Military Medal are more 'common' than others.

As a very rough guide to estimating the 'rarity' of awards, the round figures for these two Army front-line awards for 1914–18 are:

Military Cross (MC)   40,000

Military Medal (MM) 120,000

More interesting perhaps is a comparison between the numbers of awards made in 1914–18 against those for 1939–45:

Military Cross (MC) 1914–18:   40,000 1939–45:11,000

Military Medal (MM) 1914–18: 120,000 1939–45:16,000

And, reflecting the far greater role played by the Royal Navy in the Second World War, the figures for the two mainly naval awards:

Distinguished Service Cross (DSC) 1914–18: 2,000 1939–45: 5,000

Distinguished Service Medal (DSM) 1914–18: 5,600 1939–45: 7,300

Comparisons between the numbers of Air Force medals are not as appropriate, as these were instituted only in 1918. Eighteen hundred DFCs were awarded prior to 1939, and 22,000 during 1939–45. Remembering again that most pilots were officers, there were 200 DFMs pre-1939 and 6,700 1939–45.

The different nature of the Second World War led to the introduction of the George Cross in 1940, to replace the previous 'Civilian VC' – the Albert Medal – and also the Empire Gallantry Medal, a few of which can still be found on World War I memorials. It was meant to cover feats of bravery which were not eligible for the Victoria Cross because those involved were civilians or members of the services whose actions were not technically performed 'in the face of the enemy'. The George Cross would cover heroic work on mine- and bomb-disposal on the home front, as well as the bravery of those who operated in enemy-occupied territory. Several women qualified for the George Cross, most notably those who acted as secret agents while serving with the FANYs.

In some ways it is more interesting to find lesser-known distinctions appearing, and perhaps try to find out from other sources whether these awards represent some particular occasion or action.

The Croix de Guerre appears fairly regularly on British memorials, which sometimes specify whether it is a French or Belgian award. At Brora, Sutherland, there are four officer Military Crosses in a total death-roll of one woman and sixty men. Corporal A.J. Bremner has both the Military Medal and the Croix de Guerre, while Regimental Sergeant-Major J.K. Rollo has a DCM, the British MM and a Médaille Militaire.

Finally, a few points to watch out for.

Just occasionally, the abbreviation MM is used for Merchant Marine rather than Military Medal, though the context should make clear which is being referred to. MMR is not a decoration but stands for the Merchant Marine Reserve. MSM (Meritorious Service Medal) sometimes appears, presumably on those occasions when the award was made in connection with bravery, rather than its more common reward 'for Long Service and Good Conduct'.

On a few memorials one finds the awards listed in the order in which they were won, with a DCM following an MM. Technically this is wrong, as the DCM should take precedence, irrespective of the date on which it was earned.

The Distinguished Conduct Medal (DCM), though not mentioned before, takes precedence over almost all the other-rank medals. It is another award dating from Crimean days: 750 were given in that war; some 2,000 in the Boer War; 25,000 in the First World War and only 1,900 in World War II.

It has been argued that the First World War put an end to a perception of individual heroism as a social ideal, as a way in which a man should conduct himself. Is this view perhaps shared by those communities which chose not to list military honours on their memorials?

# 8 The Battles and the Places

They Won the Victor's Crown in Many Lands
Afar They Rest, At Home Their Token Stands.
Long Preston, Yorks.

In one of the best and most scholarly books about the beginning of the
First World War, *August 1914*, Barbara Tuchman describes the place of
Ypres in British Army history (p.425):

> After the incomplete victory of the Marne there followed the German retreat
> to the Aisne, the race to the sea for possession of the Channel ports, the fall
> of Antwerp, and the battle of Ypres where officers and men of the BEF held
> their ground, fought literally until they died and stopped the Germans in
> Flanders. Not Mons nor the Marne but Ypres was the real monument to
> British valour, as it was also the grave of four-fifths of the original BEF.

There must be at least another dozen battles of the Great War which
evoke some of the same sense of history for Britons that Ypres does, and
another dozen for the Second World War – and the names of many of
these battles will be found inscribed on war memorials across the
country, for it was 'The Men of This Village' who fought those battles
and died in them. Many war memorials do not mention battles; others
list all the places where men from that village or parish fought. On some
memorials, where the date of death is recorded, this may allow us to
decide in which battle or which campaign a soldier died.

Studying those war memorials which list deaths on a year-by-year basis
gives an insight into the impact casualties must have had on
communities, especially as the war went on and lists grew longer.

The first deaths in 1914 would almost certainly all be regulars, or
ex-regulars called back as reservists. Thus in the publication *Craven's
Part in the Great War* the first death recorded is that of Private Arthur
Ryder of Addingham, six miles from Skipton, in the West Riding of
Yorkshire. He was a 19-year-old regular soldier in the 2nd Battalion
Duke of Wellington's (West Riding) Regiment, killed near Mons on 23

94

August 1914. One of the last two men from Craven to be killed in action was Corporal Alfred Carey MM, from Bolton-by-Bowland, also of the 2nd Battalion Duke of Wellington's, who died on 7 November 1918.

A good deal of attention is paid to the casualties the British Army suffered on that first disastrous day on the Somme – 1 July 1916. It is a date which will recur again and again on those war memorials that specify exact dates of death. But it must always be remembered that it should be described as 'the Battles of the Somme' and that these went on for 4½ months after 1 July.

Also we must always be absolutely sure what we mean when using the term 'casualties', and of the way in which the book or war memorial we are reading is using the word too. References to casualties in a battle or campaign generally embrace all men who were killed, posted missing at the time or wounded and had to go back from their units for treatment or hospitalization. A proportion of the missing became prisoners; in the case of the German offensive in early 1918, whole battalions were 'swept into the bag', while many of the wounded would be back in action again, even qualifying again as casualties in a later battle.

It is only when you study publications such as banker Cox & Co's *List of British Officers taken prisoner in the various Theatres of War between August 1914 and November 1918* that you realize what the loss, for instance, of Kut-al-Amara in 1916 meant. It takes 5½ pages to list the 279 officers whose capture was notified to Cox & Co. In addition to General C.V.F. Townshend, there were two major-generals, four brigadier-generals, half-a-dozen full colonels and more than a dozen lt-colonels.

Even more revealing are the lists of officer prisoners taken when the Germans smashed through the Fifth Army in their 1918 offensive. The 16th (Irish) and 36th (Ulster) Divisions, which at that time contained between them just about every Irish line battalion serving on the Western Front, suffered heavily in both killed and captured. The 1st Battalion Royal Dublin Fusiliers had eleven officers captured (three of whom subsequently died), the 2nd Battalion ten. The 1st Royal Munsters lost six officers captured, the 2nd Battalion nine. The 1st Royal Irish Fusiliers lost fifteen officers, the 9th Battalion of the same regiment thirteen. The Royal Irish Rifles had twenty-four of the officers of its 12th Battalion captured, while the 15th Battalion lost its colonel and sixteen other officers as prisoners.

And so the story of those three months – March, April, May 1918 – goes on. It was, as the Duke of Wellington said of another battle, 'the nearest run thing you ever saw in your life'.

If every British historian had to make a list of a dozen battles from the First World War that were somehow eternally imprinted on the national consciousness, there would probably be general agreement on at least ten of them. There would be lots of discussion about their order of importance, but in simple terms of 'impact' and public awareness (which is the question posed), I suggest the British nominations for the dozen would probably include the Retreat from Mons, First Ypres, Gallipoli, Loos, Verdun, the Somme, Arras and Vimy Ridge, Jutland, Third Ypres (Passchendaele) and the breaching of the Hindenburg Line. After that, choose any combination of two from the battles which took place at Cambrai, Le Câteau, Messines, Hill 60, Neuve Chapelle, St-Quentin, the Argonne and 'the Advance to Victory'.

The war memorial at Shrewsbury, Salop, lists all the battles in which men from the town died. These are listed in fours on the outward-facing two sides of each of the corner-posts, with a further four single names running across on the top plinth between these corner-posts.

| | |
|---|---|
| MONS | FALKLAND ISLANDS |
| AISNE | HELIGOLAND |
| MARNE | JUTLAND |
| YPRES | ZEEBRUGGE |
| | |
| NEUVE CHAPELLE | BULGARIA |
| HOOGE | SALONICA |
| GIVENCHY | SERBIA |
| FESTUBERT | CUXHAVEN |
| | |
| DARDANELLES | LOOS |
| GALLIPOLI | VIMY RIDGE |
| SUVLA BAY | SOMME |
| ACHI BABA | HULLUCH |
| | |
| PALESTINE | HILL 60 |
| GAZA | ARRAS |
| MESOPOTAMIA | MESSINES RIDGE |
| KUT | CAMBRAI |

MONT BLIGNY
RUSSIA
ITALY
EAST AFRICA

In Edinburgh, near Haymarket Station, stands a clock memorial to the memory of players and members of the Heart of Midlothian Football Club who fell in 'the Great War 1914–19'. It lists the battles in which those men died:

| VIMY | ARRAS | MONS | MARNE |
| SOMME | LILLE | AISNE | LOOS |
| ST. ELOI | CAMBRAI | HILL 60 | YPRES |
| AFRICA | FRESNES | HOOGE | YSER |
| GAZA | STRUMA | EGYPT | JUTLAND |

At the entrance to the crypt of St Martin's-in-the-Field, off London's Trafalgar Square, there is a 'Mons to Ypres Chapel', now known as the Dick Sheppard Chapel, after a former incumbent. It is used for private prayer and meditation by visitors. Two memorial plaques explain its origin and dedication:

*This Memorial to the Force*
*which saved Britain in 1914*
*was erected in 1953 by their*
*surviving comrades – The Royal Navy,*
*The Regiments and Corps of the British Army*
*whose names are inscribed in the Roll*
*of Honour – and the Royal Air Force.*

*In Thanksgiving for the Soldiers*
*of the British Expeditionary Force 1914*
*who laid down their lives in the Battles*
*of MONS, LE CATEAU, THE MARNE,*
*THE AISNE and the FIRST BATTLE OF YPRES*
*and for the Seamen and Marines*
*who fought and died at ANTWERP.*

Whereas one would expect to find battle honours inscribed on a regimental memorial, it is perhaps worth noticing where these are also recorded in more hallowed precincts.

The 1914–19 war memorial of the London Scottish at its regimental headquarters in Buckingham Gate, London, was unveiled by the regiment's then honorary colonel, Earl Haig, on 21 January 1923. It lists twenty-four battles in which the two battalions of the 1/14th London Regiment (London Scottish) fought: the 1st Battalion in France and Flanders, the 2nd Battalion in France, Salonika and Palestine. Inscribed are the names of seventy-five officers and 1,459 other ranks who lost their lives.

The same list of battle honours is also a principal feature of the regiment's memorial in St Columba's (Church of Scotland) in Pont Street. This reads:

For God, King & Country
To the Undying Memory of the Officers and Men of
The London Scottish Regiment
Who Laid Down Their Lives
in the Cause of Freedom, Justice & Honour in
The Great War of 1914–1918.

| 1914 | 1915 | 1916 |
|------|------|------|
| Ypres | Neuve Chapelle | Gommecourt |
| Givenchy | Festubert | Somme |
| | Loos | |

| 1917 | 1918 |
|------|------|
| Salonika | Jordan |
| Vimy | Es Salt |
| Arras | El Haud |
| Ypres | Arras |
| Cambrai | Dranoutre |
| Beersheba | Cambrai St Quentin |
| Sheria | Menin |
| Jerusalem | Mons-Maubeuge |
| Shafat | |

But exactly *where* were those we see commemorated killed?

The war memorial at Milnthorpe, Westmorland, records the war zones and dates where each of twenty-one 'Milnthorpe Lads' died. This gives us a good picture of a fairly common pattern for a town that obviously had few regular soldiers. The first area and the first death is Gallipoli, June 1915. But nineteen out of that total of twenty-one were killed in France and Belgium (or 'France and Flanders', as it is always registered in *Soldiers Died* ...). The other lonely addition is a soldier who died in Turkey in January 1920.

At Casterton, a mile or so north of Kirkby Lonsdale, in the same county, the war memorial records the places of death of its six World War I dead even more exactly – all died in France and Flanders, though one presumably in hospital far from the front:

| | | |
|---|---|---|
| H.C. | CLARKE | 1917 Armentières |
| H. | HARDACRE | 1916 La Bassée |
| W. | POOLEY | 1918 Magna La Fosse |
| J.H. | SHEPHERD | 1917 Boulogne |
| W.T. | STACKHOUSE | 1915 Neuve Chapelle |
| W.E. | WILSON | 1917 Hibers |

At Edgerston, Roxburghshire, the first Scottish war memorial one encounters driving north on the A68, the nine names are also listed alphabetically, with the battle in which they fell and a date; but no record of rank or regiment. It is a simple cement cross memorial, with a fleur-de-lys interwoven, on the opposite side of the road to the Church of Scotland kirk.

## EDGERSTON

## TO THOSE WHO FELL 1914–1918

*'Their name liveth for evermore'*

| | | | |
|---|---|---|---|
| Jasper | BRIGGS | Armentieres | 1916 |
| George | BRIGGS | Montauban | 1916 |
| Adam | GLENDINNING | El Oujeh | 1917 |
| William B. | HALL | Mazingarbe | 1917 |
| Alexander M. | MACNAIR | Festubert | 1915 |
| Adam S. | TELFER | Gallipoli | 1915 |
| Andrew | THOMSON | Gallipoli | 1915 |
| Henry H. | TURNER | Lake Doiran | 1918 |
| Thomas A. | YOUNG | Guillemont | 1917 |

At Edgerston, only five died in France and Flanders; the four others fell at El Oujeh, Gallipoli (two) and Lake Doiran on the Salonika front.

Even where the war memorial does not give full details of number, rank and name, unit, place and date of death, as at Bradfield, Berks., or on a church roll of honour giving most of these details, as at Braughing, Herts., and Grasmere, Westmorland, recording the unit and date of death can soon lead one to the battle in which the death occurred.

The memorial at Outwell, Isle of Ely, Cambs., gives Christian name and surname, in most cases the exact unit, with the list arranged in the chronological order of date of death – no ranks are mentioned, no awards, no place of death. The 1939–45 list, while still not mentioning ranks, includes the date of death but is in alphabetical order.

If 1 July 1916 and the Somme are forever engraved on the nation's consciousness (and on its war memorials), 25 September 1915 and Loos are remembered particularly in Scotland.

It was at Loos that the 9th (Scottish) and 15th (Scottish) Divisions were 'blooded', along with many other New Army divisions in a series of fierce attacks which cost 60,000 casualties. The troops involved were mainly men who had volunteered as early as August and September 1914. After some nine months' training in Kitchener's Army, they were thrown into action before most of them had any idea of what fighting on the Western Front was like. Many of them landed in France only some two weeks before the battle.

Loos as a whole has been described as 'a disappointing battle'. Even though the British fought well – 15 (Scottish) Division did particularly well – and Loos itself was taken, at the end the Germans still held the key positions of Hill 70, Fosse 8 and The Dump. But its repercussions were felt all across Scotland.

With its small population, Scots tend to know each other or know of each other in a different way even from those who live in the same county in England. There was hardly a home, and certainly not a village, that did not know somebody at Loos. There were men from every Scottish regiment there, among them the 10th Argyll & Sutherland Highlanders (the battalion anonymously described in Ian Hay's book *The First Hundred Thousand*).

There were, for example, three Service battalions of the Royal Scots at Loos: 11 RS and 12 RS with 27 Brigade, 9 (Scottish) Division in Gough's I Corps on the left of the attack; and 13 RS in 45 Brigade, 15 (Scottish) Division in Rawlinson's IV Corps on the right. Other Scottish battalions were scattered throughout the attacking force. In Rawlinson's IV Corps, the regular 1st Division had in its 1 Brigade, 1st Black Watch, which would suffer 278 casualties, and 1st London Scottish, who would lose 260 dead and wounded.

It was, of course, not a Scottish battle only. London territorials were there in strength with 47 (London) Division, as were line battalions and service battalions from all over the country, suffering equally badly or worse; in 1 Division alone:

| | |
|---|---|
| 1 Loyal North Lancs | 489 casualties |
| 2 King's Royal Rifle Corps | 460 casualties |
| 2 Welch Regiment | 311 casualties |

The Army is meticulous with its definitions. *The Official Names of the Battles and Other Engagements fought by the Military Forces of the British Empire during the Great War 1914–1919 and the Third Afghan War 1919* was published and presented to Parliament in 1921.

Many other battles would follow Loos and the Somme, and equally heavy casualties would be suffered by battalions and regiments before the war was over, but 25 September 1915 and 1 July 1916 (together with other days in the weeks that immediately followed them) still make a special impact when encountered on a war memorial today.

# 9 The Causes They Fought For and How They Died

'For God, For King, For Country'

In the same way that a first fact one might notice about a war memorial is whether the dates for the First World War are given as 1914–18 or 1914–19, it is easy to note whether the slogan is as above in full or in some shorter version: 'For God and For Country', 'For King and Country' or some other variation still, such as 'They Died For England'. Is there any significance in the absence or presence of any reference to God on the memorial?

And, secondly, is it coupled with other declarations concerning the justice and rightness of the cause the soldiers died for? At Litchborough, Northants the war memorial standing by the church and opposite the Old Red Lion reads:

To Keep in Mind
Those who from this Place
Gave Their Lives
For Their Country
And for the Right
In the Great War

## 1914–1919

| | | | |
|---|---|---|---|
| Ebenezer | ARNOLD | Frank W.B. | HURLEY |
| Richard Varney | ARNOLD | Edward Gabriel | LESTER |
| William Walter | BILLINGHAM | Arthur Henry | NORRIS |
| William | DARKER | George James | WESTON |

At Wick near Pershore, Worcs., the message is:

To The Glory of God and in Ever Grateful Memory
of the Men of this Parish who Gave their Lives
for the Honour and Liberty of their Country in the Great War.

At Hanbury, Staffs., the war memorial is quite categorical: 'THEY DIED FOR FREEDOM'.

At Abbots Bromley, south-east Staffs., the war memorial standing on the village green, close to 'The Goat', declares:

To the Eternal Memory of the men of **ABBOTS BROMLEY**
Whose names are inscribed hereon
Who Gave Their Lives for England in the Great War
And of all those Others of this Parish
Who Fought Under the Flag during the same Period.
1914–1919

The inscription at Alrewas, on the other side of Lichfield to Abbots Bromley, has one interesting difference. Here the war memorial, on a small green enclave at a road-junction in Main Street, just beyond the George & Dragon, reads:

To the Eternal Memory of the Men of **ALREWAS**
whose Names are Inscribed hereon,
Who Gave Their Lives for the Empire
in the Great War,
And of all Those Others from this Parish
who Fought under the Flag during the same period.
1914–1919

Broughton in Peeblesshire boasts a nice solid restored memorial:

**1914–18**
*In Reverent and Loving Memory of Those from this Parish
Who Laid Down Their Lives in the
Great War for Liberty and Righteousness.*

| | | | |
|---|---|---|---|
| Private | Ralph | TAIT | HLI |
| Private | John | INCH | Camerons |
| 2/Lieutenant | Thomas | TUDHOPE | Scottish Rifles |
| Private | William | MACKIE | Camerons |
| Private | J.T. Scott | BELL | Royal Scots |
| Sergeant | Hugh | CRAWFORD | A & SH |
| Corporal | Gavin | SEMPLE | LIY |
| Sapper | John | BELL | Royal Engineers |
| Gunner | George | COCHRANE | RFA |
| Private | John | PRETSWELL | Scottish Rifles |
| Private | Thomas | SOMERVILLE | Royal Scots |
| Sergeant-Major | Thomas | HENSHILWOOD | Royal Highlanders |
| Private | George | IRELAND | Labour Battalion |
| Private | John | McMORRAN | Royal Scots |

| Lance-Corporal | James GRAHAM | Seaforths |
| Private | Robert HAMILTON | Machine Gun Corps |
| Private | Douglas TELFER | Royal Scots Fusiliers |
| Private | William TAYLOR | HLI |
| Miss | Anne ALEXANDER | VAD |

**1939–1945**

| Captain | D.M. FORRESTER | Cameronians |

In the parish church at Peebles a series of plaques on the wall lists the names of members and adherents who fell in the First World War. And at the end are these words:

> Not For Themselves
> For Justice Right They Fought
> And With Their Blood
> A Glorious Freedom Bought
>
> These Died In War
> That We At Peace Might Live
> These Gave Their All
> So We Our Best Should Give

What was the Cause? Was it a fight for Liberty and Righteousness, or simply a Defence of Their Country? Or both?

> For God and Country
> (Aston Abbots, Bucks and Butler's Cross, Bucks)
>
> For God and Freedom
> (Guilden Morden, Cambs.)
>
> Who Dies If England Live?
> Who Stands If Freedom Fall?
> (Kirkby Lonsdale, Westmorland)
>
> FOR BRITAIN'S WEAL THEY DIED;
> THEIR NAMES IMMORTAL RISE,
> RESPLENDENT WITH HONOUR,
> GREAT IN LOVE, SUPREME IN SACRIFICE.
> (Catrine, Ayrshire)
>
> For King and Country, For Justice and Freedom
> (Easingwold, Yorks)

For Their King and Country, and For The Freedom of the Nation
(Canonbie, Dumfriesshire)

HONOUR – FREEDOM – PEACE – JUSTICE
(Greengates, West Riding of Yorkshire)

That Freedom Might Not Perish From The Earth (1939–1945)
(Coldingham, Berwickshire)

Remember with Pride and Gratitude the True and Faithful Men
Who in Those years of War Went Forth From this Parish
To Do Battle For God and the Right
(Langholm, Dumfries, and Pershore, Worcs.)

An embroidered roll of honour in the charming Early English church at
Great Milton, Oxon, lists all those from the village who served in
1914–18. A cross and 'RIP' mark the names of the twelve who died – who
appear on the war memorial just outside the church. It is one of
comparatively few war memorials to describe the enemy.

The Names of the Officers and Men from GREAT MILTON
who for Our King and Empire
fought victoriously against German, Bulgar and Turk
MCMXIV – MCMXVIII
Deo Gratias

The inscription on the war memorial on the green at The Lee, Bucks., a
village three miles south-east of Wendover, is most unforgiving:

1914–1919

To the Glory of God
and in Memory of these men
of THE LEE
who gave their lives for
King and Country
Hearth and Home
Freedom and Honour
in Britain's War against
German Cruelty and Aggression.

And who were the Men who 'Laid Down Their Lives For Their Country'
(Ockham, Surrey) or 'Died That We Might Live' (Eynsham, Oxon, and
Fulbrook, Oxon), and how are they described on their memorial? They

are the Gallant Dead, the Glorious Dead, the Heroic Dead, the Honoured Dead. They are held in Affectionate Memory, or variously in Appreciative, Everlasting, Grateful, Honoured, Loving, Never-Dying, Never-Fading, Pious, Proud, Reverent or Sacred Memory.

> These were the Brave, Unknowing how to Yield,
> Who, terrible in Valour kept the Field
> Against the Foe, and Higher than Life's Breath
> Prizing their Honour, met the Doom of Death
> And now they Rest
> Peaceful Enfolded in their Country's Breast.

(Skipton, Yorks.)

> A people that jeoparded their lives unto
> the death in the high places of the field.

(Corbridge, Northumberland)

> Their dust is in the desert and the deep.

(Brora, Sutherland)

They fought in The Great War, the European War, the World War or The Great War of Nations (Matlock Bath, Derbys.). In the 1920s nobody knew that 'The War to End All Wars' was destined to become 'the First World War' and be followed by the Second World War.

At Shrewsbury, Salop., a large fourteen-foot red sandstone cross states:

### The Great War 1914–1918

ERECTED TO THE NEVER-FADING MEMORY OF THE GALLANT SAILORS,
SOLDIERS AND AIRMEN OF THIS TOWN
WHO MADE THE SUPREME SACRIFICE.

> 'Sons of this Place let this of you be said,
> That your live are worthy of your dead,
> These gave their lives that you who live may reap
> A richer harvest ere you fall asleep.'

And there are messages for their countrymen, who lived on:

> Live Thou For England, We For England Died.

(Deddington, Oxon; King's School, Ely, Cambs.; Silloth, Cumberland; Southam, Warwicks., and many others)

> Let Those Who Come After See To It
> That Their Names Be Not Forgotten.

(Ilkley, Yorks.)

They Died That We Might Live

(Furnace, Argyllshire)

See ye to it that these shall not have died in vain.

(Brereton, Rugeley, Staffs.)

These Men of Ours, Unselfish, Unafraid
Went to the Worldwide Fight
Forget Not How They Fought, and How They Died
For England and The Right.

(Ufton, Warwicks.)

Some of the messages are heart-breakingly sad:

Remember Us and Think
What Might Have Been.
Ye That Live On Mid
England's Pastures Green.

(Kirkby Lonsdale, Westmorland)

They Gave, We Have.

(Bloxham, Oxon.)

THEIR SUN WENT DOWN
WHILE IT WAS YET DAY.

(Talgarth, Brecon)

When You Go Home,
Tell Them Of Us, And Say,
For Your Tomorrow,
We Gave Our Today.

(Barnstaple, Devon)

Quite a few war memorials not only carry the names of those who died in the war but refer with pride and gratitude to all the men of the village or parish who served in the forces. A few war memorials actually list all the names of those who were in the forces, as well as the names of the dead. It is more usual for complete rolls of those who served to be found in other places: on a separate plaque in the church porch or on a lych-gate, or more commonly on a roll of honour on a wall inside the church.

The value of finding a complete list of servicemen is that it allows us to note the proportion between those serving and those killed, and see if it fits the usual very rough pattern of one out of every four or five dying, or if that village has been particularly lucky or unlucky. It also provides, because fuller, a more accurate picture of the surnames that are most common in the parish, giving us perhaps a better clue to the family groupings within that community.

At Gretton, Northants, all one hundred names of those who served are inscribed on a memorial wall, with the twenty-eight who did not return placed centrally and in guilded lettering. The patterns of family names here – and for 1939–45 – are particularly interesting.

A chapel in the parish church at Welford, also Northants, has been restored and dedicated to the memory of 101 men of Welford and Sulby who fought in '1914–19', twenty-seven of whom were killed; and of Dorothy Roberts of Sulby VAD Hospital who died at her post.

In the church at Northleach, Glos., we have:

### THE MUSTER ROLL OF THE MEN FROM NORTHLEACH WHO SERVED 1914–1918.
**'The people offered themselves willingly,
bless ye the Lord.'**

Six columns, with twenty-six names on all but one of them, give us a total of 153 serving from this village. Sixteen are listed on the Northleach war memorial as having died.

At Chalgrove, south-east Oxon, the war memorial, on a green enclosure on the main street, is dedicated:

### TO THE GLORY OF GOD AND IN MEMORY OF
Joe ATKINS
Ernest BELSON
Jesse BELSON
Francis BROWN
Joseph CLEMENTS
James FRANKLIN
Ernest HICKS
Stanley HICKS
Thomas HICKS
George HURST
Albert KING
Horace LACEY

### WHO OF THE 61 MEN WHO WENT FORTH FROM THIS PARISH TO SERVE IN THE GREAT WAR GAVE THEIR LIVES
**1914–1919**

'Their Name Liveth for Evermore'

At Worlington, West Suffolk, thirty-three served, eleven died.

The roll of honour of the parish of St Mary Magdalene, Duns Tew, Oxon., mentioned before, lists those who *served* and specifies all who were casualties of any kind, including those who were invalided out.

| | | |
|---|---|---|
| ALDSWORTH, Daniel - | Cavalry | Wounded |
| ALDSWORTH, Ernest | Cavalry | |
| BENNETT, Albert Edward | OBLI | Killed |
| BOLTON, James | Royal Artillery | |
| DASHWOOD, Robert Henry S. BM | 2/1st Inf. Bde | Wounded |
| DASHWOOD, Wilfrid James, 2 Lt | Grenadier Guards | Killed |
| DASHWOOD, Lionel Albert, 2 Lt | OBLI | Killed |
| DASHWOOD, Henry Godfrey, 2 Lt | OBLI | |
| FRENCH, John, L/Cpl | OBLI | |
| GILLAM, Charles John | Gloucestershire Regt | Killed |
| GILLAM, Albert Edward | East Surrey Regt | Killed |
| GILLAM, Charles William Reeve | Guards MGC | |
| HARRIS, Henry | OBLI | Invalided |
| HOLTON, John | OBLI | |
| HUDSON, Christopher | Oxford Heavy Artillery | |
| JARVIS, Fred | Worcestershire Regt | |
| JARVIS, Percy | Royal Ordnance Corps | |
| MOBBS, James | London Irish Rifles | Killed |
| MOLE, Albert | OBLI | Invalided |
| PULLEN, Laurie | Royal Navy | |
| REEVE, Frank | Labour Corps | |
| ZIEKEL, Frank DCM, Sgt | OBLI | Wounded |

'Their name liveth for ever more'

Many of those commemorated on war memorials did not die in battle. They died of wounds in Casualty Clearing Stations (CCS) at the front; in hospitals in France, Britain, Egypt or India; or from the effects of their wounds or gassing, often well after the war ended.

In most cases, no distinction is made between those killed in action and those dying of wounds, or in accidents, from drowning, or simply from natural causes while on active service. On some memorials, however, full details are given, including the number of the CCS or the location of the hospital in which they died, or the name of the transport or hospital-ship from which they were buried at sea.

As John Keegan points out in *The Face of Battle*:

The wounds suffered by the human body on the Somme were of a far greater variety and degree of severity than any Waterloo surgeon would have seen. Edged-weapon wounds would almost have disappeared ... the best statistic available is that [they] were a fraction of one per cent of all wounds inflicted in the First World War.

Bullet wounds were far more frequent, (generally) amounting to about thirty per cent of all new wounds. Shell and bomb wounds ... usually amounted to about seventy per cent of those inflicted. Shell wounds were the most to be feared, because of the multiple effects shell explosion could produce in the human body.

John Keegan's chapter on 'The Wounded' is well worth reading, for its analysis of the wounds received by front-line soldiers and for his account of the way in which doctors coped with these new types of injuries. He also gives an excellent description of the whole infrastructure of the medical services at the Front, and how they were adapted to the vast numbers of men who had to be catered for.

From the point of view of war memorials, it is worth tracing the passage of a wounded man through the Regimental Aid Post (RAP) where the battalion's medical officer (RAMC but attached to a unit) sorted out the casualties; through the Casualty Clearing Station, the Advanced Dressing Station and Collecting Post, to the Base Hospital.

In *Craven's Part in the Great War*, which was published in 1920, of the 1,563 names appearing, forty-six died after the Armistice, several in the post-war influenza epidemic while still in uniform. These post-Armistice deaths include that of the only woman in the Craven roll of honour, VAD Nurse Doris Proctor of Settle, and that of Private Richard Foster, also of Settle, who was believed to have been taken prisoner in April 1918 but was never seen again and was finally officially presumed dead on 19 January 1920.

Some memorials actually record the passing of veterans who died as a direct result of war, but whether these names appear as an integral part of the war memorial or have been clearly added later will depend on which year the memorial was erected.

War memorials, and even rolls of honour, seldom reveal details of a man's death when this was as a result of an error by his own side – such as the accidental shooting by a sentry of members of a returning patrol, or negligent behaviour with a hand-grenade, leading to death.

Major M. Barne DSO of the Scots Guards (formerly of the Suffolk Yeomanry, and who thus appears twice in *Officers Died* ...) is simply given as killed in action on 17 September 1917. In Eton's roll of honour he is described as having 'Died of Wounds in accident'.

Major Barne, who had been a regular in the Scots Guards before leaving the Army, rejoined his old regiment in the spring of 1915. In the autumn of that year, during the Battle of Loos, he was temporarily in command of the 1st Battalion Scots Guards and acted as commanding

officer again on several occasions during 1916/1917. He was killed when
a crew-member of a friendly plane, preparing to crash-land after a flight
over enemy lines, jettisoned a live bomb. This fell in the Scots Guards
transport lines, killing one soldier and wounding four others, including
Major Barne, who died of his wounds next day. It is said that he had seen
more continuous service with his battalion than any other Scots Guards
officer.

Company Sergeant-Major Hayes DCM of the same regiment died in
February of that same year 1917 in an accident on the brigade
bombing-ground. He had gone to France with his Scots Guards battalion
at the very start of the war and served for two years in the hazardous trade
of bombing before his fatal accident.

The term 'Died on Active Service' is sometimes used for those who
died abroad from disease, in ordinary accidents or even by suicide.

The 1st Garrison Battalion of the Cameronians (Scottish Rifles) was
formed at Hamilton, near Glasgow, in February 1916 and was on its way
to India by the end of the same month. It served as a garrison battalion in
India for three years and was not involved in any fighting, but
twenty-one of its other ranks died there – in 1917 and 1918.

One can get some sort of picture of that garrison battalion from the
mini-obituaries of those twenty-one men in *Soldiers Died* …. Nineteen of
them were Scots, and sixteen had served previously in other Scottish
regiments (five in the Highland Light Infantry and four each in the Black
Watch and the Argylls).

A number of Territorial Force battalions also went to India to relieve
regular battalions stationed there. An account of how the 2/5th
Battalion (Prince Albert's) Somerset Light Infantry fared on garrison
duty in India and Burma is given in a very readable book called *A Strange
War* by C.P. Mills, grandson of one of the men. The battalion's first
casualty came on the voyage out, when Private Ernest Charles Williams
died of ptomaine poisoning. Eight men died during the twenty-eight
months 2/5th SLI spent in Burma, and twenty-three more in India. Their
taking over such unglamorous garrison duties for the duration (many men
left Britain in December 1914 and did not get back till late 1919) made
possible the formation of the regular 29th Division, which would so
distinguish itself at Gallipoli and later in France. The book serves as a
memorial to these men of Taunton and Somerset.

# 10 Religion

Greater Love Hath No Man Than This
St John 15:13

There are grounds for a good deal of theological argument over the phrases that so often appear on war memorials:

'Laid Down Their Lives'

'Gave Their Lives'

'Made The Supreme Sacrifice'

The parallel with Christ's knowing sacrifice of His life may have been apparent to leaders of the Church and to the writers of leading articles in the press, but it seems unlikely that many front-line soldiers saw themselves in this sacrificial light. While recognizing the fact that there was a good chance that they would lose their lives, for the evidence was all around them the moment they set foot in the trenches, after a few days or weeks or months what many of them hoped for was 'a good Blighty' – an honourable wound that would take them home, and even out of the war altogether.

The Joan Littlewood musical play, and subsequent Richard Attenborough film, *Oh What A Lovely War*, made telling critical points about the belief by all the belligerents that God (and Justice) was on their side. Prayers to this effect, said in services just behind the lines, and in the home parishes of all the belligerent nations, may have varied their messages somewhat, but almost all saw themselves as fighting a Just and Holy War.

And some, as at Warmington, Warwicks., were grateful to God: 'THANKS BE TO GOD WHICH GIVETH US THE VICTORY.'

Once again, taken all together, what war memorials offer is a comprehensive insight into how the war was seen from a religious point of view. It is generally a post-war, 1920s vision, and in most cases from the point of view of the Established Church – the Church of England in the south and the Church of Scotland in the north. But, by and large, war memorial inscriptions do provide us with a valid contemporary picture.

We know that Lutyens deliberately avoided incorporating a cross in the Cenotaph, because he felt that Indian and Muslim troops in the Victory Parade would not want to salute this Christian symbol. The same would apply to other religions and even to some Christian denominations, as well as to Jews and agnostics. Indeed, many war memorials are deliberately sited just outside consecrated ground, in an enclave in the churchyard itself, for this very reason. Nonetheless, one suspects that a goodly number of those commemorated under a cross memorial may have been Jewish, Mohammedan or unbelievers. As a side-issue, it would be interesting to know if there were many cases of relatives refusing to have the names of their loved ones included on a war memorial for religious or denominational reasons.

In many churchyard memorials the tribute is to 'Men of This Parish', and though a parish was sometimes a political and geographical boundary, rather than exclusively a churchly demarcation, those who lived in villages did have this unifying feature.

But we should recognize a point made about parish boundaries by Richard Muir, in his excellent *Shell Guide to Reading The Landscape*: ' "Field" churches were established to serve some of the communities which lived within the ambit of each minister and the field churches duly became tied to a parish and diocese. The parishes themselves however seldom seem to result from a planned carve-up of ecclesiastical territory. Most existed as estates or village-centred land units in pagan, Roman or prehistoric times and the estate boundary simply provided a convenient demarcation for the later parish.'

The sacrifice theme is illustrated by the war memorial cross at Brailes, South Warwicks., which carries the traditional 'Greater Love' inscription but is one of the minority to source it to the Gospel according to St John.

THESE MEN ALSO MADE
THE SUPREME SACRIFICE, LAYING DOWN
THEIR LIVES THAT WE MIGHT LIVE.

'Greater Love Hath No Man Than This
That A Man Lay Down His Life For His Friends.'
St John XV, 13

Another war memorial giving the source is at Halkirk, Caithness. At Priors Hardwick, Warwicks., an obelisk memorial reads:

TO THE MEMORY OF
Private G.H. Haynes
Private E.T. Haynes

## Private W. Taylor

WHO GAVE THEIR LIVES IN THE GREAT WAR

'Their Glory Shall Not Be Blotted Out
But Their Name Liveth for Evermore'
Ecclesiasticus XLIV 13/14

It will take a better theologian, or a better-read Christian, than I to analyse why verses were chosen from the Old or New Testaments, or in this case from Ecclesiasticus in the Apocrypha. This passage comes from the forty-fourth chapter, known to many for its 'Let us now praise famous men, and our fathers that begat us' theme; then it turns to those who have no memorial:

> And some there be, which have no memorial; who are perished as though they had not been, and are become as though they had not been born; and their children after them. But these were men of mercy, whose righteous deeds have not been forgotten. With their seed shall remain continually a good inheritance; their children are within the covenants. Their seed standeth fast, and their children for their sakes. Their seed shall remain for ever, and their glory shall not be blotted out. Their bodies were buried in peace, and their name liveth to all generations.

It is surely good practice to go back to the source of any quote and read the chosen extract in context. An oft-recurring one is: 'The men were very good unto us, they were a wall unto us both by night and by day.'

At Harlech, Merioneth, it is adapted and sourced:

They Were A Wall Unto Us Both By Night And Day
And We Were Not Hurt (I Samuel 2)

It is part of a fairly complicated story about David and Saul and the Philistines, and how David is provoked by Nabal's churlishness till Abigail intervenes with David on her husband's behalf. Well worth re-reading, from at least I Samuel 21 onwards.

Some of the epitaphs appearing on memorials are not from the Bible but are obviously there for their religious overtones.

At Alveston, Warwicks., Earl Haig is credited with his quote which appears in full or in part on so many memorials. Here the war memorial is a small cross on a triangle at the approach to the village.

AND BY THE LONG ROAD THEY TROD
WITH SO MUCH FAITH AND WITH SUCH
DEVOTED SELF-SACRIFICING BRAVERY
WE HAVE ARRIVED AT VICTORY
AND TODAY THEY HAVE THEIR REWARD
Earl Haig
(Moreton Corbet, Shropshire)

Proving themselves worthy, sleep and rest, and resurrection in Christ: these are themes which run through the inscriptions, reflecting the views of parishioners, the squire or the vicar.

God proved them and found them worthy for Himself
[Stoke Lyne, Oxon.]

They loved not their lives unto the death (Revelations 12:11)
[New Galloway, Kirkcudbright; Alsager, Ches.]

Be Thou Faithful Unto Death and I will give Thee a Crown of Life
[or simply] 'Faithful Unto Death' (Revelations 2:10)
[Pershore, Worcs; Tadmarton, Oxon; Datchet, Berks.]

'Lo, these are They from Suff'rings great'
[Lochmaben, Dumfries]

The doctrine of Resurrection is understandably strongly represented, especially in view of the 'Greater Love Hath No Man Than This' theme of so many war memorials. It is variously expressed.

At Sarsden-cum-Churchill, West Oxon, a rather gloomily Gothic and mausoleum-style war memorial carries the words:

I am the Resurrection and the Life,
He that believeth in me shall never Die.

At war memorial ceremonies on 11 November a bugler marks the end of the Two Minutes Silence by sounding 'Reveille'. This is the trumpet-call, sounded each morning, which exhorts soldiers to wake up and start the day. This theme of awakening from sleep in response to Reveille is found on many war memorials.

R.I.P. (Requiescant in Pace)

Grant Them, O Lord, Eternal rest, and
let Light Perpetual Shine upon Them
(Great Torrington, Devon)

Eternal Rest grant them O Lord
(Buckland, Oxon; Horley, Oxon.)

He giveth his beloved sleep
(Benwick, Isle of Ely)

And in this rest always that expectation of Immortality.

In the sight of the unwise they seem to die,
yet is their hope full of immortality
[Wimbledon, Surrey]

Their Hope Is Full of Immortality (Wisdom III.4)
[Saham Toney, Norfolk]

Mourn Not For Them, For They Can Never Die
[Datchet, Berks]

Dying, and Behold We Live'

But, above all, that hope of resurrection ...

UNTIL REVEILLE

In Loving Memory and Sure Hope of Life Eternal
this Tablet was erected by Fellow-Parishioners
to the Men of TENBURY
who fell in the Great European War 1914–19

The King of the World shall raise us up
Who have died for his Laws unto Everlasting Life
(Hollybush, Worcs.)

Be Thou Faithful Unto Death,
And I Will Give Thee A Crown of Life.
(Great Milton, Oxon.)

In addition to what the war memorials said, and perhaps reflecting the spirit of an age more religious than our own, many endowments to churches were made after the First World War by way of memorials to those who had died – and even to those who had served and returned. At Hinton-on-the-Green, Worcs., the east window and the clock in the tower of the parish church were given as a memorial of the 1914–18

War. A plaque inside the doorway of the church says it honours the following men from Hinton-on-the-Green who joined His Majesty's Forces:

### THESE DIED FOR THEIR COUNTRY

S. Diston
J.W.R. Gould
C.W. Taylor

### THESE SERVED AND RETURNED

| | | | |
|---|---|---|---|
| F.L. | Barnes | P.C. | Griffin |
| W. | Brooks | W.E. | Griffin |
| C.E. | Betteridge | W. | Hunt |
| W. | Clinton | J.D. | Johnson |
| H.J. | Cotton | H.H. | Lampitt |
| A. | Diston | F. | Pulley |
| W. | Diston | C.G. | Rimell |
| C.F. | Freeman | J.H. | Rowland |
| E.J. | Freeman | S.J. | Rowland |
| W.J. | Freeman | G.H. | Smith |
| E.G. | Gregg | S.G. | Walcroft |
| J. | Gregg | H. | White |
| T.H. | Gregg | | |

At Shelfanger, Norfolk, a village two miles north-west of Diss, a tablet on the wall under the clock at All Saints' Church reads:

The above CLOCK
was given by the Inhabitants of **SHELFANGER**
and Friends in the Year 1919
TO THE GLORY OF GOD
and in Memory of the following men
who gave their lives for King and Country
in the Great War 1914–1918

William PAGE
Frederick Charles BOWEN
Arthur George HUGGINS
Frederick FULCHER
Edward Last WARD
William Sidney WELTON
Alexander Charles SHULVER
Spencer Henry BOND
Christopher William ROUT

'Greater Love Hath No Man Than This,
That A Man Lay Down His Life For His Friends.'

**R.I.P.**

At Troutbeck, Westmorland, a parish and village three miles south-east of Ambleside, the bells at Jesus Church are a memorial. A plaque reads:

The Peal of Chiming Bells on this Tower was presented
by Arthur Brook DUNLOP of The Howe, and his daughter Ingha,
in loving memory of his only two sons Eric and Lindsay,
who gave their lives in the Great War
as Officers in His Majesty's Forces
– the former in 1917, the latter in 1916.

Church lych-gates are often used as a war memorial instead of a cross. It is at the lych-gate outside the church that a coffin awaits the clergyman's arrival during a burial service.

At Marchington Woodlands, Staffs., the lych-gate is inscribed '**IN MEMORIAM**', and it has two panels at ground level, one with a dedication, the other with the names:

**TO THE GLORY OF GOD AND IN MEMORY
OF THE MEN OF MARCHINGTON WOODLANDS
WHO GAVE THEIR LIVES IN THE GREAT WAR
1914–1919**

| | | |
|---|---|---|
| H.S. | GRIFFIN | KRRC |
| W.H. | HOLLINGSWORTH | West Yorks |
| A.W. | ROWE | West Yorks |
| W.H. | THORLEY | RFA |
| A. | TUNNICLIFFE | Grenadier Guards |
| E. | WHEAT | North Staffords |

The lych-gate at the Church of St Peter's at Sibton in east Suffolk is a war memorial:

To The Glory of God and in Memory
of the Men of SIBTON
who Gave Their Lives for Their Country
in the Great War 1914–1918
and 1939–1945

| | | | |
|---|---|---|---|
| F. | CRICKMER | A. | SPRINGTHORPE |
| C.W. | GODDARD | S.H. | THREADGALE |
| H. | MAYHEW | G. | WEAVERS |
| D. | SHEPHERD | S. | WOODWARD |
| A.H. | TEAGO | A.G. | WHINCOP |
| C.W. | WALKER | | |

'Lest We Forget'
S. WOODARD
G. EMERSON

The restoration of chapels within a church, as memorials to those who lost their lives, seems more common after the Second World War.

The Church of St Giles at Stoke Poges, Bucks., two miles north of Slough, is most famous for being the place where the poet Thomas Gray wrote 'Elegy – Written in a Country Churchyard'. It is a fine church with Saxon remains, Norman pillars, Early Gothic reconstruction, Tudor additions and a Second World War memorial window at the back:

> To the Glory of God and in Grateful Memory
> of the Men of this Church and Parish
> who Fell in the War **1939–1945**

> John Leslie BEESON
> Frederick William BRIGHT
> John Stuart DEVEREUX
> James William EDMONDS
> John William HARTLEY
> Harry HAZELL
> James Alfred George PITKIN
> Walter Edward WINTER

But there is also the Hastings Chapel, a Tudor addition of red brick and stone mullioned windows on the outside of the church. It was built as an oratory for those living in an almshouse near the church, and as a burial-place for the Hastings family. The chapel was included within the church in the eighteenth century, and restored in 1946 by Colonel Wallace Devereux.

> **This Chapel founded and built by Edward Hastings,**
> **2nd Earl of Huntingdon AD 1558,**
> **was restored by Colonel Wallace C. DEVEREUX**
> **in Memory of his son**
> **John Stuart DEVEREUX**
> **Pilot Officer R.A.F.**
> **Killed on Active Service 29 September 1944**

At St Mary's Church in Lambeth, London, which is now the home of a gardening association, the Tradescant Society, a chapel dedicated to the fifth Earl of Chichester, a former rector of St Mary's, was turned into a World War I memorial chapel. It has a wooden altar-piece with the names of the 1914–18 dead on it, as well as a marble carving of St George dedicated to the fourth son of the fifth Earl, a regular soldier who was killed in 1914. At the entrance to this chapel, carved in wood on either side:

Alleluia * Praise God for the Men of this Parish who Gave Their
Lives in the Great War 1914–18. Their Name Liveth For Evermore.

'I sent you out with mourning and weeping, but God will give you
to me again with joy and gladness for ever' (Baruch IV)

(A marble carving of St George, with another marble plaque beneath.)

In Praise to God for
Herbert Lyttleton PELHAM
Fourth son of Francis Godolphin, 5th Earl of Chichester,
sometime Rector of Lambeth, and Alice, his Wife.

Adjutant, 2nd Bn. Royal Sussex Regiment
Croix de Chevalier, Legion d'Honeur [sic]
born 3 April 1884
Killed in the forefront of the Battle of the Aisne 14 September 1914
Vincit Amor Patria

To the Glory of God and in Loving Memory of
Edward Charles DAUN
Lieutenant & Assistant Adjutant, 2nd Bn. Royal Sussex Regiment
beloved and only son of Charles J. and Ada M. DAUN
born 15 June 1885
Killed at the Battle of the Aisne in France 14 September 1914
aged 29 years
There is no death.

In addition to actual endowments for church improvement, another form
of war memorial often encountered in cathedrals, minsters and major
churches is the tablet which records the names of former members of the
choir who died in the First World War.

Ely Cathedral has such a tablet:

WE REMEMBER BEFORE GOD THE CHORISTERS OF THIS
CATHEDRAL WHO GAVE THEIR LIVES FOR THEIR COUNTRY
1914–1918.

J.W.  BLAKE
F.L.  CLARKE
R.A.  CLARKE
P.F.C. FOX
H.  LAWRENCE
W.  NEWTON
J.V.  THOMPSON, MM
T.E.T. WOODROFFE
E.C.  WOODROW

This Tablet was Dedicated by their Fellow Choristers.

Among the many individual memorials at churches are the gates at Holy Trinity Church, Claygate, Surrey, inscribed:

These gates were erected in 1959
In Memory of
Hugh ROSSITER of Devoncroft, Claygate
Who died at Colyton, Devon
21 October 1955 aged 69 years

(and of his son)

Captain David ROSSITER M.C.
Queen's Royal Regiment
killed in action in Italy
13 September 1944 aged 24 years
**R.I.P.**

As *The Churchyards Handbook*, published by the Council for the Care of Churches puts it, 'Every churchyard should have a properly defined entrance, well-designed and welcoming; nineteenth-century architects were particularly successful at designing lychgates ....' At Kilmartin, Argyllshire, a village eight miles north-west of Lochgilphead, the war memorial is a stepped-arch gateway in front of the church.

THEY DIED
THAT WE
**1914**     MIGHT     **1919**
LIVE

| Captain Jas. M. | McLACHLAN, MC | Lieutenant Gavin | BOYD |
|---|---|---|---|
| Sergeant A. | McKELLAR | Sergeant A. | McNAIR |
| Corporal A. | McFADYEN | Corporal H. | McLEAN |
| Private W. | BALLANTYNE | Private A. | CAMPBELL |
| Private J. | CAMPBELL | Private A. | CRAWFORD |
| Private D.C. | McKAY | Private J. | McEWAN |
| Private C. | McKELLAR | Private J. | McLELLAN |
| Private D. | McKELLAR | Private B. | McLELLAN |
| Private A. | McINTYRE | Private D. | McVEAN |

At Newchurch, Staffs., six miles west of Burton-on-Trent, a gateway arch in front of the New Church is inscribed:

This Arch was Erected in Honour
of the Men of the Parish who
Served Their King and Country in the Great war
1914–1919

Also in Memory of the three who Died in Action

James MYATT
William PAYNE
Fred EASON

At St Olave's, Hart Street, near the Tower of London, the church porch was presented as a war memorial. An inscription reads:

Let all who pass through this porch
Remember with honour those who lost their lives
Through acts of war 1914–1918 and 1939–1945.

This Memorial Porch is the gift of
The Wine and Spirit Trade of the British Isles.

'These stones shall be a memorial for ever'

St Olave's was the church of Samuel Pepys (1633–1703), and a tablet on the outside wall marks the entrance to the South Gallery and the Navy Office pew often mentioned in Pepys's diary. (The tablet was erected in 1891.) In a small garden nearby a plaque marks the site of the Navy Office in which Pepys worked and which was destroyed by fire in 1673.

There is a certain historical continuity in the memorial plaques which you will encounter as you read the war memorials of Britain.

# 11  *Local Affiliations*

*Hedd perffaitth hedd*
*Gus am bris an la*

I referred in the opening chapter, when talking about the memorial to the Eyemouth fishermen who died in the Great Storm of 1881, to a sense of place, the feeling of belonging to a home town or ancestral village. I see this as accompanying an acceptance of the life-style and mores of that place as one's own, for life.

This may be hard for present generations to appreciate. Much more mobile than our predecessors, weaned as many of us were on radio and later television, accustomed to cheap holiday travel, we need to make an effort to remember how localized life was before 'the Great War'. In 1914 most working-class people never travelled much beyond the next village or market town, or the urban parish in which they lived. The idea of travel for pleasure was almost non-existent, or limited to a short trip to the sea on the few Bank Holidays there were or during a Fairs Week each year.

The more you read accounts written at the time by working-class soldiers, the more often you encounter their real surprise at the strangeness and unintelligibility of other people's accents. Whereas they might have encountered a few 'posh' accents in their lives, even a travelling Irish tinker or a job-searching Scotsman, most Geordies had never met a West Countryman, a Yorkshireman a Man of Kent, or a Cumbrian a Cockney. With no radio to accustom people to non-local sounds, no television or pop-music lingua franca to bind all young people together, regional accents were a considerable barrier to communication. People are time and time again identified by accent, by where they came from.

One of the many, almost certainly apocryphal stories told to account for the rumours of trainloads of Russians travelling through Britain in 1914 with 'snow on their boots' involves the Lovat Scouts. It is said that Gaelic-speaking Lovat Scouts, travelling south by rail with their shaggy Highland ponies, were asked where they came from. When they said 'Ross-shire', their reply was taken as 'Russia'.

Even as late as 1939, one squadron of about 120 Lovat Scouts was almost entirely composed of Gaelic-speakers for whom English was still very much a second language. The fact that half of them were also called Macleod led to other problems of identification, solved in the usual way by adding an occupational title: Willie Macleod the Postie, Willie Macleod the Dominie (schoolmaster) or Willie Macleod the Piper.

The identification by place which we see on war memorials is also sometimes necessary to distinguish men with exactly the same name. *Soldiers Died* ..., giving an army number and place of birth and residence, is needed to make certain which Willie Macleod it is.

In *Craven's Roll of Honour* – which I have mentioned before – are recorded the names of 1,562 men and one woman from the area of the Skipton parliamentary division who fell in the First World War. Of these, some 348 names are identified as coming from Skipton itself. This roll of honour accounts for over ten per cent of the 3,000-odd inhabitants of military age in Skipton.

A war memorial which could be used to illustrate points made in several chapters is the one at Llangefni, Anglesey. It lists the Christian names and surnames of thirty-four men from the district who were killed or died of wounds between 1914 and 1918. The names are listed in the order in which they died, with the first man killed in 1916, surprisingly late.

The battles in which each man died also feature, as well as the campaign areas in which the men of Llangefni fought. The battles are interesting in themselves for including so many of the engagements and places that are part of British military history of World War I: Albert, the Somme, Mametz, Delville, Givenchy, the Ancre, Ypres, Messines and Armentières. Of the thirty-one whose places of death overseas are recorded (two of the total of thirty-four are listed simply as dying of wounds, and one died in Scotland), only six died elsewhere than on the Western Front (four in Palestine, one in Mesopotamia, one in Italy).

The memorial itself is a fine one of a soldier, with arms reversed, sculpted by a local man, John Griffiths of Llangefni.

Two features about this memorial stand out: the Welshness of the names, and the local affiliations. There are six Joneses (including a Lloyd-Jones); five Owens, five Roberts and five Williams, two Hughes and two Evans; and among the nine others are a Davies, a Griffiths, a Meredith, a Parry and a Thomas. The Christian names are much in the pattern of the top names for England and Wales but include Tegerin, Iorwerth and Gwilym.

But it is when you study the list of places from which the men came that you get an overwhelming feeling of place, of community. Only seven of the thirty-eight are Llangefni-born. About a dozen are from the north and east coast of Anglesey, including five from Amlwch and three from Marian-glas. Another group comes from along the railway-line (Llanfair, Gaerwen, Bodorgan, Ty-croes) or what is now the A5 to Holyhead (Gwalchmai, Heneglwys). Yet another grouping can be made of those from well south of Llangefni, from places along the Menai Strait, such as Brynsiencyn, or from the Malltreath marsh area (Malltreath, Trefdraeth, Llangaffo).

Anglesey remains a very different and very Welsh part of Wales. Eighty-three square miles of the island are now designated as an area of outstanding natural beauty for conservation purposes.

Finally, in reading the Llangefni memorial you will have noted, amidst all those Anglesey place-names, that Iorwerth Griffiths was from Bootle, and David R. Williams from Liverpool.

## LLANGEFNI, Anglesey

Market town, urban district and parish, Anglesey.
Fine war memorial statue of a soldier.

### THE GREAT WAR
*Killed*

| | | | |
|---|---|---|---|
| Tegerin HUGHES | Llanerchymedd | St Eloi | 1916 |
| Henry OWEN | Brynsiencyn | (Died of wounds) | 1916 |
| Edward PARRY | Llanerchymedd | (Died of wounds) | 1916 |
| Iorwerth GRIFFITHS | Bootle | Albert | 1916 |
| David R. WILLIAMS | Liverpool | Somme | 1916 |
| Arthur WILLIAMS | Llangefni | Mametz | 1916 |
| Albert E. JONES | Trefdraeth | Mametz | 1916 |
| Lewis R. WILLIAMS | Benllech | Somme | 1916 |
| Hugh JONES | Marian-glas | Delville | 1916 |
| Edward OWEN | Brynsiencyn | Delville | 1916 |
| Richard EVANS | Llangristiolus | Givenchy | 1916 |
| Robert J. ROBERTS | Pentraeth | Somme | 1916 |
| Thomas ROBERTS | Marian-glas | Ancre | 1916 |
| Evan JONES | Ty Croes | Merville | 1916 |
| John WILLIAMS | Gaerwen | Somme | 1917 |
| Griffith OWEN | Marian-glas | Mesopotamia | 1917 |
| Victor ROBERTS | Llangefni | Ypres | 1917 |
| Owen ROBERTS | Llangaffo | Ypres | 1917 |
| Thomas J. JONES | Penrhoslligwy | Messines | 1917 |
| John W. MEREDITH | Llangefni | Ypres | 1917 |
| Albert V. HALLSWORTH | Gwalchmai | Gaza | 1917 |
| Edward Lewis JONES | Cemaes | Palestine | 1917 |
| William R. BLACK | Llanfair | Armentieres | 1917 |
| John R. OWEN | Amlwch | France | 1917 |
| Richard G. PIERCE | Gwalchmai | Italy | 1917 |

| | | | | |
|---|---|---|---|---|
| William | OWEN | Benllech | Wimereux | 1917 |
| William | ROBERTS | Amlwch | Palestine | 1917 |
| Arthur | THOMAS | Gaerwen | Palestine | 1917 |
| W. Ivor | WILLIAMS | Amlwch | Armentieres | 1918 |
| John J. | GARLAND | Llangefni | Armentieres | 1918 |
| Gwilym | DAVIES | Llangefni | Hazebrouck | 1918 |
| Arthur | LLOYD-JONES | Heneglwys | Germany | 1918 |
| George R. | EVANS | Amlwch | Haussy | 1918 |
| John | HUGHES | Amlwch | Ayrshire | 1918 |

**1914–1918**

[Four names added outside plaque and very hard to read.]

*Also Died*

| | | | |
|---|---|---|---|
| Hugh P.J. | HUGHES | Malltraeth | |
| O.C. | EDWARDS | Llangefni | |
| Royle | JONES | Llangefni | |
| Robert A. | WILLIAMS | Bodorgan | 1919 |

(John Griffiths, Sculptor, Llangefni)

In the case of 'the Men of Harlech', the place from which they came is the *only* additional fact given on the war memorial, a shrine at a bend in the road near the centre of town. The inscription and the Bible quotation at the end may be in English, but the names of all those listed there are truly Welsh.

## ROLL OF HONOUR

### IN MEMORY OF THE MEN OF HARLECH
### WHO FELL IN THE GREAT WAR 1914–1918.

| | | |
|---|---|---|
| Gwilym | BEVERS | Tremorthin |
| Douglas | DAVIES | Caereinion |
| Evan | EVANS | Brwynllynau |
| William J. | HUGHES | Dan'rallt |
| David W. | HUMPHREYS | Station House |
| Thomas | JONES | Llechwedd Canol |
| Edward | JONES | Hendre |
| Evan | LLOYD | Tynymaes |
| Ellis | OWEN | Moriah Terrace |
| R. Lewis | OWEN | Moriah Terrace |
| George | OWEN | Fforddgroes |
| William | OWEN | Fforddgroes |
| Mathew | OWEN | Waterloo House |
| William | OWEN | Llechwedd Canol |
| Owen | PARRY | Grogan Terrace |

| | | |
|---|---|---|
| Leon Rees | ROBERTS | Bronwen Terrace |
| Morris | THOMAS | Grogan |
| J. Griffith | WILLIAMS | 2, Bronwen Terrace |
| Richard | WILLIAMS | Rosslyn House |
| Robert R. | WILLIAMS | Ty'nybuarth |
| Griffith | JONES | Llechwedd |

### 1939–1945

| | | |
|---|---|---|
| Hugh C. | EDWARDS | Pencerrig |
| Colin J. | GRIFFITH | Tregwylan |
| Clarence G. | HAMMOND | St. David's Hotel |
| Robert Ll. | LEWIS | Brynteirion |
| Ivor | LLOYD | 1, Ael-y-bryn |
| Robert D. | LLOYD | Gwyndy Bach |
| Emlyn | ROBERTS | 4, Rock Terrace |
| John | ROBERTS | Isgaer |
| Owen | ROBERTS | Grogan |
| Meirion | THOMAS | 2, Porkington Place |
| John H. | WILLIAMS | Isallt |

'They Were A Wall Unto Us Both By Night And Day
And We Were Not Hurt'

I Samuel 25

Comparing the 1939–45 names and places, one notes minor new trends in Christian names and that only one place-name is a repeat.

This same sense of place, of its being important where a man comes from, is true of Scotland and of parts of rural England. At Liddlesdale, in Roxburghshire, on the road down from Hawick, at a very minor road-junction, there is a small war memorial.

### THE GREAT WAR
### 1914–1919
IN FOND AND LOVING MEMORY OF THESE YOUNG MEN
WHO AT THE HIGH CALL OF DUTY WENT FORTH FROM THIS VALLEY
ON ACTIVE SERVICE AND GAVE THEIR LIVES FOR THEIR COUNTRY
IN THE GREAT CAUSE OF FREEDOM

| | |
|---|---|
| 2/Lieutenant Walter BARRIE | Berryfell |
| Private James BURNETT | Barnes |
| Private Andrew CURRIE | Greenbraeheads |
| Gunner James DICKSON | Winningtonrig |
| Private Henry ELLIOT | Flex |
| 2/Lieutenant Walter HADDON | Colislinn |
| Lieutenant A.R. MACFARLANE-GRIEVE | Penchrise Peel |
| Private Thomas R. OLIVER | Winningtonrig |

Private Thomas REDPATH  Newmill
Private James W. TELFER  Earlside
Private Robert WRIGHT  Fleety
Private David WYLIE  Flex

**1939–1945**
Sergeant James CORRY  Adderstoneshiels

The 1939–45 memorial of the parish of Daviot and Dunlichity, Inverness-shire, a solid, castle-shaped memorial, stands by the old A9 road from Aviemore to Inverness:

SACRED TO THE MEMORY OF THE MEN FROM THIS PARISH
WHO GAVE THEIR LIVES IN THE SECOND WORLD WAR
1939–1945.

| | |
|---|---|
| Major-General M.B. Beckwith SMITH, DSO MC | Aberarder |
| Sergeant/Air Gunner George E.R. LATIMER | Daviot |
| Sergeant-Pilot Malcolm F. MACLEAN | Culloden Moor |
| Private David ALLAN | Daviot |
| Private Thomas P. FERGUSON | Farr |
| Private Malcolm MACKINTOSH | Daviot |
| Driver William REID | Farr |
| Trooper Lachlan SMITH | Dunlichity |
| Able Seaman Murdo D. SCOTT | Culloden Moor |

*'Gus am bris an la'*

On 22 May 1915 the worst train-crash ever on Britain's railways occurred near Gretna Green. One of two troop trains carrying the 1/7th Battalion of the Royal Scots (TF) from Larbert in Stirlingshire to troopships at Liverpool, waiting to take them to Gallipoli, ran into some empty carriages of a local train. The troop-train, which was carrying the battalion's headquarters staff, and A (Major J.D.L. Hamilton) and D (Captain A.M. Mitchell) Companies of the 1/7th battalion, overturned. A minute later, a northbound London-Glasgow express ploughed into the wreckage, which caught fire.

Three officers, twenty-nine NCOs and 182 men were killed or burned to death. Major Hamilton, Captain J.M. Mitchell and Lieutenant C.R. Salvesen, from the famous Leith ship-owning family, were killed. Another five officers (including another Salvesen) were among the 246 injured.

This was a case where a battalion's tragic losses particularly impinged on one local community, as the 1/7th Royal Scots (the Leith Battalion of

Territorials) had been recruited mainly from the burgh and seaport of Leith, which forms part of north Edinburgh, and had joined up to serve together.

A memorial to the dead was unveiled on 12 May 1916 at Leith Rosebank Cemetery by the Honorary Colonel of the battalion, Lord Rosebery.

War memorials can be used to help define linguistic maps of both Wales and Scotland, and often illustrate a sense of place too.

The first thing to notice is if they carry inscriptions in the Welsh language or in the Gaelic. If they do, do they also carry a translation, and if so, which of the two languages takes precedence?

Once again, because no central authority was responsible for war memorials, in each case the decision about the language to use will have been a local one. Each use of a language other than English must indicate an ability by some people to speak the second tongue. Their use on a public monument must reflect Welsh or Scottish nationalism, not in its narrowest sense but in pride of origin.

With this use of Welsh or Gaelic often went a strong emphasis on place, on where the men remembered came from. Two interesting examples are the memorials at Talsarnau, Merioneth, and Talwrn, Anglesey, which follow. At Talsarnau there is no translation of the Welsh inscription, though one notices that two of the 1914–18 place-names are 'Station' and 'Crossing', while for 1939–45 Corporal Maybury is described as of 3 Bryn Street.

At Talwrn, where the war memorial is a fairly simple plaque by the B5109 road from Llangefni to Pentraeth, the inscription is again all in Welsh, with the 1914–18 men all dying in 'Ffrainc', but at the bottom is an addition in English:

## TALSARNAU, Merioneth

War memorial in front of Christ Church (Eglwys Crist)

### Y RHYFEL MAWR 1914–1918

| | |
|---|---|
| Lt. Colonel J. Stuart WORTLEY | Maeseneuadd |
| Captain Lewis LLOYD | Bron Wylfa |
| Sergeant W.S. JONES | Beudy Bach |
| Corporal J. JONES | Brynteirion |
| Private Thomas HUGHES | Crossing |
| Private W. HUGHES | Bryneirin |
| Private J. Rees JONES | Tyn y berth |
| Private W.T. JONES | Brynmair |

Private W. JONES      Ty'n twll
Private W. PRITCHARD      Station
Private Robert WILLIAMS      Talsarnau

*Dymuniad ardallwyr bro*
*Talsarnau ydyw, am i'r golofn*
*Hon trosglwyddo i lawr i'r*
*Desau a ddel goffawdwriaeth*
*Y dewrion o'r plwyf hwn a*
*Aberthodd cysuron a'u bywydau*
*Ar allor rhyddid*

## Y RHYFEL MAWR 1939–1945

Sergeant (AG) R.G. WILLIAMS      Derwydd
Corporal D.B. MAYBURY      3, Bryn Street
Quartermaster R.H. GRIFFITH      Bryntirion

*'Newn angof ni chant fod'*

## TALWRN, Anglesey

## CODWYD Y MAYEN COFFA HWN GAN DRIGOLION Y PLWYF A'R CYLCH, ER COF ANNWYL AM YR RHAI A GWYMPASANT YN Y RHYFEL MAWR
## 1914–1918

| | | | |
|---|---|---|---|
| Hugh THOMAS | Caecrin | Ffrainc | 1915 |
| Henry JONES | Minffordd | Ffrainc | 1915 |
| Richard OWEN | Nyth Clyd | Ffrainc | 1916 |
| Henry OWEN | Bryn Goleu | Ffrainc | 1917 |
| Owen HUGHES | Pen y bryn | Ffrainc | 1918 |
| Evan Oswald THOMAS | Bryn Gors | Ffrainc | 1918 |

**1939–1945**

| | | | |
|---|---|---|---|
| Hugh JONES | Bron alar | Collwyd | 1940 |

## 'EU HABERTH NID A HEIBIO – A'U HENWAU ANNWYL NID A'N ANGO.'

This piece of land was presented
by Cyril P. Vivian, Esq.,
from Plas Llanddyfnan.

Edinburgh, as a national capital, is perhaps not a true example of the kind of local affiliations we have been looking at. However, the range of memorials and monuments the city contains, to people from Edinburgh killed in Britain's wars and to Scots in general, makes it worth special mention.

Above all, there is the Scottish National War Memorial at Edinburgh Castle. Here are recorded the names of the soldiers who died in the Scots Guards and the nine Scottish infantry regiments (Royal Scots, Cameronians and Scottish Rifles, Royal Scots Fusiliers, King's Own Scottish Borderers, Black Watch, Highland Light Infantry, Seaforth Highlanders, Cameron Highlanders, the Argyll & Sutherland Highlanders). Volumes list the infantry dead and those of Scotland's cavalry regiment (Royal Scots Greys) and other Scottish units throughout the Army. Listed too are the names of Scots who died in English, Irish and Welsh regiments, in the Royal Navy, Royal Marines, Royal Flying Corps and the Royal Air Force, as well as Scots in the Merchant Marine, the women's services and the nursing services.

Several of Edinburgh's memorials are pre-First World War, going back to the Crimea, the Indian Mutiny and Afghanistan; there are many for regiments which lost men in the Boer War, and for the Scottish Horse which was formed in South Africa; and on through memorials commemorating the two World Wars to a very rare acknowledgement of Scots who died in the International Brigade in the Spanish Civil War (a roughly cut block of stone in East Princes Street Gardens).

Another interesting war memorial is the Scottish-American First World War frieze in West Princes Street Gardens. It was erected in 1927 by the Scottish American Association, as a reminder of wartime ties between the peoples of Scotland and the USA at a time when relations between Europe and America were in danger of falling apart.

St Giles Cathedral in Edinburgh is typical of the principal church in a garrison town in housing numerous regimental memorials. Many of them are to battalions of Edinburgh's regiment – the Royal Scots or First of Foot, the senior infantry regiment in the British Army. There are 1914–18 plaques to most of the Territorial Force and (Service) battalions of the Royal Scots, as also to other Edinburgh units, such as the Edinburgh Field Company, Royal Engineers. There is a memorial to Scots of the RAMC and to Scottish nurses (1914–19).

A pattern of regimental chapels, laid-up regimental colours and memorial plaques to individual units and those who died with them, is found throughout the country. All provide valuable information about local social and military history.

# 12 Empire and Commonwealth

Simple Service, Simply Given
To His Own Kind In Their Common Need

Kipling

(On the Royal Newfoundland Regiment cross in Wandsworth Cemetery)

First World War memorials in Britain carry the names of many men who died while serving in the forces of other countries in the British Empire and in those of the United States of America.

We should remember that in those days the British Empire encompassed a total of 13 million square miles, with a population (1911) of 434,286,650. The status of each country within that British Empire varied considerably, from self-governing dominions such as Canada (though Newfoundland was still a colony) to a complicated mixture of protectorates (such as Bechuanaland, Somaliland, Uganda), leased territories (the New Territories of Hong Kong and Wei-hai-wei) and every size and shape of island, from Ceylon and Cyprus to Trinidad & Tobago and Tristan da Cunha.

The British Isles comprised the United Kingdom of Great Britain and Ireland (both north and south), the Isle of Man and the Channel Islands. South Africa was coloured red on the maps, as were Australia and New Zealand. Britain's Indian Empire included Burma, and as reference books of the time delicately put it, three other countries – Nepal, Bhutan and Afghanistan – were considered to be 'within the Indian Sphere of Influence'.

In the First World War, in addition to 702,410 dead from the British Isles, another 200,000 men from the British Empire lost their lives. Casualty figures for the First World War never wholly agree, but for the purposes of this book I take it that in round terms the British Empire lost a million dead:

702,410 from Britain
64,449 from India
59,330 from Australia

131

57,843 from Canada
16,711 from New Zealand
7,121 from South Africa
507 from British Colonies

Unlike the Second World War, in which Empire and Dominion soldiers died fighting close to their homelands (in the South Pacific, in Malaya, in Burma and in Africa), the largest proportion of First World War Empire deaths occurred in the mud and blood of France and Flanders.

A point that does, however, get overlooked is that many of the servicemen in the Anzac divisions, and those who were serving in the Canadian Expeditionary Force, were British-born. Many were expatriates returning by choice from overseas, not necessarily emigrants to the dominions and colonies. It truly was a case then of men of British stock (and others) rallying to the support of the Mother Country, of helping their own kind, in an hour of common need, far away across the sea.

War memorials throughout Britain testify to their local birthplaces, by listing them with their kinsfolk (and brothers) at home.

The war memorial at Dunvegan, in the north-west of the Isle of Skye, is a good example:

In Affectionate Memory of The Glorious Dead
**1914–1918**
from DUNVEGAN, ROAG, HARLOSH and BAY

'Agus bheannaich an sluagh na daoine uile a thairig
iad fein gu toileach'

NEH. 11:2

**DUNVEGAN**

| | | | |
|---|---|---|---|
| Captain | D.F. | MACKENZIE | Camerons |
| Lieutenant | J. | BOYD | Camerons |
| 2/Lieutenant | J.J. | MATHESON | Camerons |
| Lance-Sergeant | D. | MACDONALD | Camerons |
| Private | K. | ROSS | Camerons |
| Private | P. | MACKINNON, MM | Camerons |
| Private | J. | MACLEAN | Camerons |
| Private | J. | MACDONALD | Camerons |
| Private | N. | MACMILLAN | Camerons |
| Private | J. | JOHNSTON | Camerons |
| Private | J. | WILSON | Camerons |
| Private | H. | MACPHEE | Camerons |
| Private | M. | CAMPBELL | Camerons |

| Lieutenant | I.B. MACLEOD | Black Watch |
| Private | D. GRANT | Scots Guards |
| Private | A. GRANT | Rhodesian Rifles |
| Private | H. MACDONALD | NZ Infantry |
| Private | J. MACDONALD | Canadian MR |
| Private | A. MACDONALD | Seaforths |
| Gunner | W. MACLEOD | RGA |
| Seaman | A. SHAW | Mercantile Marine |

## ROAG, HARLOSH and BAY

| Captain | G. GRANT | Mercantile Marine |
| Private | N. MACINNES | Camerons |
| Private | D. MACLEAN | Camerons |
| Private | A. FERGUSON | Camerons |
| Private | N. MACLEOD | Camerons |
| Private | E. MACKINNON | Camerons |
| Private | M. MACMILLAN | Lovat Scouts |
| Private | A. MACMILLAN | Lovat Scouts |
| Corporal | W. TAYLOR | Seaforths |
| Private | N. MACLEAN | Seaforths |
| Corporal | K. MACKAY | SA Scottish |
| Lance-Corporal | M. MACASKILL | AIF |
| Lance-Corporal | A. FERGUSON | AIF |
| Lance-Corporal | A. MACASKILL, MM | R Innisk. Fus. |
| Private | J. MACLEOD | Royal Scots |
| Deckhand | D. MACPHEE | RNVR |
| Able Seaman | J. MACDONALD | Mercantile Marine |
| Gunner | J. MACLEOD | RNR |

## 1939–1945
## DUNVEGAN

| Flight-Lieutenant | A.F. MACQUEEN DFC Bar | RAF |
| Private | A. CAMPBELL | Camerons |
| Sapper | N. MACDONALD | Royal Engineers |

## ROAG, HARLOSH and BAY

| Guardsman | J. CAMPBELL | Scots Guards |
| | J. MACKENZIE | Merchant Navy |
| Private | J. MACLEAN MM | Gordons |
| | | |
| Flying-Officer | R.A. MACKENZIE | RAFVR |

As the memorial makes clear, Skye, then in Inverness-shire, was in the recruiting area of the Cameron Highlanders, even though the Cameron base was in Inverness, right on the other side of Scotland.

Also worth noting is that in Egypt, in September 1916, two dismounted yeomanry regiments (which also recruited in the Highlands and Islands) the 1/1st and 1/2nd Lovat Scouts, would be merged to form the 10th (Lovat Scouts) Battalion TF, the Cameron Highlanders.

But the most interesting point to emerge is the way in which Skye-born men were to be found in the overseas forces of the Empire: a Grant in the Rhodesian Rifles, a Mackay in the South African Scottish, a Macdonald in the New Zealand Infantry and another in the Canadian Mounted Rifles, and a Macaskill and a Ferguson in the Australian Imperial Force.

It is also interesting to see how memorials note this overseas participation. In some cases, exact battalions and units are given, in others a man is simply described as being with the 'Canadians' or the CEF or in the New Zealand Expeditionary Force (NZEF) or AIF.

A poignant symbol found on a number of Army headstones in Britain is the Caribou badge of the Royal Newfoundland Regiment. Coupled with the quotation from Kipling which introduces this chapter, it marks a special relationship between some of those from overseas who died in the First World War and their Mother Country, Britain.

Newfoundland is a large, triangular-shaped island, lying off the north-east coast of Canada, of which it is now part. It was at the time Britain's oldest colony, its acquisition dating from 1583. The soldiers of the Royal Newfoundland Regiment – known as 'the Blue Puttee-Boys' from that distinctive feature of their uniform – served as an integral part of the British Army and not in the CEF.

A set of Army headstones in Wandsworth Cemetery says more about the sacrifice made by Empire soldiers in 1914–18 than any words of mine can. They are those of Newfoundlanders who died in London hospitals, mostly from wounds received at Gallipoli or in France. Note the ages and their preponderantly Anglo-Saxon names.

| 2201 Private | A.J. | ABBOTT | 1 May 1917 | (22) |
|---|---|---|---|---|
| 700 Private | F.D. | BASTOW | 12 October 1916 | — |
| 1053 Private | P.J. | BROWN | 18 July 1916 | (20) |
| 1031 L/Corporal | Thomas | CARTER | 3 May 1917 | (23) |
| 1251 Private | S. | EDGCOMBE | 11 July 1916 | — |
| 450 Private | John Charles | EDWARDS | 21 July 1916 | (24) |
| 1697 Private | P. | GILLETT | 20 June 1917 | (23) |
| 1166 Private | A.G. | HEATH | 24 April 1917 | (20) |
| 1362 Corporal | R. | LEBUFF | 11 August 1916 | (25) |
| 1303 Private | C. | MERCER | 14 November 1915 | (19) |
| 934 Private | H.J. | MILES | 18 March 1916 | (18) |
| 1656 Private | E. | PECKFORD | 29 August 1916 | (20) |
| 1235 Private | S.G. | PIKE | 10 August 1916 | (25) |

| 2195 Private | A. QUINTON | 19 November 1916 | (20) |
| 761 Private | A. REID | 18 August 1916 | (21) |

| and | Nurse B. BARTLETT died 3 November 1918 | (23) |

Voluntary Aid Detachment (Newfoundland Contingent)
'She Died For Those She Loved'

The first real coming-together of troops from the Empire happened some fifteen years before the First World War – in the South African War, or, as it was dubbed by the popular press, the Boer War (1899–1902). This war was also the first in modern times in which Militia and other volunteers were used to supplement British regulars overseas. Previous wars in British military history were fought by professional soldiers or by mercenaries hired for the occasion.

The Boer War – in which an irregular force of some 60–70,000 Boer farmers fought against a British Army which eventually numbered some 300,000 – exposed many Army shortcomings. Where lessons were learned, these undoubtedly helped Britain win the European war which followed. The Boer War provided many soldiers in the British Army with battle experience against a European enemy, a factor absent from frontier clashes in India and Africa. It is not the place of this book to examine what was and what was not learned from the fighting in South Africa. Its value to our study of war memorials is that the memorials erected after the Boer War often served as models for those of the First World War.

Some of these Boer War memorials carry the kind of information that is discussed for the First World War memorials: names, ranks, battles and regimental details. They are generally found in garrison towns and main centres of population, rather than in villages and small town market-squares. In terms of numbers, the British lost 5,774 killed in the Boer War (and 22,829 wounded) against that million dead of World War I.

A Boer War memorial which was actually re-used for 1914–18 and 1939–45 is that erected to the Lothian & Border Horse at Dunbar, a royal burgh and seaport town twenty-nine miles east of Edinburgh. A red sandstone obelisk war memorial carries the inscriptions:

To The Memory of those Members of the LOTHIAN'S AND BORDER HORSE YEOMANRY who fell during the Two World Wars 1914–1918 and 1939–1945.

Their names are recorded on The Rolls of Honour
in The SCOTTISH NATIONAL WAR MEMORIAL at Edinburgh Castle.

This Memorial is erected in Memory of those Members of the 19th Company and The Lothians and Berwickshire Imperial Yeomanry who fell in South Africa during the War 1900/1901.

'They Bravely and Willingly gave their lives at the Call of Duty
for their Queen and Country.

Their Sorrowing Comrades and Friends desire
throughout All Time to Commemorate their Splendid Devotion.'

*Dulce et decorum est pro patria mori*

| | | | | |
|---|---|---|---|---|
| Trooper | C.R. | PEDDIE-WADDELL | February 1901 | Johannesburg |
| Trooper | G. | STOBO | October 1900 | Krugersdorp |
| Trooper | D. | TURNBULL | 1901 | Pretoria |
| Trooper | Ian | FLETCHER | May 1901 | Winburg |
| Trooper | J. | McGUIRE (Colt Gun Sec) | April 1900 | Stellenbosch . |
| Corporal | J. | McLAUGHLAN | April 1902 | Steinkop |
| | | | | |
| Lieutenant | Alfred | COCHRAN-CAMPBELL 13 December 1900 | Shot at | Nooitgedach |
| Sergeant | W.W. | ROMANEL | February 1901 | Johannesburg |
| Corporal | G.R. | McGIBBON | October 1900 | Welverdend |
| Corporal | G.M. | ADDIE | October 1900 | Frederikstad |
| Trooper | A.A. | COWAN | April 1901 | Brandfort |

A fine Boer War memorial, consisting of a wall with a brass plaque giving
the names of the men from the York and Lancaster Regiment who died in
South Africa, is to be found in Weston Park, Sheffield, behind the
regiment's even finer memorial to those who died in 1914–19 and
1939–45.

Most of the volunteers and militiamen who fought in the South
African War served within regular units of the British Army. A few
locally raised formations were exceptions to the rule, but they too were
generally officered by regulars or ex-regulars, rather than by militia
volunteers.

It was not until the First World War that units of the Territorial Force
and the volunteer battalions of Kitchener's New Armies went overseas as
complete fighting units to serve under their own officers. Indeed, not
very long into the war, after the slaughter of the British Expeditionary
Force in its first year, the 'Saturday-night soldiers' of the Territorial Force
and Kitchener's citizen volunteers outnumbered the regulars in the field.
This state of affairs came about because policy allowed the highly trained
and professional BEF to be 'wasted' throughout 1914. Hindsight makes it
clear that it would have been wiser to retain cadres from the regular
Army to train and eventually lead into action the massed citizen land
armies needed for a Continental war. The decision to send most of the

available British forces overseas at once was dictated partly by the need to support France as quickly as possible against the advancing German armies, in a war that most people expected to be 'over by Christmas', but is also attributable partly to the belief held by most generals that wars could be fought only by regulars – that is, by professional soldiers like themselves.

Pre-First World War war memorials, and particularly those pre-1900, are mainly tributes to regular soldiers who died for their country. A few of them antedate the formation of the county regiments, with their strong territorial associations, but nevertheless point the way to those affiliations we have looked at in previous chapters.

Even before regiments were named, they generally had established recruiting areas, so that the battalions listed as 'the 1st of Foot' or 'the 5th Fusiliers' would respectively have contained a goodly number of Lothian Scots from Edinburgh and its surrounds, or men from Northumberland, and, of course, in each case many Irishmen, who provided the British Army of the nineteenth century with some nine per cent of its strength. The Scots provided well over seven per cent.

A nineteenth-century war memorial worth looking at is the obelisk sited in Royal Hospital Gardens, between the Chelsea Pensioners' home and the Embankment on the Thames. It commemorates 255 officers, non-commissioned officers and privates of the XXIVth Regiment who died in the Battle of Chilianwalla on 13 January 1849.

Chilianwalla was fought by a strong British-Indian force of 12,000 men and sixty guns under Lord Gough, against 40,000 Sikhs led by Shir Singh, in what is now known as the Second British-Sikh War. It was a closely fought battle, with the British losing 2,300 men killed and wounded in three hours' fighting. Although Lord Gough drove the Sikhs from the field of battle, he had to withdraw his force later, owing to lack of water.

This Chelsea war memorial lists the names of all the 255 men who died from the XXIVth Regiment. The officers are carefully separated from the NCOs, and the NCOs from the private soldiers. The distinction is driven home further by giving the officer dead in order of rank, Christian name first and then surname, whereas the NCOs and men are by rank, surname and Christian name last.

## CHILIANWALLA

TO THE MEMORY OF
TWO HUNDRED AND FIFTY-FIVE
OFFICERS, NON-COMMISSIONED OFFICERS AND PRIVATES
OF THE XXIV REGIMENT
WHO FELL AT
CHILIANWALLA 13 January 1849

This Monument has been erected by their surviving comrades. AD 1853

### 1849 JAN XIII

| | | | | |
|---|---|---|---|---|
| Lt-Colonel BROOKES, | Robert | Sjt-Major | COFFEE, | John |
| Lt-Colonel PAYNTER CB, | How.l | Col-Sjt. | COLLINS, | James |
| Lt-Colonel PENNYCUICK, | John | Col-Sjt. | DAVIS, | William |
| Major HARRIS, | Henry R. | Col-Sjt. | YOUNG, | William |
| Captain LEE, | Charles | Serjeant | LEAR, | Thomas |
| Captain TRAVERS, | Robert Wm. | Serjeant | WEBSTER, | John |
| Captain HARRIS, | Charles R. | Corporal | BUGDEN, | William |
| Captain SHORE, | John S. | Corporal | EAMES, | George |
| Lieutenant PHILLIPS, | George | Corporal | HOWELL, | Francis |
| Lieutenant PAYNE, | O.B. | Corporal | PATTENDEN, | William |
| Lieutenant WOODGATE, | James A. | Corporal | RUNCHEY, | William |
| Ensign PHILIPS, | William | Corporal | SHERRIFF, | James |
| Ensign COLLIS, | H.C.V. | Corporal | WEBB, | Henry |
| Ensign PENNYCUICK, | Alexander | Corporal | WILKS, | John |
| Drummer DOUGHTY, | Edward | | | |

| | | | | |
|---|---|---|---|---|
| | | Private EDMONDS, | Robert | |
| Private ALLSWORTH, | William | Private EDWARDS, | James | |
| Private AMOS, | John | Private EGAN, | Garr.t | |
| Private ANDREWS, | Stephen | Private EGGINTON, | Joseph | |
| Private ANSON, | Robert | Private EHEMELY, | William | |
| Private ARMETT, | Joseph | Private ELLIOT, | James | |
| Private ATKINSON, | Thomas | Private ELLIS, | Thomas | |
| Private ATWELL, | Jonah | Private ENGLISH, | Samuel | |
| Private BAILEY, | William Henry | Private ENRIGHT, | John | |
| Private BAILEY, | John | Private EVANS, | George | |
| Private BARBER, | James | Private EVEREST, | Edward | |
| Private BARNES, | Charles | Private FARNER, | Henry | |
| Private BARNETT, | William | Private FERGUSON, | John | |
| Private BARR, | Edward | Private FLETCHER, | Will | |
| Private BARRINGTON, | George | Private FLYNN, | James | |
| Private BARRY, | John | Private FLYNN, | Patrick | |
| Private BEETLESTON, | Francis | Private FOWKE, | Philip | |
| Private BENTLEY, | James | Private FRANCIS, | William | |
| Private BETSON, | Michael | Private FRY, | Edward | |
| Private BIBB, | John | Private GARDNER, | William | |
| Private BIDDLE, | Thomas | Private GEORGE, | George | |

| Private | BINGHAM, | Sam | Private | GIBSON, | George |
|---|---|---|---|---|---|
| Private | BIRD, | George | Private | GILES, | William |
| Private | BOMAN, | James | Private | GOODCHILD, | James |
| Private | BONE, | Will | Private | GRANDY, | Thomas |
| Private | BRADBROOK, | John | Private | GRAY, | James |
| Private | BREWER, | James | Private | GREEN, | Gordon |
| Private | BURCHETT, | Richard | Private | GREEN, | James |
| Private | BURGESS, | John | Private | HALL, | Thos.Sm. |
| Private | BURTON, | James | Private | HANLON, | James |
| Private | BUTCHER, | James | Private | HANSCOMBE, | Thomas |
| Private | BYERS, | Joseph | Private | HARDING, | Richard |
| Private | BYRNE, | Thomas | Private | HARDMAN, | George |
| Private | CAMPBELL, | Robert | Private | HARRIS, | George |
| Private | CARPENTER, | Thomas | Private | HARRISON, | George |
| Private | CARRIER, | John | Private | HASTON, | James |
| Private | CARTER, | Samuel | Private | HAWKINS, | Joseph |
| Private | CARTER, | John | Private | HEBSON, | William |
| Private | CHAPPEL, | Thomas | Private | HENRY, | Bart'mw |
| Private | CLARKE, | James | Private | HENSHAW, | John |
| Private | CLIFFORD, | Daniel | Private | HICKS, | James |
| Private | CLUNEN, | Thomas | Private | HILL, | John |
| Private | COATS, | Richard John | Private | HOPKINS, | William |
| Private | COCKERTON, | Robert | Private | HORSFALL, | John |
| Private | CONNOLLY, | James | Private | HOULSTON, | Dan |
| Private | CORK, | Henry | Private | HUCKER, | William |
| Private | COULT, | William | Private | HUGHES, | Thomas |
| Private | CRESSWELL, | Thomas | Private | HUNTER, | John |
| Private | CROSS, | William | Private | HUTTON, | George |
| Private | CUTHBERTH, | William | Private | INDLE, | Edward |
| Private | DALEY, | Patrick | Private | INTON, | John Edw |
| Private | DAVIS, | William | Private | JERVIS, | William |
| Private | DEANE, | George | Private | JOBLIN, | Thomas |
| Private | DELMAGE, | James | Private | JOHNSON, | Edward |
| Private | DEVANEY, | Patrick | Private | JOHNSON, | Benj.mn |
| Private | DUDLEY, | James | Private | KELLY, | James |
| Private | DUFFAN, | Wm.Sands | Private | KENNING, | John |
| | | | | | |
| Private | KELSON, | Thomas | Private | PRIEST, | Thomas |
| Private | KILLEEN, | James | Private | PULLING, | Nathaniel |
| Private | KING, | James | Private | QUIRK, | Patrick |
| Private | LAKE, | John | Private | RAMPLING, | William |
| Private | LAKIN, | William | Private | REGAN, | Thomas |
| Private | LAMB, | John | Private | RYDER, | William |
| Private | LANCASTER, | James | Private | RIDDLE, | James |
| Private | LANCASTER, | Thomas | Private | ROCHFORD, | Christian |
| Private | LANG, | Francis | Private | ROBINSON, | Thomas |
| Private | LAING, | Robert | Private | ROSTER, | Thomas |

| | | | |
|---|---|---|---|
| Private LANDER, | Charles | Private ROXBERRY, | Joseph |
| Private LAWRENCE | Charles | Private SANDERS, | George |
| Private LIST, | Thomas | Private SANDERS, | Lonc.James |
| Private LLOYD, | Oliver | Private SAVAGE, | Thomas |
| Private LOMAS, | Thomas | Private SANDFORD, | Richard |
| Private McCULLOCH, | John | Private SELBY, | William |
| Private McRARY, | John | Private SHARPE, | Joseph |
| Private McMULLEN, | Joseph | Private SHEA, | Daniel |
| Private MACKAY, | Thomas | Private SHEA, | Edmund |
| Private MACOLEY, | Peter | Private SHAW, | James |
| Private MAGILL, | Benjamin | Private SIERS, | Walter |
| Private MANGAN, | Patrick | Private SIMMONDS, | Wm.Gro.vr |
| Private MARCHANT, | Thomas | Private SIMPSON, | Charles |
| Private MAYO, | Charles | Private SLADEN, | William |
| Private MEAD, | Edwin | Private SLATTERY, | James |
| Private MEDLUM, | William Henry | Private SMITH, | William |
| Private MEEDS, | Henry | Private SMITH, | George |
| Private MITCHELL, | Charles | Private SMITH, | Samuel |
| Private MOHAN, | John | Private SMITH, | Richard |
| Private MOOR, | Michael | Private SOMERSGILL, | John |
| Private MORRISH, | Thomas | Private SOVACHAN, | John |
| Private MORRIS, | Evan | Private TERRY, | John |
| Private MORRIS, | James | Private TEBBLE, | John |
| Private MORTON, | Joseph | Private THOMPSON, | William |
| Private MURPHY, | Philip | Private TOBYN, | William |
| Private MURPHY, | John | Private TOWNEND, | James |
| Private MURPHY, | Ted.e. | Private TULLEY, | James |
| Private MURTHER, | James | Private TWIGG, | Joshua |
| Private NEWMAN, | Joseph | Private TYERS, | John |
| Private NEVARD, | William | Private WAKEFIELD, | John |
| Private NICHOLS, | William | Private WALKER, | Joseph |
| Private OAKLEY, | William | Private WALKER, | William |
| Private O'CONNOR, | James | Private WALSH, | William |
| Private O'DONOGHUE, | Ty. John | Private WARREN, | James |
| Private OSBORNE, | Thomas | Private WEIGHTMAN, | Henry |
| Private OVERTON | John Mor.1 | Private WELTON, | William |
| Private PATIENCE, | James | Private WELCH, | John |
| Private PARKER, | Thomas | Private WELDON, | Alfred |
| Private PEARSON, | William | Private WESTNEAT, | Peter |
| Private PHEALAN, | Michael | Private WHEELER, | Daniel |
| Private PHILLIPS, | James | Private WHITTLE, | Ambrose |
| Private PITTMAN, | James | Private WHITEHEAD | James |
| Private POCOCK, | Thomas | Private WILLIS, | William |
| Private PORTER, | Robert | Private WILLIAMS, | James |
| Private PRATT, | Robert | Private WINDLE, | Richard |
| Private PRATT, | John | Private WOOD, | John |
| | | Private WORLEY, | Charles |

As mentioned, memorials to those killed in the Boer War tend to be found in garrison towns or in towns closely affiliated with a particular regiment or corps. Most are on a regimental basis, as in the case of the memorial to the VI Dragoon Guards (the Carabiniers) on the Ranelagh Gardens side of the Chelsea Embankment, not far from the Chilianwalla memorial just mentioned. But many of those killed in the Boer War are also commemorated in cathedrals and churches. In the crypt of St Paul's in London, an elaborate frieze and plaque list the names of officers, non-commissioned officers and men of the Royal Dragoons who lost their lives during the South African War 1899–1902.

At Winchester Cathedral there is a memorial window:

> This Window was Erected by the County of Hampshire
> to the Sacred Memory of the Officers, Non-Commissioned Officers
> and Men of the Hampshire Regiment and other units belonging
> to the County who fell in the Service of their Country
> during the South African War 1899–1902.

> The Names of Those to Whom this Memorial
> is Dedicated are inscribed on the adjacent Tablet.

More humble plaques in village churches, as at St James the Great, Snitterfield, Warwicks., list militia men and volunteers who died:

> This Tablet erected by their fellow-parishioners perpetuates the
> names of
> Trooper George TIMMS
> 5th (Warwickshire) Company Imperial Yeomanry
> and
> Private James Edwin HADLAND
> 6th Royal Warwickshire Regiment
> both of Snitterfield
> who died valiantly fighting for their country
> in the South African War AD 1900–1901

For an historian, the more revealing details of 'deaths in service' are the often ornate marble plaques or brass memorials to pre-1914 Army officers. These are often valuable to a First World War military historian for their pinpointing of family connections within a regiment, connections which will be relevant again in 1914–18. Cathedrals are often full of such plaques as these at Winchester:

To The Glory of God and in Affectionate Remembrance
of Barry Nugent YELVERTON, 5th Viscount Avonmore
Captain, 1st Battalion Hampshire Regiment
who whilst on duty with the Nile Force
died at Kirbekan on 13 February 1885, aged 26 years

In Affectionate Remembrance of
Edward Henry LE MARCHANT,
Lt-Colonel commanding the 1st Battalion
who was shot by a fanatic at Peshawur,
23 March 1899, aged 45 years

This tablet was erected by the Officers,
NCO's and Men of the Hampshire Regiment.

A Crimean plaque in Winchester Cathedral is interesting for two
features: mention of an award that would have been made had the officer
survived, and the fact that the officer (by then a major-general) had
commanded his regiment for fourteen years. It reads:

Sacred to the Memory of
Major-General Sir John CAMPBELL, Bart.
(named for the honour of KCB had he survived)
who fell at the head of his Brigade
in launching it to the Assault at Sevastopol
18 June 1855

This Tablet has been raised by the Officers,
NCO's and Soldiers of the 38th Regiment,
in which he served for 33 years
and commanded for 14 years
as Testimony of their Respect,
their Sincere Affection and Esteem.

His body lies in the cemetery on Cathcart's Hill, near Sevastopol.

One thing worth noting is that not only was the British Army in 1914 a
volunteer army – with conscription introduced only in 1916 – but so
were all the armies coming from the British Empire overseas. A memorial
tablet in St Paul's Cathedral sums it up in the case of the Indian Army:

**1746–1947**

This Tablet commemorates 201 years of faithful service given by British, Indian and Gurkha soldiers, who, as comrades, served in

**THE INDIAN ARMY**

in the employ of the Honourable East India Company, and, after 1858, under the Crown. The Indian Army served in the former Indian Empire and overseas in Peace and War.

Since its first overseas expedition in 1752 its soldiers took part in 31 expeditions and fought in 83 frontier campaigns.

In the First World War this army sent over one million soldiers overseas. In the Second World War two millions were on active service during this conflict. The Indian Army served alongside the British and Allied forces in East Africa and Asia.

In its two centuries of service here commemorated this was

**A Volunteer Army.**

# 13   Civilians

'Patriotism is not enough.'

Nurse Edith Cavell

A statue of Nurse Edith Cavell probably qualifies as a memorial to a civilian killed in World War I. The matron of a Brussels hospital, Edith Cavell stayed on after the German occupation of Belgium. She was shot by the Germans at dawn on 12 October 1915 as a spy, for her efforts in helping British soldiers and others to escape.

A tall memorial to her, with a statue by Sir George Frampton RA of her in nurse's uniform, is in St Martin's Place, opposite the National Portrait Gallery, just off Trafalgar Square in London. It was erected in 1920, and her last words – 'Patriotism is not enough. I must have no hatred or bitterness for anyone' – were added four years later.

Civilians of both sexes who were serving with British or Allied Red Cross units, or with organizations providing hospital care or comfort for the troops, and who were killed or died overseas, are often included on British parish war memorials.

Most of the nurses who were killed or died while working in service hospitals at home or abroad appear on their local memorials. Occasionally one finds a special plaque or tablet dedicated to them in churches and cathedrals, or in the hospitals in which they nursed.

I shall include the recording of the deaths of all servicewomen and nurses on war memorials in this chapter labelled Civilians. This is not because their contribution to the war effort was 'civilian' in nature, though they were, of course, officially non-combatants in both wars. It is simply that the way in which members of the women's services and nurses are treated on war memorials is generally very similar to the treatment accorded civilians who were killed. That is, in many cases women's names (like those of the civilians) are listed separately from those of the men who were killed on active service. This is particularly true of the First World War, which – as I must keep reminding readers – was the reason why most of the war memorials in Britain were built in the first place, and which was where patterns of precedence and presentation were set.

A Christ Crucified Calvary in a Northamptonshire village: 'Erected by Ella Harrison/to the Memory of the Men of Paulerspury/Who Fell in the Great War/for God, King and Country 1914–1918.'

Most war memorials are inscribed in roman-type capitals. This lower-case type on the war memorial at Bakewell, Derby., is particularly pleasing – and legible.

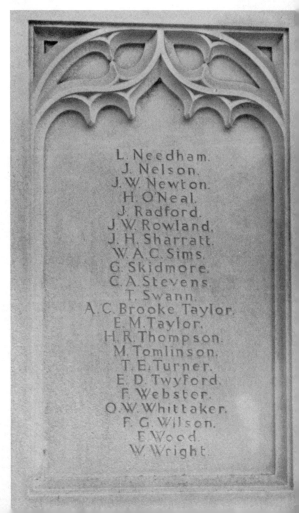

L. Needham.
J. Nelson.
J. W. Newton.
H. O'Neal.
J. Radford.
J. W. Rowland.
J. H. Sharratt.
W. A. C. Sims.
G. Skidmore.
C. A. Stevens.
T. Swann.
A. C. Brooke Taylor.
E. M. Taylor.
H. R. Thompson.
M. Tomlinson.
T. E. Turner.
E. D. Twyford.
F. Webster.
O. W. Whittaker.
F. G. Wilson.
E. Wood.
W. Wright.

THEY DIED
FOR
OUR FREEDOM

NORTH STAFFORDSHIRE EX FAR EAST
PRISONERS OF WAR ASSOCIATION

TO THOSE WHO SERVED IN THE FAR EAST IN
THE 1939–1945 WAR AND DIED IN JAPANESE
PRISON CAMPS OR LATER AS RESULT OF CAPTIVITY

An example of a plaque with strong significance: this late addition to the 1914–18 memorial at Hanley is in memory of those who suffered as prisoners of the Japanese in World War II.

The Newfoundland Corner in Wandsworth Cemetery, London – with the Caribou badge on the large granite cross and on the individual Newfoundland headstones.

The fine war memorial at Skipton, West Yorks., with a figure at the foot breaking his sword across his knee.

At Knighton, in Radnorshire, a Cenotaph-shaped war memorial in a plaza, with the names particularly clearly printed.

The war memorial at Alnwick, Northd., in foreground; overlooking it, a tall column with the Percy lion. The Ninth Duke of Northumberland is among the 1939–45 war dead.

At Coldstream in the Borders, birthplace of the Coldstream Guards; though surprisingly not a single one of the fifty Great War or the eighteen Second World War dead served with the Guards.

The war memorial at Auchterarder in Perthshire. The largest number of names are from the 1/6th (Perthshire) battalion, Territorial Force, The Black Watch.

Another Perthshire war memorial with, as would be expected, again a large proportion of Black Watch names – at Crieff.

A fine memorial obelisk, at Catrine in Ayrshire. The bulk of names on the memorial are Royal Scots Fusiliers.

A memorial hall at Tempsford, Beds., provided by Colonel Dugald Stuart and his wife, in memory of their only son, a second lieutenant killed on the Somme, aged twenty.

A clean well-kept roadside memorial, at North Ferriby, near Hull, in what was then the East Riding of Yorkshire.

A lych-gate war memorial – at Marchington Woodlands, Staffs.: on one side a memorial inscription, on the other the names of six villagers who were killed.

The war memorial in the main square at Portree, on the Isle of Skye. It was then in Inverness-shire, a recruiting area for the Cameron Highlanders.

The memorial at Dunvegan on the Isle of Skye, with a Gaelic quote on it and all the Mc's spelled 'Mac'.

In the First World War, women (and civilians) were on the whole exposed to danger to a far lesser extent than they were in the Second World War. Nurses and ambulance-drivers in 1914–18 were among the most vulnerable, and the names of nurses who were killed or died in the line of duty are listed with pride on many memorials.

The same comparison of the amount of danger to which non-combatants were exposed in the two wars applies equally to civilians. Deaths from bombing in Britain during the First World War were extremely few when compared with the casualties civilians suffered in the Second.

In the First World War, Britain was bombed by both Zeppelins and aircraft. According to H.A. James and Sir Walter Raleigh, in *The War in the Air 1914–1918*, the Zeppelins dropped 196 tons of bombs and killed 557 people, German aircraft dropped 73 tons of bombs, killing 857 people. A total of 8,578 bombs were recorded as dropped on the British mainland during the First World War, and in addition to the total of 1,414 dead mentioned above, a further 3,416 people were injured.

*Pear's Cyclopedia* (1960) tell us that in the Second World War the United Kingdom had 357,116 killed:

> 264,443 in the armed forces
> 624 in the women's auxiliary forces
> 1,206 in the Home Guard
> 30,248 in the Merchant Navy and Fishing fleets
> 60,595 civilians

In other words, forty-five civilians were killed in World War II for every one civilian killed in World War I.

German VI and V2 rocket attacks on Britain, mainly on London and the south-east, alone killed 8,958 people and seriously wounded some 24,500. That is, even this particular last-minute form of unpleasantness killed six times as many civilians as the total civilian dead for the whole of the First World War.

Incidentally, though people tend to think of the VI and V2 rockets as Hitler's ultimate revenge weapon directed against Britain, we should remember that over half the German rockets fired were aimed at Antwerp, Liège, Brussels and other targets in the Low Countries.

Statistics can be made to prove almost anything, but it is fair to remind ourselves of the great difference between the losses Britain suffered in the two world wars: a million British dead in the First World War, less than a third of a million killed in the Second.

If we accept the probably unfair expedient of lumping the Merchant Navy dead in with the civilians (for, after all, many seamen fought in actions against U-boats and surface-raiders, and most were serving at sea as their form of wartime service) and if we then add the servicewomen in with the civilians, it allows us to argue that almost one in three of the British dead in 1939–45 were non-combatants. The wartime cliché about everybody being in the front line in the Second World War thus rings true. Remember that figure: nearly one in three of the dead were not in the armed services.

A theory I have not yet had time to pursue, but which readers might like to consider as they look at war memorials, is that the civilian dead of World War II get much less recognition than their numbers deserve. Mention of the civilian dead often seems to be added as an after-thought, and they are seldom listed by name.

What, I think, accounts for this lies, once again, in the fact that almost all the war memorials of Britain were built in the 1920s to honour the 1914–18 service dead. The patterns were thus set, and the names of those killed in the Second World War were generally simply added to the World War I memorial, few of which had any civilians listed.

I also feel that by the end of the Second World War people wanted to forget the bombings. While willing to carry out the now-recognized ritual of honouring servicemen who did not return, they did not feel the same responsibility towards the civilian dead. Some of this I attribute to that pattern set by the First World War memorials, which had very few civilian dead and only a handful of servicewomen or nurses to record. Another reason is that the deaths from bombing were unevenly distributed throughout the country. It was London and the southern counties which were most heavily bombed, together with many industrial towns in the Midlands and North. But even here, certain areas suffered disproportionately. The one thing lacking was the village-by-village, street-by-street involvement in death which occurred in the First World War.

Nonetheless, it is always worth keeping an eye out for mentions of civilian dead for what they might tell us about a town's history.

The war memorial in Hertford, municipal capital of a county bounded on the north by Cambridgeshire, on the east by Essex, on the south by what was Middlesex and on the west by Buckinghamshire, has entries on its war memorial for civilians killed in both wars.

| *Killed in Air Raid*<br>(13 October 1915) | | **1939–1945**<br>*Civilians* | |
|---|---|---|---|
| CARTLEDGE | G. | BATTELL | W.C. |
| COX | A. | BRETT | Mrs. B. |
| GAME | C.S. | JOHNSON | A.E. |

| | | | |
|---|---|---|---|
| GREGORY | D.L. | NEWMAN | Mrs. |
| HART | A. | WRIGHT | Miss E. |
| JEAVONS | J.H. | | |
| JOLLY | C.T. | | |
| SPICER | C. | | |
| WALLER | C. | | |

An impressive tall war memorial obelisk at Scarborough, Yorks., standing on Oliver's Mount, a high hill overlooking the town, commemorates over 700 people. Included in their number are eight men, nine women and three children, who were killed in the two German naval bombardments of the town, in 1914 and 1917.

| *Men* | | *Women* | | *Children* | |
|---|---|---|---|---|---|
| BEAL | A | BENNETT | J. | BARNES | G.J. |
| BENNETT | A.F. | CROSBY | E.E. | RYALL | S.J.S. |
| ELLIS | L. | CROW | A. | WARD | J.C.H. |
| FRITH | H. | DUFFIELD | A. | | |
| HALL | J. | MERRYWEATHER | E.L. | | |
| HARLAND | H. | McINTYRE | B. | | |
| TAYLOR | G.H. | PAINTER | A. | | |
| PICKUP | T.T. | PRUE | M. | | |
| | | SCOTT | E. | | |

Scarborough's obelisk carries several of the popular quotes: 'And Lo They Passed Over And All The Trumpets Sounded For Them On The Other Side' and 'They Were A Wall Unto Us, Both By Night And By Day'; and also 'They Shall Grow Not Old' (in full). The lists are rigidly compartmentalized. There are twenty-three panels, each with thirty-three names (except for two which total fifty-one) for the dead from the Navy, Army and Air Force. Then there are the civilians killed in the bombardments. Then there are four VADs:

| | |
|---|---|
| McLAUGHLIN | M.M. |
| McLAUGHLIN | E.W. |
| SELLORS | E.P. |
| TAYLOR | E.E. |

– and twenty-nine lost at sea with the Merchant Marine.

For 1939–45 the panels with names are headed:

### In Memoriam – People of SCARBOROUGH
### Who Gave Their Lives in the Second World War
### 'Greater Love Hath No Man Than This'

There are three panels of servicemen and women, half a panel for the

Merchant Navy, and a panel for those Killed in air raids.

The civilian dead are fifteen men, fourteen women and thirteen children, including one 'Bigden (Baby)' who presumably died before being christened.

An example of a more neglectful attitude after the Second World War is a memorial in Wandsworth Cemetery, London. Tucked away by the railway, it has broken bits of other memorials stacked beside it.

**1939–1945**
[With Wandsworth Borough badge]

TO THE MEMORY OF THOSE CITIZENS OF
THE BOROUGH OF WANDSWORTH WHO ARE
LAID TO REST HERE HAVING LOST THEIR
LIVES THROUGH ENEMY ACTION DURING
THE WORLD WAR 1939–1945 AND WHOSE NAMES
ARE PERPETUATED ON THIS MEMORIAL

Charles ADAMS            William David THORPE
Arthur BREWSTER        Florence Louisa TREDRAY
and 24 Others Unknown

Civilians in areas subjected to bombing in the Second World War do often get a general mention on their borough war memorials. At Putney, Surrey, an oldish war memorial in the front courtyard of the parish church of St Mary the Virgin, by Putney Bridge, has an additional plaque:

**1939–1945**
IN HONOURED MEMORY OF
THE CIVILIANS OF PUTNEY
WHO LOST THEIR LIVES IN
THE SECOND WORLD WAR

Wimbledon honours the service dead of two world wars, adding:

In Honoured Memory of the Civilians
of Wimbledon
who lost their lives
in the Second World War 1939–1945.

Christchurch Gardens, Battersea, London, are dedicated to the borough's civilian dead. After the borough motto – '*Non mihi, non tibi, sed nobis*' – a plaque reads:

To the Memory of the
Men, Women and Children of **Battersea**
who lost their lives in the World War 1939–1945.

One category of civilian often included on war memorials is that of munition workers. Many front-line troops had some reservations about munition workers, who they felt drew excellent wages while even going on strike at crucial moments in the war. However, where local men and women died in accidents and explosions in munition factories they were generally found a place on the village or parish memorial.

At Furnace, Argyllshire, the last name on the First World War memorial is that of munitions worker A. Munro. In Suffolk, munitions worker John Gissing is listed among 'the eighteen Brave Men of WESTLETON Who gave their lives for their Country in the GREAT WAR 1914–1918'.

At Silloth, Cumberland, on the Solway Firth, J. Corry, munitions worker, is listed. Silloth's war memorial is one of those with a wide spread of services and regiments. Its only 1914 casualty was Assistant Clerk C.T. Martin of HMS *Monmouth*, sunk with all hands. Five of the ten 1915 dead are men of the Royal Naval Division, presumably killed at Gallipoli. By 1916, most of the names (seven out of eleven) are from the local Border Regiment; but the list for Silloth dead in 1917 shows a surprisingly wide spread.

### 1917

| | | |
|---|---|---|
| Private | J. HOLLIDAY | London Rifle Brigade |
| 3rd Officer | W.G. IRVING | SS Sycamore |
| Sergeant | F.W. ACCLETON DCM MM | Royal Field Artillery |
| Sergeant | B. BARTON | Duke of Wellingtons |
| L/Corporal | F.M. OSBORNE | Border Regiment |
| L/Corporal | G. WANNOP | MG Section |
| Private | D.J. GRAHAM | Border Regiment |
| Private | T. BELL | Border Regiment |
| Private | A. BARTON | Cheshires |
| Private | G. HOWE | Canadian Field Ambulance |
| Private | W. HOWE | Border Regiment |
| Private | R. SAUNDERS | Manchester Regiment |
| Private | .B. WIGHTMAN | Australians |
| Fireman | J.J. KAVAGHAN | Transport 'Treverbyn' |
| ———— | J.H. CORRY | Munitions Worker |

and this continues for 1918 too:

| | | |
|---|---|---|
| Lieutenant | A.E. WHITE, MC | Canadians |
| Chief Officer | D. McCALLUM | HMT 140 |

| | | | |
|---|---|---|---|
| Cadet | J.H.B. | KAYSS, MM | Canadians |
| Cadet | N.G. | DIXON | RA Force |
| Sergeant | W.D. | ELLIOTT | Border Regiment |
| Corporal | T. | PIGG | Border Regiment |
| Private | J.B. | LITTLETON | Australians |
| Private | W. | ARCHER | West Yorkshires |
| Private | N. | DAND | Canadians |
| Stoker | F. | ELLIOTT | RN HMS SPIRAEA |
| Private | F. | GRAHAM | Border Regiment |
| Private | Max | AIKIN | Border Regiment |
| Private | E. | EMMERSON | Canadian Light Infantry |
| Lieutenant | J.A. | WHEATLEY | RN HM Submarine L10 |

At Hanbury, Staffs., five miles north-west of Burton-on-Trent, there is a framed memorial list of all those who died in the Hanbury munitions explosion of 27 November 1944:

| | | |
|---|---|---|
| APPLETON | John | |
| BARKER | Edward | |
| BEARD | James | |
| BELL | Joseph | |
| BOWRING | Fred | |
| BRASSINGTON | James | |
| CARTER | Harold | |
| CARTWRIGHT | Frank | |
| CARTWRIGHT | Reginald | |
| CARROLL | Fred | |
| CHAWNER | Sidney | |
| COCKAYNE | Lawrence G. | |
| COOPER | Joseph | |
| COOPER | Percy | |
| DANIELS | E.W. Gustave | |
| FELL | Edgar | |
| FELL | Benjamin | |
| FORD | William | |
| FROW | Lewis D. | |

| | |
|---|---|
| GENT | William |
| GILBERT | Elm Omar |
| GOODWIN | Maurice |
| GOODWIN | Mary |
| HARRIS | Arthur |
| HARRISON | F.W. |
| HILL | Henry John |
| HILL | Sarah L. |
| HOGG | Charles Edmund |
| HUDSON | Thomas |
| KIDD | William |
| MARR | Gerald A. |
| MELLOR | Albert W. |
| MILES | J. Russell |
| NICKLIN | Frederick |
| PAGE | Errold Alfred |
| PAGE | George |
| PAGE | Philip |
| PATTERSON | Ambrose |

| | |
|---|---|
| PICK | Samuel |
| POWELL | George H. |
| PRIESTLEY | George |
| REDFERN | John |
| ROCK | F. George |
| SANDERS | Tom |
| SHEPHERD | Hilary |
| SHEPHERD | William H. |
| SHIPLEY | Alfred A. |

| | |
|---|---|
| WEST | John W. |
| WEST | Stephen |
| WOOLEY | Edmund |
| WORTHINGTON | — — — — |

*** Mrs Lilian Emma CROOK
and Mrs Nellie FORD
died subsequently

| SKELLETT | J.W. | | *Servicemen* | |
|---|---|---|---|---|
| SLATER | F. William | Sergeant | Stanley G. | GAME |
| SMITH | Elizabeth | LAC | Henry C. | FAIRBANKS |
| SMITH | George | LAC | John T. | BAILEY |
| STANLEY | Bert | Corporal | Alan S. | DUROSE |
| WAGSTAFF | Robert | LAC | W. | DEUCHARAS |

By the Second World War, the involvement of servicewomen was much greater too, and their appearance on war memorials is always of interest. By 1939, women were serving on airfields, at army and naval headquarters and at other military establishments.

They were in action in mixed anti-aircraft batteries and in signal units; they flew in greater numbers as ferry-pilots and served as transport drivers and staff-car chauffeurs. And, again, many of them worked in hospitals at home and abroad.

In the Second World War, the women of the three services were as vulnerable to bombing as any soldier, sailor or airman, for they were often employed in Britain at prime-target sites, such as dockyards and RAF stations. About 400 members of the women's Army, the ATS (Auxiliary Territorial Service), died on active service in 1939–45.

Some servicewomen died at sea when journeying to overseas stations; others (mainly enrolled for the purpose in the FANYs – First Aid Nursing Yeomanry) were dropped behind enemy lines as agents and wireless-operators. Several of them would die in concentration camps or at the hands of the Gestapo.

The First Aid Nursing Yeomanry was founded in 1907 to provide nursing services for the Army in the field. When war broke out in 1914, the War Office decided not to use them, so many went overseas to work for the Belgian and French governments instead. In the Second World War, the FANYs took on many roles: several thousand working with the Army in twenty-five motor transport companies. Others were interpreters, drivers and teachers with the Polish Army.

Outside St Paul's Church in Knightsbridge, London, there is a tablet to members of the Women's Transport Service (FANY) who died in the Second World War. Readers of books about Occupied Europe will note familiar names. The number and quality of the awards recorded on the plaque – the George Cross and the Croix de Guerre – are added testimony.

## WOMEN'S TRANSPORT SERVICE (FANY)
In Honoured Memory of Those Members of
The Women's Transport Service (FANY)
Who Gave Their Lives for Their King and Country.

| | | | |
|---|---|---|---|
| M.W. | ANDERSON | M. | DAMERMENT L.de H. C.de G |
| Y.E.M. | BEEKMAN C.de G. | B.M. | DICKIE |
| D. | BLOCH | B.E. | EBDEN |
| E.M. | BOILEAU | M. | HEATH-JONES |
| A. | BORREL | J. | HILDICK-SMITH |
| M.S. | BUTLER | N. | INYAT-KHAN GC |
| M. | BYCK | C. | LEFORT |
| C.E. | CLERK-RATTRAY | V.E. | LEIGH |
| C.D. | CROOKE | C.M. | LOPRESTI |
| K. | CROSS | D.M. | MANNING (**née** PORTMAN) |
| | | | |
| M.L.M. | McKENZIE MILLIGAN | E.G. | SADLER |
| D. | MORGAN | H.I.P. | SALMON |
| R.E. | NELSON | J. | SHEPLEY |
| M.C. | PEAKE | L.M. | STALKER |
| E.S. | PLEWMAN C.de G. | E.P. | STANGER |
| B.E. | RAMSAY | N.C. | STAPYLTON |
| F.L. | RAWLINS | B. | SWINBURNE-HANHAM |
| L.V. | ROLFE C.de G. | V.R.E. | SZABO GC C.de G. |
| T.H. | ROWDEN C.de G. | M.J. | THOMPSON |
| Y. | RUDELLAT | P.C. | WOOLLAN |

(In Japan)
C.M.  BRADFORD 7 March 1947

### W.T.S. (EAST AFRICA)

| | | | |
|---|---|---|---|
| B.M. | AUSTIN | B. | KENTISH |
| A. | CALLISHER | F.F. | MOOJEN |
| H.C. | CAMERER | M. | SYKES |
| B. | DUNBAR THOMSON | P.H. | LE POER TRENCH |
| W. | GREY | R. | SOUTHEY |
| S. | HOOK | | |

## THEIR NAME LIVETH FOR EVERMORE
## 'ARDUIS INVICTAE'

Most of the memorials for the Great War are for nurses. In the cathedral at St Asaph (formerly Llanelwy, Flintshire) there is a wall-plaque:

To the Glory of God and in Memory of
the Welsh Nurses attached to the
Queen Alexandra's Imperial and Military Nursing Service (Reserve)
and the Territorial Force Nursing Service
who Fell in the World War 1914–1918.

| | | |
|---|---|---|
| Frances Ethel | BRICE | |
| Jane | ROBERTS | Staff Nurses |
| Margaret Dorothy | ROBERTS | QAIMNS |
| Margaret Evans | THOMAS | Staff Nurse |
| Eleanor May | ROWLANDS | Assistant Nurse TFNS |

Apart from specialist memorials, such as those for nurses or FANYs, I find the most interesting feature is how each individual community decides to list women on their war memorials.

A first problem those responsible for inscribing war memorials encountered was finding an overall phrase that encompassed women. On the memorial at Sulgrave, Northants, Lilian A.M. Taylor is listed among 'The Men of This Village' who fell in the war. At Wrotham, Kent, the war memorial in the courtyard of St George's Church carries the inscription:

**TO THE
GLORY OF GOD
AND IN MEMORY OF
THE MEN OF WROTHAM
1939–1945**

with only initials given for the names on the memorial. Examining the roll of honour in the church reveals that M. Breeds is, in fact, Margaret Breeds, who is thus included among 'the Men of Wrotham'.

Kenilworth, Warwicks, solves the problem by its inscription:

In Grateful Memory
Of Those From KENILWORTH
Who Gave Their Lives
In The Great War 1914–1919

This formula embraces Constance Seymour, the only one whose Christian name is spelt out in a sea of initials, and she appears in the correct alphabetical order among the men.

At the village of Pilsley in Derbyshire, near Chatsworth Hall, one of the noblest houses in England, a distinction is made in the wording of the commemorative plaques for 1914–18 and 1939–45. The first pays tribute to 'the Men of this Village who fought in the Great War', the second to 'the Men and Women of this village who served during the Second World War'.

Another difference of phrasing to be noted on war memorials is how often the First World War use of the sacrifice theme ('Gave Their Lives'/'Laid Down Their Lives') is changed to 'Lost Their Lives' for World War II, when bombs and rockets removed any element of choice.

A majority of 1914–18 war memorials place the women at the end, but on several occasions they are listed first. At Brora, Sutherland, WAAC Williamina Matheson has pride of place in an otherwise alphabetical listing; but at Broughton, Peebles, Miss Anne Alexander VAD and, at New Galloway, Kirkcudbright, Nurse Jane A. Medwell VAD both appear at the foot of the bill. However, at Inveraray, Argyllshire, Sergeant Violet Ross of the WAAC appears in her proper alphabetical and hierarchical placing as a sergeant in the 1914–18 list. She thus appears between Sergeant Lewis Fredrick Munroe of the Argyll & Sutherland Highlanders and Sergeant Malcolm Sinclair of the Royal Scots Fusiliers.

After the Second World War, when women's names were seen more often on war memorials, their inclusion in a non-discriminatory alphabetical order was much more accepted.

At Mildenhall, Suffolk, the women's names on the war memorial (1939–45) are still separated and listed at the bottom. While the thirty-three men's names are listed alphabetically in two columns, with only their initials given, the names of the three women who lost their lives appear with their Christian names.

| | |
|---|---|
| Martha | BRIGHTWELL |
| Gertie | HUTCHINSON |
| Evelyn | PALMER |

At Canonbie, Dumfriesshire the inscription reads:

TO THOSE WHO IN THE SAME NOBLE SPIRIT
OF SELF-SACRIFICE GAVE THEIR LIVES
IN THE SECOND WORLD WAR 1939–1945

| | |
|---|---|
| 3rd Officer Isabel Mary MILNE-HOME | WRNS RN |
| Miss Eleanor Teresa Pearson ARMSTRONG | British Diplomatic Sta |
| Bombardier William James BYERS | Royal Artillery |
| Private John CAMPBELL | QO Cameron Hdrs |
| Able Seaman Walter DARGUE | HMS St Angelo |
| Sergeant (AG) Walter Thomas DOUGLAS | RAF |
| Corporal Walter Dickson FLETCHER | Border |
| Pilot Officer Robert Wallace KOMISKY | RAF |
| Private George Thomson PATERSON | RSF |
| Ordinary Seaman Murdoch McLean SOLMAN | HMS Hood |
| Gunner Andrew VERE | Royal Artillery |
| Private John WIGHTMAN | Border |

Third Officer I.M. Milne-Home of the Women's Royal Naval Service is not only listed at Canonbie but appears on the Second World War list at the nearby main town of Langholm, Dumfriesshire. Here she takes her place among the Ms (though not strictly alphabetically) between Private J. Main of the KOSB and Fusilier N. Maxwell of the Royal Scots Fusiliers.

War memorials have once again provided us with social comment. They do show a change in attitude to the standing of women in war. Women are no longer accorded a special 'ladies first' placing or relegated to the bottom of the list but have won their way by the 1940s to at least equal alphabetical status with their male companions in death.

The same can hardly be said for civilians, who on the whole get fairly minimal recognition on the war memorials of Britain. Perhaps their memorial lies in the rebuilt Coventry Cathedral. Coventry suffered one of the worst bombings of the Second World War, on 14 November 1940, and the Cathedral Church of St Michael was almost completely destroyed. Sir Basil Spence incorporated remnants of the old building into the new, and it has become a centre of pilgrimage and reconciliation. So perhaps civilians do have their own memorial after all, even if little room was found for them on those first built in the 1920s.

# 14   The Royal Navy and the Merchant Marine

'The Lord hath done great things for us.'

The British are an island race and in recent history have relied on the Royal Navy to ensure their freedom and independence. But 1914–18 was, above all, a land war, a bloody conflict between huge continental land armies massed against each other.

Nearly a million British and Empire soldiers died on battlefields in France and Flanders, and elsewhere round the world. By contrast, total naval deaths, even including 10,000 men of the Royal Naval Division who died fighting on land, were fewer than 33,000, to which can be added 12,000 men of the Merchant Marine lost at sea.

It was said of Admiral Jellicoe that he was the only man who could lose the war in an afternoon. If he hazarded the British Fleet and lost, German victory would inevitably follow. If he managed to keep the German High Seas Fleet bottled up or make it run for home on most of the occasions on which it ventured out – as he did, the Royal Navy's contribution to eventual victory was assured.

The one big naval engagement of the war, the Battle of Jutland on 31 May 1916, is generally regarded as having been inconclusive. Admiral Jellicoe's Grand Fleet met the German High Seas Fleet in a battle which both sides expected to settle the course of the war.

The controversy over Jutland continues among historians to this day. The British certainly lost more ships and men than the Germans. The Germans sank three of Admiral Beatty's battle-cruisers (*Indefatigable, Invincible, Queen Mary*), three armoured cruisers (*Black Prince, Defence, Warrior*) and eight destroyers (*Tipperary, Ardent, Fortune, Nestor, Nomad, Shark, Sparrowhawk, Turbulent*). The British sank a battleship, a battle-cruiser, four light cruisers and five destroyers. The British lost 6,097 men, the Germans 2,551. Jellicoe never achieved the full-scale battle and triumph he wanted, but the German High Seas Fleet never emerged in force again, until it was time to surrender at Scapa Flow in November 1918.

There are two reasons for limiting discussion of the naval content of

156

war memorials to a single chapter. One is the comparatively small number of naval casualties to be found; the second is that the Royal Navy was run on a far less territorial basis than the Army and therefore has less to say to us from the point of view of social and regional history. (Admittedly the Royal Navy was based on a handful of major home ports – such as Belfast, Chatham, Devonport, Plymouth, Portsmouth, Rosyth – drawing many of its men from them. Its ships were commissioned from one or other of the manning ports, towards which seamen felt a divisional loyalty, but it was not a county-by-county system.)

Few people outside naval circles would be aware of how ships were commissioned; most public interest would be on the ships themselves. This is where naval names on war memorials are nearly always of interest, by giving us the name of the ship on which a man served. Naval activities being always well documented, a ship's name on a war memorial will usually trigger off access to details of an exciting engagement or a famous disaster.

Typical of the latter is the appearance of the names of the three ancient cruisers (*Aboukir, Cressy* and *Hogue*) sunk in the Dogger area of the North Sea on 22 September 1914 with the loss of 1,459 lives, and those of two ships (*Good Hope* and *Monmouth*) sunk with all hands in the British defeat off Coronel in Chile on 1 November 1914.

The sinking by *U-9* of those three old cruisers in the North Sea, in less than an hour, is well chronicled in accounts such as *Three Before Breakfast* by Alan Coles. Less than a month later another ancient cruiser, HMS *Hawke*, was torpedoed and lost after stopping to exchange mail with another ship. All but twenty-one of the *Hawke*'s crew died. Two weeks later the sea-plane carrier HMS *Hermes* was torpedoed, and on New Year's Day 1915 the pre-dreadnought battleship HMS *Formidable* was sunk by submarine in the Channel, with 547 lost. Many of those lost in the North Sea and at Coronel were reservists recalled for war service. There were also teenage midshipmen aboard, youngsters who would otherwise still have been at Dartmouth Naval College. Their names will be found on war memorials and in detail in the early *All Ranks Rolls of Honour*, discussed in Chapter 17.

Naval losses (and successes), except on the few occasions when these were kept secret, can easily be traced in newspapers of the time or in the naval history books. Naval affairs always provided better 'copy' for newspapers than the steady slaughter of the trenches.

Three examples of where the date of death, coupled with the name of a warship, helps to identify the likely naval occasion of a seaman's death appear on the village war memorial at Otford, Kent.

Able Seaman S. Wise of HMS *Chester*, dying in May 1916, was clearly a Jutland casualty. This light cruiser ran into a squadron of German cruisers sailing ahead of Hipper's battlefleet and took a crushing punishment. An early salvo put HMS *Chester's* guns out of action. She was hit eighteen times and had to pull out of the battle. It was on the *Chester* that Boy John Travers Cornwell won his VC.

Ordinary Seaman S. Bearman of Otford died aboard HMS *Vanguard*, which was also at Jutland. But the July 1917 date on the memorial ties his death to the *Vanguard's* loss at Scapa Flow, when unstable cordite blew the battleship apart. Another *Vanguard* casualty (the *Craven Roll of Honour* tells us) was Boy 1st Class Frank Pollard of Skipton, one of only two 17-year-olds on that list.

Another wartime death recorded at Otford, that of Boy W. Farmer of HMS *Impregnable*, is a useful reminder of one naval custom, for HMS *Impregnable* was not a seagoing ship at all but a shore training establishment. So we must remember that deaths occurring 'aboard', for example, His Majesty's Ships *Excellent, Ganges, Pembroke, President, Vernon* and *Victory* were all probably the result of accidents during training, or from illness or natural causes, and only very occasionally perhaps from earlier wounds at sea.

Naval traditions and 1914–18 trench warfare come together in the story of the Royal Naval Division, a force unique to the First World War. Before the war, there were plans to form a brigade of Royal Marines. They would be used for home defence or for capturing ports overseas for the Navy or airports for the Royal Naval Air Service to use. There were also to hand more than 20,000 naval reservists for whom there were no ships. Together with other surplus volunteers, these men were formed into two additional naval brigades.

The Royal Marine brigade and the two naval brigades allowed the formation of an extra division of disciplined men – albeit untrained as infantry – to support the original small six-division British Expeditionary Force sent to France. Later, in a context of seventy or so New Army divisions, this odd-man-out one-division naval force would be an embarrassment, at least to the orthodox military mind.

The Royal Marine Brigade consisted of a battalion each from Chatham, Plymouth and Portsmouth; and a fourth from the RM Artillery depot. The two Naval Brigades would be led by cadres of petty officers from the Royal Navy and instructors and sergeants from the Royal Marines. Retired Guards officers would provide needed infantry experience.

The battalions were built up with Royal Naval Volunteer Reserve men and those spare stokers and other reservists available. There were also Army volunteers, many of them miners from the north-east of England who had not found immediate places in Kitchener battalions.

Once again, with hindsight it is clear that it was a complete waste to use trained naval reservists and high-calibre volunteers of the RNVR as infantrymen. Many of them were soon needed for ships or for shore training cadres. By then, though, they were already committed to trench warfare at Gallipoli, where many of them died. On the other hand, they proved a tough and intelligent fighting division, which never let the Army down. As Churchill said, the gallant Guards officers were among the first to fall, together with many RNVR men who would be sadly needed elsewhere later on, particularly in submarines and destroyers.

Before Gallipoli, the Royal Naval Division was involved in a singularly unsuccessful attempt to hold Antwerp. Most of one battalion lost its way in a retreat and was interned in the Netherlands. Then came Gallipoli, where it suffered heavy losses. Reformed after Gallipoli and used very much as an ordinary infantry division, the RND again suffered heavy losses. In an attack on Beaucourt and in the Ancre Valley, the division lost one-third of its strength. It would suffer again in the German spring offensive of 1918 and incur further losses in The Advance to Victory. Many of the naval names on war memorials are men of the Royal Naval Division – who never fought at sea and did all their dying on land.

The names of men who lost their lives at sea while serving in the Merchant Marine (the 1914–18 name) or in the Merchant Navy (the term used by 1939–45) appear on war memorials across Britain. Obviously names will be found mainly in the memorials of seaports or the home bases of the fishing fleets, but occasionally a merchant seaman's name appears unexpectedly in some remote inland village.

Apart from men of the Royal Naval Reserve who rejoined for service or who manned ships taken over for use as warships, supply-ships or auxiliaries and merchant seamen serving on vessels commandeered or converted for war service, such as troopers and hospital-ships, one might ask whether merchant seamen strictly qualify as members of the armed services, at least in 1914–18.

Unlike World War II, when there was a national mobilization of manpower from the very start, and men could be directed to serve as merchant seamen as their contribution to the war effort, most of those aboard merchant vessels at the start of the First World War were carrying on their ordinary civilian trade. They faced danger and hardship, certainly when German U-boats engaged in unrestricted submarine warfare, but it was very different from the kind of death faced by soldiers in the trenches. Seen from the trenches, merchant seamen remained civilians and earned civilian rates of pay (plus war bonuses). They lived in comparative civilian comfort for most of their service and were not subject to the full rigours of military discipline.

Early on in the Great War, ships were seldom sunk without warning and a chance for crews to take to the boats. Ships were at that stage seen as transport vehicles, to be denied to one's opponent's war effort certainly, but not by treating the seamen sailing in them as enemy 'soldiers' to be killed, to stop them ever sailing again. Neutral vessels might be searched, and war contraband seized, but the old-fashioned courtesies and traditions of the sea prevailed for many months into the war.

When defensive guns were added to British and Allied vessels, and anti-submarine Q-ships and German raiders went into action disguised as merchantmen, the rules necessarily changed.

By the time the convoy system had been belatedly introduced by Lloyd George in 1917, over stern opposition from a conservative and hidebound Admiralty, it could be said that every merchant seaman belonging to one of the belligerent nations was now a serviceman. By then too, the Germans had decided that one of their best hopes – even at the risk of bringing the United States into the war – was to sink every ship taking food and war supplies to beleaguered Britain. Ships were sunk without warning, and very little provision could or would be made to save their crews.

Memorials to the merchant seamen of each war who were lost at sea and have no known grave stand together in Trinity Gardens, opposite the Tower of London. They commemorate 12,000 who died in the First World War, and double that number – 24,000 – lost in the Second World War. The names of the 1914–18 dead are found on brass panels on a series of arches in front, by the road. The dead are listed under the name of the ship in which they were serving. The 1939–45 names are registered in the same way, except that instead of being attached to a building, their brass panels run round a sunken courtyard garden.

Exact figures for losses in the merchant services are hard to find. There was no central agency charged with keeping records of deaths and injuries, which mainly remained a responsibility of the individual ship-owners. Ships which were attacked but not sunk often had casualties. Ships which were mined, but beached, appear in the 'Ships Attacked' lists, rather than as outright losses.

A recent re-publication of four volumes for naval and merchant losses in each war, now combined into one volume, is an invaluable reference. *British Vessels Lost At Sea – 1914–1918 and 1939–1945* is a sort of ships' equivalent of *Soldiers Died ...*, though the book does not record individual names of seamen, only those of the ships. The figures for men lost on each ship are often at variance with the numbers named on the main memorial, the latter possibly more accurate. The ships lost in 1914–18 are recorded alphabetically, as are the names of their crews, except for the Master (Captain) or Skipper (in the case of the fishing-vessels) who always heads the list.

## GEO
(Registered in London)

| | |
|---|---|
| McINTYRE | J.W. (*Master*) |
| BROWN | W.J. |
| CATTLEY | L.A. |
| COSTARIS | D. |
| COUTTS | C.A. |
| FREEMAN | A.E. |
| HADIELUKA | S. |
| HALFORD | J. |
| McCALLUM | D. |
| MacDOUGALL | A. |
| MARTIN | J.L. |
| MOSSOP | J.W. |
| PARKER | T. |
| PURKISS | J. |
| ROMANIDIS | C. |
| VASILION | G. |

## ROMEO
(Registered in Hull)

| | |
|---|---|
| NEALE | J. (*Master*) |
| ALLEN | J. |
| ANDERSON | H. |
| BARGEWELL | G. |
| BIRKINSHAW | R. |
| BLAIR | G. |
| CARNEY | A. |
| CARR | J. |
| CROWTHER | C. |
| DEADMAN | R.M. |
| FROMM | T.H. |
| GUSTAFSON | H. |
| HARVEY | J. |
| HELM | R.J. |
| HINES | T. |
| KEARNEY | J. |
| LEE | M. |
| LINACRE | J.E. |
| LONGLEY | J.B. |
| McLOUGHLIN | D. |
| MIDDLETON | J.W. |
| MOLLOY | P. |
| NUGENT | J.A. |
| O'BRIEN | A. |
| O'GORMAN | T.C. |
| PARRY | J. |
| PITTS | A. |
| WHITE | W. |
| WILLIAMS | B.P. |

The presence of Greek and Scandinavian names in these ships is perhaps worth noticing, as are the possible family connections among the crews of the fishing-smacks which follow.

## *FISHING FLEET*

## BOY JACK
(Registered in Lowestoft)

| | |
|---|---|
| CLAXTON | T.J.T. |
| CROUCHEN | T.F. |
| SIMONS | F.A. |

## BOY SAM
(Registered in Lowestoft)

| | |
|---|---|
| ROSE | H. (*Skipper*) |
| MEADOWS | W. |
| ROSE | C.S. |
| WELCH | P. |
| WINK | J. |

**BOY PERCY**
(Registered in Lowestoft)

| BACON | W. (*Skipper*) | **BREADALBANE** | |
| CLARKE | E. | (Registered in Granton) | |
| FREEMAN | L. | | |
| STURMAN | E. | McINTYRE | J. (*Skipper*) |
| STURMAN | R.H.R. | TURNBULL | J. |

In the 'Merchant Shipping (Losses)' part of *British Vessels Lost At Sea* we find total casualties for the war given as 14,287 for those on merchant vessels, plus a further 434 fishermen. Another 592 died aboard the vessels which were attacked but not sunk.

In the case of our examples, the Geo was torpedoed and sunk on 29 January 1918 off Sicily in the Mediterranean, with the loss of twelve lives, including her master. (On the memorial sixteen names appear.)

The *Romeo* was also torpedoed and sunk by a submarine, on 3 March 1918, seven miles south of the Mull of Galloway, southernmost point of Scotland. Her losses are given as twenty-nine, including her master, which corresponds to the number of names on the memorial. Both vessels were sunk without warning; both carried defensive guns.

The *Boy Percy* and *Boy Sam* were sunk together by a submarine on 17 May 1916, the *Boy Jack* on 26 July 1918. The only casualties listed in *British Vessels Lost At Sea* are those of the *Boy Jack*. The *Breadalbane* does not appear in that publication.

Much the same system is used for the names of the 1939–45 dead, with the ships of the Merchant Navy arranged in alphabetical order and with special panels for the fishing fleets and the men of the lighthouse and pilotage services.

Registers containing all the names of those commemorated on the memorial are held at the office of the Corporation of Trinity House in the square and by the Commonwealth War Graves Commission (2 Marlow Road, Maidenhead, Berkshire) who maintain the memorial. An inscription says:

**1939–1945**
RESPECT THIS SANCTUARY WHICH
BEARS THE NAMES OF TRUE MEN
LOST AT SEA.

The 24,000 of the Merchant Navy and Fishing Fleets
whose names are honoured on the walls of this garden
gave their lives for their country and
have no grave but the sea.

**CLAN MACFADYEN**
(Registered in Glasgow)

| | |
|---|---|
| WILLIAMS | P.E. (*Master*) |
| BODDINGTON | A.J. |
| BULLOCK | G.S. |
| CARTER | D.G. |
| CARTER | H.C. (MBE) |
| HUTCHISON | A.M. |
| IRVINE | H. |
| LEE | J. |
| LOW | W. |
| LOWDEN | F. |
| MacLEAN | A.McD. |
| MURCHIE | J.A. |
| SCOTT | D.A. |
| SHEPHERD | D.G. |
| STIRLING | T.W. |

**CLAN MACFARLANE**
(Registered in Glasgow)

| | |
|---|---|
| ALLAN | H. |
| DALZIEL | T. |
| FERGUSON | A.D. |
| JEFFREY | S. |
| McCALLUM | M. |
| MILNER | C.W. |
| MUNN | A. |
| WELSFORD | J. |

**CLAN MACKINLAY**
(Registered in Glasgow)

| | |
|---|---|
| LYLE | W.E. |
| WHEATLEY | H.F. |

## FISHING FLEET

**BOY BILLIE**
(Registered in Rye)

| | |
|---|---|
| COUSSENS | D.J. (*Skipper*) |
| MUGGRIDGE | J.E. |
| PAGE | C. |

**LEACH'S ROMANCE**
(Registered in Shoreham)

| | |
|---|---|
| CROCKER | E.A. (*Skipper*) |
| FISK | W.R. |
| HINDES | G.A. |
| HOWE | E.C. |

When the names of merchant seamen appear on village war memorials, it is interesting to note where these names are placed. They may appear in their ordinary alphabetical placing, treated exactly as though they were service casualties, or in a naval section. In the case of Royal Naval Reserve men, many of whom were probably serving out of their home ports on armed trawlers or on other auxiliaries, they tend to be grouped together. This is so at Pittenweem, Fife, on the Firth of Forth, where the first names on the memorial appear under 'NAVY' and are all Royal Naval Reserve: the one officer heading the list, the rest of the names alphabetically.

## NAVY

Lieutenant David MUIR RNR
Deckhand Thomas ANDERSON RNR
Deckhand Peter BOWMAN RNR
2nd Hand Robert C. BOWMAN RNR
Gunner Thomas GAY RNR
Gunner James HUGHES RNR
Deckhand George LINDSAY RNR

Deckhand John LINDSAY RNR
2nd Engineer Alex. M. MACKENZIE RNR
2nd Hand John SMITH (FLEMING) RNR
Deckhand John M. WOOD RNR
Deckhand William WOOD RNR

Afterwards follow forty men listed under 'ARMY', including a private in
the Royal Flying Corps, an Australian corporal and a Canadian private,
while at the end, under 'MERCHANT MARINE' we have:

Master Mariner John H. BROWN
Master Mariner James ELDER
Seaman James GALLOWAY

The pattern for the Second World War names at Pittenweem is similar to
those for the First, with seven Navy names heading the list:

**REMEMBER ALSO THE CITIZENS OF THIS BURGH
WHO GAVE THEIR LIVES IN THE 1939–1945 WAR.**

**NAVY**
Stoker John BOWMAN
Able Seaman James GARDINER
Able Seaman Alex. E. HUGHES
Gunner Andrew HUGHES
Able Seaman William HUGHES
Ldg. Seaman Andrew WATSON
Able Seaman Thomas B. WATSON

This is followed in 1939–45 by the names of five men of the Royal Air
Force and only three Army but seven Merchant Navy, including two
captains (not masters), all listed alphabetically, and right at the end, an
Army chaplain:

**Merchant Navy**
Captain George BONNER
Quartermaster William GAY
Carpenter Alexander JAMIESON
Captain Wilfred MURRAY
Skipper David SMITH
Able Seaman William R. SUTHERLAND
Captain Alfred TRAVIS

**Royal Army Chaplains Department**
The Rev. Robert McPHERSON

Sometimes merchant seamen are grouped collectively, sometimes in their proper alphabetical position. At Dunnet, Caithness, five names are listed together as 'NAVY', after twenty-six Army names:

## NAVY

Captain James SWANSON SS Brantingham
Captain Ed MUIR SS Princess Royal
Seaman John DUNNET SS Trinidad
Seaman John ROBERTSON Royal Naval Reserve
Seaman George SIMPSON SS Brantingham

At nearby Castletown, John Brotchie, 'Shipmaster, Merchant Marine', heads an altogether alphabetical list which includes a Canadian, a South African and an American soldier.

In many places merchant seamen's names or those of naval reservists appear in the normal alphabetical order and with their ship's name, as at Silloth in Cumberland described in the previous chapter.

The eighteen 'Brave Men' of Westleton, Suffolk, who died in the First World War include five who died at sea. They are interesting for their variety:

| | | | |
|---|---|---|---|
| BROWN | Leonard A. | Skipper 'Silver Queen' | Dover Patrol |
| NOY | Arthur J. | Leading Deck Hand | HMS Blackthorne |
| POTTER | William J. | Seaman Gunner | HMS Cressy |
| ROUS | Oscar | Engineman RNR 'Fisherboy' | Trawler Section |
| SPINDLER | David | Stoker | HMS Cressy |

Note that two of them were aboard HMS *Cressy* and were probably reservists. The three Bacchante-class cruisers sunk in those fateful minutes on 22 September 1914 were full of naval reservists recalled before or at the start of the war.

Presumably there are many cases too where both the naval dead and merchant seamen lost at sea appear anonymously on the memorials which simply list a man's initials or Christian names and surname.

It is hoped that all 'Those That Go Down To The Sea In Ships' are remembered on 11 November with those who died on the battlefields, whether their memorial carries details of their ship or not.

# 15   Other Kinds of War Memorial

*Memorial halls, hospitals, homes, houses*

Soldier rest! Thy warfare o'er.
(Castlerigg St John's and Wythburn, Cumberland)

Many communities, or their social leaders and more affluent members acting on their behalf, sought to leave something more tangible than a village cross or church roll of honour to commemorate the dead. The alliterative listing at the head of this chapter covers just a few of the possibilities, which overflow into the following chapters, where several other kinds are also discussed.

The memorial hall was perhaps the most symbolic. The idea was that a community would use it to perpetuate the camaraderie and levelling companionship of the war years, with a place that would be a memorial to those who had not returned, and be used by those who had served together and come back, and the families of them all. It was a chance to build a new village hall or establish one where there had not been one before.

They took many shapes, from genuine community centres of some size to small British Legion clubhouses, from buildings for which everyone had subscribed to others given by the squire in memory of a fallen son. Some continue to fulfil a useful purpose, others sadly have degenerated into being derelict blots on the landscape, their community usage falling victim to competing centres of attraction for succeeding generations, and to the domestic entertainment values of television and video.

An example of a memorial hall presented to the community is that at Tempsford, Beds., beside the A5, where a square block memorial stands in a gravelled enclosure in front of the building:

## STUART MEMORIAL HALL

Erected and Presented to the People of TEMPSFORD
according to the intention of
Colonel William Dugald STUART of Tempsford Hall
and of Millicent, his wife, and carried out by her after his death.

To the Memory of their Only Child
William Esmé Montagu STUART
2/Lieutenant, 6th Royal West Kent Regiment
killed in action near Geudecourt, Somme
7 October 1916, aged 20.

Also to the Honour of the fourteen men of TEMPSFORD
who Gave Their Lives in the Great War 1914-1918
For God, King and Country.

REMEMBRANCE – Until the Reveille
**1914–1918**
To The Glorious Memory of

| | | |
|---|---|---|
| Gunner | L.F. BARLOW | Royal Field Artillery |
| Sapper | F. BARNES | Royal Engineers |
| Private | T. BASON | 2nd Bedfords |
| Sergeant | F.T. DARLOW | Borderers Regiment |
| Private | S.F. HARDWICK | 8th Royal West Surreys |
| L/Corporal | T. HARRIS | 6th Bedfords |
| Private | L.A. HARVEY | 7th Bedfords |
| Private | H.S. HUMPHRIES | 7th Bedfords |
| Corporal | F.A. IBBITT | 4th Bedfords |
| Gunner | W.H. MASON | Royal Garrison Artillery |
| Stoker | F. NORTH | HMS FORMIDABLE |
| Private | T. PARTRIDGE | 13th Royal Irish Rifles |
| 2/Lieutenant | W.E.M. STUART | 6th Royal West Kents |
| Drummer | C. WILSON | 2nd Suffolks |
| Private | A. WOOTTON | 7th Yorks |

WHO IN THE GREAT WAR
GAVE UP THEIR LIVES THAT
OTHERS MIGHT LIVE IN FREEDOM

'Their Name Liveth For Evermore'

**1939–1945**
ALSO IN GRATEFUL MEMORY OF
Kevin Joseph BETTLES
missing in action 3 August 1944.

Another example of a building designed to serve as a memorial is:

## *SUTTON HOUSE, Hackney*

This Building was given to The National Trust
by W.A. ROBERTSON in Memory of his Brothers
Norman Cairns ROBERTSON, Captain 2nd Bn. Hampshire Regiment
who died 20 June 1917 at Hanover, Germany
and of Laurance Grant ROBERTSON, 2/Lieutenant 2nd Bn K.O.S.B.
who was killed in action in France
during the Battle of the Somme
in or near Delville Wood, 30 July 1916.

A stone and plaque with the same inscription can be found on the Downs near Dunstable, Beds., where W.A. Robertson gave land to the National Trust in memory of his two brothers, now known as Robertson Corner. We know more about the Robertson brothers from the *Record of Old Westminsters*, a biographical list of all those educated at Westminster School in London. There is also a memorial brass to the brothers in Upper School.

William Alexander Robertson, who presented these several memorials, was the eldest of four brothers. After Westminster, he was a scholar of Christ Church, Oxford, and a barrister of the Inner Temple. He was born in 1871, and another brother, Reginald, was born two years later, Norman following in 1876. Norman joined the Inns of Court OTC in 1914, became a captain in the Hampshire Regiment and was taken prisoner near Monchy on 23 April 1917. He died a month later in a German military hospital at Hanover. The youngest of these four Westminster brothers (there was at least one Robertson brother at the school between 1884 and 1895) was Laurence Grant Robertson, born in 1877. A chartered accountant in local government, he became a Second Lieutenant in the Army Ordnance Department, was attached to the KOSB in July 1915 and a year later was killed in action at Delville Wood on the Somme. (*Officers Died* ... incidentally follows the Westminster roll in spelling Laurence with an 'e', as opposed to the 'a' of the plaque, and has him serving with the 9th Battalion KOSB – a reminder, once again, that sources often conflict over details.)

Building memorial hospitals or continuing to maintain wartime establishments as a tribute to those who died or served is an obvious form of commemoration. These range from entire hospitals, as at Chipping Norton, Oxon., or memorial wings, to the endowment of beds. All are now absorbed into the National Health Service, or what is left of it.

The Sandon Estate memorial (comprising Sandon, Gayton and Marston) in Staffs., where eighty men joined the forces in 1914–1918. Twenty-three died and eighteen were wounded.

The war memorial at Inveraray, seat of the Dukes of Argyll. Its dead include seven officers and thirty-one Argyll & Sutherland other ranks.

A war memorial gate at Muirkirk in eastern Ayrshire, with a stone memorial brought in from nearby Glenbuck.

At Ullapool in the far north-west of Scotland. A well-kept floral display decorates an elaborate memorial.

A piece of true Victoriana: the war memorial at Glenelg on the Scottish mainland, looking over the sea to Skye.

A roll of honour, on a British Legion hall at Ripley, Surrey, put up by The Comrades of the Great War, one of the original constituents of what is now the Royal British Legion.

A plaque on an outside wall at St Paul's Church, Knightsbridge, dedicated to FANYs who gave their lives for King and Country. Many of them were murdered by the Gestapo or died in concentration camps after capture on secret missions.

A 1939–45 example is the Canadian Memorial Hospital at Taplow, Bucks. A plaque in front of the main building reads:

This hospital which stands on land lent by Lord Astor and
subsequently presented by him to the National Trust
was built and equipped by the Canadian Red Cross Society
with monies subscribed by the people of Canada and handed over
for operation to the Royal Canadian Medical Corps on 1 July 1940.

After the war the hospital was presented by the Canadian Red Cross
Society and the people of Canada with its full equipment
for use as a National Research Centre for Rheumatism in Children
– and other purposes.

In Kent, the market town and Cinque Port of Deal, eight miles from Dover, built a war memorial hospital by public subscription. The names of those who gave their lives in the 1914-18 War are recorded on boards inside the building, and a volume listing the names of those who died in World War II is on display.

A pleasant example of a hospital-bed endowment is registered on the back of the war memorial at Boroughbridge, W. Yorks.

The committee of the Boroughbridge Nursing Institution
on behalf of the inhabitants of the district
desire with grateful appreciation
to record on this war memorial
the endowment of a ward of three beds
in the Harrogate Infirmary
for the use of the district
in memory of
Captain C.S. Haslam

A tablet has been placed in the ward which reads:

In memory of
Charles Stanley HASLAM,
Captain, Yorkshire Hussars
of Heaton House, Boroughbridge
killed in action November 10th 1917

In the London borough of Hackney, in a small park in front of the church of St John of Hackney, there is a cenotaph structure. A knight in armour, his sword pointing down, is embedded in it. Underneath the knight are the words:

COURAGE
SACRIFICE
[On the back]

The houses in
Wattisfield Road
Millfields
erected for the use of Disabled Sailors and Soldiers
are a further tribute from the Borough
to the Memory of the Fallen.

Caroline Dakers, in *The Countryside at War* (p.207), tells the story of a country house that was built as a kind of war memorial, though the full intention was never realized:

> Wyke Manor in Worcestershire is one of the few country houses built immediately after the war. It was designed as a memorial to the past rather than a home for the future, built in memory of Lieutenant Hudson, killed at the battle of Messines in 1917.
>
> His tomb rests in an oratory constructed in the northeast corner of the house. Wyke Manor, a fake sixteenth-century yeoman's hall, was meant also to be at the centre of a scheme to help disabled ex-soldiers. Two long rows of almshouses were to be built to provide accommodation. However, only the house was completed. Most of the work available for architects (at this time) was in the nature of memorials: some simple crosses, few as elaborate a memorial as Wyke Manor.

But it is probably in the public schools of Great Britain that the full flowering of memorial building is to be seen. There were memorial halls (Bedford Grammar School – 454 Old Boys killed); memorial libraries (Aldenham School, Herts – 160 Old Boys killed) and combined memorial libraries and museums (Berkhamsted School, Herts – 231 dead, and Felstead School, Essex – 225 dead). Harrow, which lost 600 Old Boys in the war, now has a complete War Memorial Building, including a shrine. The building was opened on 3 June 1926 at a ceremony attended by the Prime Minister (Stanley Baldwin) and the Archbishop of Canterbury.

New classrooms were added at some schools, chapels built or improved; there were memorial gateways and elaborate walls and friezes carrying the names of the dead, and war memorial crosses of every kind. Portora Royal School at Enniskillen (seventy Old Boys killed) built a sanatorium.

As usual, the social and military historian will find most interest in the rolls of honour of those killed, and in studying their careers and circumstances before they enlisted, their service records and where and how they died – and perhaps speculating on what might have been.

One of the finest forms of memorial mentioned in *British Public Schools War Memorials* appears at Glasgow Academy. In addition to recording the names of 327 Old Boys who died, on carved oak panels in a gallery in the school, and the building of an ornate wall memorial outside, the school itself was endowed. This meant buying all the shares of Glasgow Academy Co, winding up the company and founding the Glasgow Academicals' War Memorial Trust – which thus came to own the school.

But the names are what matter. At the Royal Belfast Academical Institution the school service roll lists a total 703 names: 132 were killed and 121 wounded. They earned one VC, sixteen DSOs, forty-six MCs and twenty-four foreign decorations. Also a tablet carries the names of the 132 Instonians who lost their lives.

## ROYAL BELFAST ACADEMICAL INSTITUTION

To The Memory of Those Instonians
Who Gave Their Lives in The Great War 1914–1918

| | | | |
|---|---|---|---|
| ADRAIN | W.K. | ELLIOTT | G.K. |
| ASHMORE | R.H. | ELLIOTT | T.B.J. |
| AUSTIN | James | ERSKINE | W.R. |
| BAILLIE | H.M. | FISHER | H.B. |
| BANNISTER | H.S. | FORBES | J.D. |
| BARLOWE | J.A.B. | FORBES | W.F. |
| BENNET | T.M. | FRANKLIN | F.R. |
| BILL | J.A.P. | GALWAY | J.C. |
| BOAS | E.G. | GALWAY | J.L. |
| BOSTON | Thomas | GORDON | A.W. |
| BOYD | Brian | GRAHAM | W.R. |
| BOYD | W.G. | GREEN | A.V. |
| BROWN | Hugh | GUNNING | B.T. |
| BROWN | John B. | GUNNING | J.St C. |
| BROWN | Thomas F. | HAMILTON | R.V. |
| BROWNE | M.H. | HANNA | F.L. |
| BUCHANAN | T.G. | HEWITT | Ernest |
| BURNSIDE | E.E. | HEWITT | Holt |
| CAMBRIDGE | Robert | HEWITT | William |
| CAPPER | A.C. | HOLLYWOOD | Arthur |
| CHAMBERLAIN | H.N. | HOLLYWOOD | James |
| CLARKE | John | HOUSTON | W.W. |
| CRYMBLE | C.R. | HUGHES | J.L. |
| CRYMBLE | J.G. | IRELAND | James |
| CURRAN | Herbert | IRELAND | Ralph |
| CURRY | W.G. | IRWIN | W.J. |
| DAVIDSON | J.S. | JACKSON | Balfour |

| | | | |
|---|---|---|---|
| DEANE | Arthur D. | JACKSON | George |
| DESPARD | C.B. | JOHNSTON | Sidney |
| DICKSON | J.H. | KENNEDY | James |
| DUNLOP | Charles | KENNEDY | William |
| DUNWOODY | T.C. | KERTLAND | E.B. |
| EKIN | F.W. | LEES | J.L. |
| | | | |
| LEGATE | Charles | McMULLEN | E.H. |
| LEGATE | George | NEILL | J.D. |
| LEGG | Charles | O'FLAHERTY | D.H. |
| LEGG | W.N. | OSBORNE | H.C. |
| LEONARD | F.P.M. | OSBORNE | W.J. |
| LETTS | B.C. | PETTIGREW | R.MacC. |
| LYNESS | Harold | POLLOCK | Paul |
| MacCOLL | G.E. | RAMSEY | John |
| MacCORMAC | J.S.D. | REA | H.F. |
| MACILWAINE | Julian | READ | S.T. |
| MACKAY | James | REILLY | A.M. |
| MACREADY | O.H. | RIGGS | J.S. |
| MARKS | J.G. | ROSS | W.S.B. |
| MILLER | H.T. | SEYMOUR | W.M. |
| MILLIKEN | James | SINCLAIR | G.S. |
| MITCHELL | A.G. | SMYTH | G.D.L. |
| MOORE | D.S. | STANLEY | R.O. |
| MORRIS | W.O.E. | STEVENSON | H.G. |
| MORROW | H.G. | STEWART | A.L. |
| MYDDLETON | H.W. | STORY | L.P.StJ. |
| McBURNEY | J.W. | TAYLOR | A.S. |
| McCANN | W.R.A. | TAYLOR | Nathaniel |
| McCLINTON | J.S. | THOMSON | A.M. |
| McCONNELL | R.B. | TODD | E.V. |
| McCULLAGH | E.S. | TURNBULL | A.M. |
| McCULLOUGH | John | TYRRELL | J.M. |
| McCULLOUGH | F.J. | TYRRELL | W.A. |
| McCURRY | W.T. | VANCE | Ezekiel |
| McDOWELL | John B. | WALKER | C.A.L. |
| McFARLAND | George | WARWICK | W.N. |
| McINTYRE | R.W. | WHITE | Thomas |
| McKINNEY | T.G. | WILSON | R.H. |
| McKINSTRY | J.McN. | WRIGHT | Robert |

### And In Honour Of Those Who Served & Returned

The idea of practical memorials designed to help soldiers and ex-soldiers after a war is a recent one. The first perhaps was the Union Jack Club, opened by King Edward VII as a tribute to servicemen killed in the Boer War.

The First World War saw the founding of a Veterans' Club in Holborn, London, originally for ex-servicemen. It later became the Allenby Club, after General Allenby, and finally the Victory Services Club.

After the First World War, four organizations set up to cater for ex-servicemen eventually joined together as a national body. The constituent units were the National Association of Discharged Sailors and Soldiers, founded in Blackburn, Lancs., in 1916 and inspired mainly by the Trade Union and Labour movement, the National Federation of Discharged and Demobilised Sailors and Soldiers (Liberal Party), the Comrades of the Great War (Lord Derby and the Conservatives) and the Officers' Association. Out of them came the British Legion, non-political, non-sectarian and open to ex-servicemen of any rank. British Legion clubhouses were established in many villages and towns, and the organization remains best known for its annual Poppy Day on 11 November.

Special hospitals and foundations were established: St Dunstan's for the Blind; the Royal Star & Garter Home for Disabled Sailors, Soldiers and Airmen (named after a nearby pub in Richmond, Surrey); and the Sir Oswald Stoll Foundation – practical memorials all of them.

Often war-memorial plaques, or descriptions of the services they commemorate, are to be found inside or outside the club buildings. At Ripley, five miles north-east of Guildford, Surrey, we have the British Legion Memorial Hall – **1914–18**, with a plaque outside:

### The Comrades of the Great War – Ripley Branch

### ROLL OF HONOUR

| | | |
|---|---|---|
| Private | A. BROWNING | Notts & Derby Regiment |
| Private | A. CHANDLER | East Kent Regiment |
| Sergeant | F. CLARK | Royal West Surrey Regiment |
| C.P.O. | J. FAGENGE | Royal Navy |
| Lieutenant | H.S. FLEMING | Royal Flying Corps |
| Rifleman | A. GADD | Rifle Brigade |
| Gunner | S. GADD | Royal Garrison Artillery |
| Trooper | F.J. HEATH | Household Battalion |
| Rifleman | D. HYDE | Rifle Brigade |
| | | |
| Major | W. JONES | Royal Field Artillery |
| Private | A.J. DILLEY | Royal West Surrey Regiment |
| Telegraphist | A. NASH | Royal Navy |
| Private | G. NASH | Royal West Surrey Regiment |
| Rifleman | E. NEW | Rifle Brigade |
| Rifleman | F. PARFETT | Rifle Brigade |
| Sergeant | S. PLOWMAN | East Surrey Regiment |

| Private | L. | SINK | London Rifle Brigade |
| L/Corporal | N. | SMITHERS | Military Police |
| Rifleman | R. | SPOONER | Rifle Brigade |
| Rifleman | H.J. | TAPPIN | Rifle Brigade |
| Private | R. | WATSON | Royal West Surrey Regiment |
| Telegraphist | E. | WHAPSHOT | Royal Artillery |
| Rifleman | J. | WOOLGAR | Rifle Brigade |
| Rifleman | C. | WORSFOLD | Rifle Brigade |
| Lieutenant | M. | YOUNG | KOSB |

### 1939–1945

| Bombardier | J. | BEASLEIGH | Royal Artillery |
| Sergeant | R. | CARTER | RAF |
| Sergeant | H. | PARROTT | RAF |
| Sergeant | L.J. | STANSFIELD | Royal Tank Regiment |

A war memorial building that is somewhat different from the usual run is the Sandham Memorial Chapel, at Burghclere, Hants. A plaque explains what you see there:

The Chapel and Almshouses were built in 1926
by Mr and Mrs J.L. Behrend, Burghclere,
and given with an endowment to the National Trust in 1947.

The paintings are by the late Sir Stanley Spencer, CBE, RA for
which he had made designs in 1919 shortly after being demobilised.
The Chapel was built to enable him to carry them out.
This he did in the space of 6 years, entirely unaided.

Whatever one feels about Spencer as a painter, the subjects portrayed and the mood expressed in them are very moving. The pictures stem from Spencer's experience during the First World War, from when he served as an RAMC hospital orderly in Bristol in 1915–16, and later when he was a private in the Royal Berkshire Regiment in Macedonia, 1916–18. He apparently thought out the ideas for the paintings and a sanctuary to house them in while in the Army, and then worked on the Burghclere paintings for six years. The chapel and the paintings are also now a memorial to the artist:

IN MEMORY OF SIR STANLEY SPENCER, Kt., CBE, RA
born at Cookham 30th June 1891
died at Cookham 14th December 1959
Worked at Burghclere 1926–1932

# 16 More Kinds
## Playing-fields, gardens, trees ...

Nature provides the best monument.
The perfecting of the work must be
left to the gentle hand of time,
but each returning spring will bring
a fresh tribute to those whom it is
desired to keep in everlasting remembrance.

*On a war memorial in gardens near Putney, London*

Although this book is concerned principally with the archetypal war memorial, the simple cross on village green or market square, some are sited on playing-fields or as part of a memorial garden. These represent that larger effort by a local community to commemorate their dead with a tribute designed to benefit the living. There is something quintessentially British in siting a war memorial to overlook a cricket green, and incorporating imperial sentiments on gates leading to playing-fields or leisure gardens.

The public schools, which suffered disproportionately by supplying so many subalterns to front-line units, also led the way in memorials which incorporated playing-fields and accompanying cricket pavilions.

Bradfield College, Berks (257 Old Boys killed), built a memorial pavilion and new playing-fields; so did Christ College, Brecon (fifty-seven dead), and Elizabeth College, Guernsey (108 dead from 662 serving). The City of London School acquired twenty acres of playing-fields at Grove Park as a memorial, while Hurstpierpoint College, Sussex, not only built a new cricket pavilion but inaugurated it with a School versus ex-Servicemen Old Boys' cricket match in July 1921. Edinburgh's Loretto School (143 Old Boys killed) added two rugby fields and a cricket pitch as part of its war memorial.

Off the A3, near Putney Vale Cemetery and up Stag Lane, on the north-west corner of Wimbledon Common, there is a large granite war memorial cross. It consists of three plinths as a base, set on a square block. The cross sits among trees, overlooking playing-fields. This war

175

memorial seems originally to have carried names, but these have been removed or were on individual plaques which fell out. Instead there are inscriptions on either side – the one which introduces this chapter, and:

The land around
– 42 acres –
is dedicated to public use
in Memory of all those who, having
been resident or belonging to
families resident in the adjoining
districts, Gave their Lives in the
Great War 1914–1918.

Another example of a war memorial embodying playing-fields is at Addlestone, Surrey, where 'Victory Park' houses playgrounds, tennis-courts, a cricket-pitch and putting and bowling-greens. The war memorial proper comprises the gateposts at the entrance, paid for by subscriptions by the local inhabitants, the land being donated by County Councillor G. Doresa in memory of his wife, who died on 21 April 1922. The gift of the land is recorded separately on a plaque on a drinking-fountain just inside the grounds.

The names on these gateposts deserve the same scrutiny one would give the traditional war memorial sited in town or village centre. For example, at Addlestone we note that, though the names are mainly in alphabetical order, on several occasions where the same name occurs, it is separated from its fellow, or from some of its fellows. Thus we get one Allen in its proper alphabetical placing, but the second Allen comes at the end of the As. In the Cs, Gilbert Cooper is separated from two other Coopers (Dan W. and Albert J.), who are out of order alphabetically. Two Elliot, three Field and two Green names follow each other, but their Christian names do not dictate their alphabetical placing. Further on, we find three Miles, two Noakes and two O'Farrell placed together, but Fred Stevens is some way from Wilfred T. Stevens, and Charles P. White is separated by a Woodger from James White.

Are those grouped-together members of the same family, deliberately separated from namesakes who were not related? Are those grouped together possibly in some sort of family order of age seniority or are their placings decided by date of death? Is the separation of the sound-alike Dedman and Deadman deliberate?

It is worth noting how the names of those who died are listed here: surname and Christian name and initials only. No ranks are given, no regiments or units, no decorations – and yet their simple listing does give us a feel for the surnames (and first names) of these men from Surrey who died for their country.

## ADDLESTONE WAR MEMORIAL 1914–1919
## VICTORY PARK

The names of those who died listed on the two gateposts

| | | | |
|---|---|---|---|
| A'COURT | Leonard | HEAD | Charles |
| ADAMS | Arthur J. | HIGGS | William |
| ADAMS | Stanley | HOADE | Reginald W. |
| ALLEN | William | HOARE | John |
| AUSTIN | Ronald G. | HORROD | George |
| AWCOCK | Frederick C. | HUNER | John B. |
| AYRES | Henry | HORNE | Percival G. |
| ALLEN | Herbert | JOYCE | Arthur |
| BAILEY | George A.W. | JOYCE | Herbert G. |
| BATCHELOR | Edward | KEMP | Harry W. |
| BARTRAM | James | KINGTON | Edwin |
| BASSON | Harry W. | LIGHT | Frank |
| BAVIN | William J. | LANGFIELD | Frank |
| BEAUMONT | Sydney D. | LEWINGTON | William E. |
| BOVINGTON | Alfred | LITTLEPROUD | William F. |
| BUTLER | Vincent M. | MACE | George |
| BURGESS | Lawrence F. | MANSER | Victor G. |
| BRYAN | Norman | MILES | Alfred G. |
| BOLTON | Philip L.A. | MILES | William H. |
| BAXTER | Charles | MILES | Charles E. |
| CHANDLER | Harry E. | MATTHEWS | Edward H. |
| CHATFIELD | Charles | MASTERS | Percy |
| CHANDLER | William S. | NEW | Edward |
| CHALCROFT | Arthur | NOAKES | Nelson W. |
| CLARK | William J. | NOAKES | Albert T. |
| COOPER | Gilbert | OWEN | John E. |
| COLE | William J. | O'FARRELL | Joseph F. |
| COX | Valentine | O'FARRELL | Thomas C. |
| CRANSTON | Percival | PERRY | Walter |
| CRANSTON | George | PLOWMAN | Samuel |
| COOPER | Dan W. | POOK | Harold |
| COOPER | Albert J. | PROCTOR | Lewis |
| CROFT | Victor S. | RIGBY | Charles |
| COLLIER | Robert G. | ROBERTS | Charles H. |
| COTTON | William A. | ROBERTS | John |
| DEDMAN | Newbart F. | ROGERS | William R. |
| DEAN | Ernest H. | ROSHIER | William J. |
| DURRANT | William J. | SHUTTLE | George |
| DIVES | William | SIZMUR | William |
| DREW | George H. | SNOOKS | Charles |
| DEADMAN | Frank W. | SPENCER | William J. |
| DOREY | Arthur B. | SPONG | Alfred J. |

| | | | |
|---|---|---|---|
| EAGLES | George S. | SPONG | Frederick J. |
| ELMS | William G. | STEER | Reuben W. |
| ELLIOTT | George F. | STEVENS | Fred |
| ELLIOTT | Bertie V. | SKEATS | George W. |
| ETHERINGTON | William | STICKLEY | Herbert A. |
| EDWARDS | Colin H. | SWEENEY | Patrick |
| FIELD | Thomas | SCHUMACHER | Samuel |
| FIELD | Alfred J. | STEVENS | Wilfred T. |
| FIELD | George | SMITHERS | Henry C. |
| FREEMAN | Frederick | SYMES | Thomas J. |
| FUIDGE | James C. | SANDS | Henry |
| GAY | James H. | TICKNER | Edward |
| GOSDEN | George H. | TINBLICK | Henry |
| GRANT | Frank | TULLIDGE | Robert M. |
| GREGORY | Albert | TULLIDGE | Bernard H. |
| GREEN | Claud | TURNER | Bert |
| GREEN | Arthur P. | TURNER | Arthur |
| GRIMM | Archibald | TURNER | Ernest |
| GRIMM | Arthur | TURRELL | William J. |
| GURNEY | George T. | TALBOT | Joseph |
| HILEY | Charles | WAKEFIELD | John B. |
| HADDEN | Archibald R. | WATTS | William J. |
| HADDEN | Eustace W.R. | WEEDING | Thomas |
| HAINES | George H. | WELLS | Frederick T. |
| HALEY | Albert L. | WEEDING | John R.B. |
| HALL | Frederick F. | WHEELER | Henry |
| HAMPTON | Arthur L. | WHITE | Charles P. |
| HAWKINS | Arthur C. | WOODGER | Walter T.S. |
| HIGHAM | Eric E. | WHITE | James |

There are memorial playing-fields or the equivalent of Addlestone's Victory Park all over the country. Generally there is a plaque on the side of a building, a cricket pavilion or a clubhouse which explains the purpose to which the grounds are dedicated. Sometimes the affiliation goes unexplained, and only a careful search of local newspapers or council records will tell us the whole story.

Sometimes the details can be found on a nearby war memorial. The memorial at what was Langley Marsh, Bucks., but is now Langley and encompassed by Slough, Berks., reads:

This Memorial was erected and the adjoining Field acquired
in Memory of **LANGLEY** Men Who Gave Their Lives
in the Great War 1914–1919
'Their name liveth for evermore'

There are Memorial Fields at Garsington, Oxon., and at Wiveliscombe, Somerset, where a cairn carries the inscription:

THIS WAR MEMORIAL RECREATION GROUND
opened on 3 June 1920
was provided by Public Subscription
by the inhabitants of **WIVELISCOMBE**.

At Great Kingshill, Bucks, there are two plaques on the side of the village hall which overlooks the village green and cricket field:

| IN MEMORY OF | IN MEMORY OF |
|---|---|
| R. ADAMS | K.J. CHESHIRE |
| F.H. BENNETT | H.A.N. COLLIER |
| A.F. BUNCE | F.J. HAWES |
| F.A. COPELAND | J.W. JANES |
| J. CRUTCHFIELD | A.H. LACEY |
| K. GAUNT | F.E. TUCKER |
| F.J. JANES    A.H. JANES | H.J. WALLACE |
| A.G. JANES    P. JANES | I.R. PURDIE |

J. LANGSTON
A.C. PHILLIPS
J.R. TILBURY
W.H. TIMPSON
E.A. TIMPSON

| OF THIS VILLAGE | OF THIS VILLAGE |
|---|---|
| WHO FELL IN THE GREAT WAR | WHO FELL IN WORLD WAR TWO |
| 1914–1918 | 1939–1945 |

Considering what a tree-loving and horticulturally minded society Britain is said to be, on the whole trees and flower-gardens do not figure very prominently in war-memorial terms.

Just behind the York and Lancaster regimental war memorial in Weston Park, Sheffield, is a tree planted in honour of another unit.

Planted by Members of the
2/3rd West Riding Field Ambulance
Old Comrades' Association.
In Memory of their Fallen Comrades
1914–1918.

The Earl of Wemyss and March and his wife Mary lost two sons in the First World War, including his heir, Lieutenant the Lord Elcho of the

Gloucestershire Yeomanry. The Earl presented the parish council of Aberlady, the village closest to his Gosford estate outside Edinburgh, with some land lying between the bowling green and the church. It was to be used as a garden of rest. A South African war memorial was freshly engraved and moved to the same site, as was an old Venetian well, given to the village by the tenth Earl in memory of his first wife.

The Aberlady memorial garden was dedicated by Mary Wemyss on All Saints' Day 1919. In addition, a birch tree and a service tree were planted for remembrance. The service tree (*Sorbus domestica*) was planted by her two young grandchildren, David (who would become the 12th Earl of Wemyss and March) and Martin Charteris (who became private secretary to the Queen and, as a life peer, Lord Charteris of Amisfield). The service tree was accompanied by a notice: 'The service tree is planted as a token to remind us, that for many a year, we shall all have to render service, in order to make good the evil and the waste caused by the cruel war – not greedy service, not grumbling service, but loving service, service for love of England and for loyalty for those who died for her.'

Caroline Dakers in *The Countryside At War 1914–1918* (p.207) quotes from the speech Lady Wemyss made when she dedicated another memorial at Gullane nearby: 'I like to think that when our names are forgotten these names will live in their glory – and will remain as long as this little church remains and even if an earthquake were to destroy the church (or if the Kaiser sent a Zeppelin) their names would not be forgotten. They live in our hearts.'

The use of trees and gardens does seem to be more frequent after 1939–45 than after 1914–19. In some cases, existing park space or a garden was converted into war memorial gardens by the inclusion there of the town's already-existing war memorial cross. Of course, an obvious reason for this is that a war memorial cross already existed, so the addition of gardens or trees represented something more than an added plaque for 1939–45.

At Amersham, Bucks., there are memorial gardens in front of the parish church of St Mary. In them is a 1914–19 war memorial cross and a bronze plaque with 1939–45 names. Inside the church there are two memorial rolls of honour. A message in the gardens makes it clear that the gardens are a World War II addition.

At Barnstable, North Devon, the war memorial was built in the existing civic park to make the whole area a centre for remembrance. In the park there is a rose-bed given by the North Devon branch of the Burma Association, 'To The Memory of Our Comrades Who Fell in the Burma Campaign 1942–1945'. The accompanying plaque carries one of the most poignant of the war epitaphs, one that the men of the 'Forgotten Army' made their own:

When You Go Home,
Tell Them of Us, And Say,
For Your Tomorrow,
We Gave Our Today.

In front of the regimental museum of the Royal Hampshire Regiment at Winchester, is a tree planted in memory of Brigadier H.W. Le Patourel VC (1916–79). Major Herbert Wallace Le Patourel, a Jerseyman, won his VC at Tebourba in Tunisia on 3 December 1942 while with the 2nd Battalion Hampshire Regiment (Royal Jersey 11th).

The gardens in front of the museum are also a memorial:

A Garden of Memory to the Men of
The Royal Hampshire Regiment
who have Fallen in Battle.

*The Churchyards Handbook*, that excellent, common-sense guide to the business of 'Remembrance', has some views on which trees might be used and, at the risk of a slight digression, I include its advice:

Whether evergreen or deciduous trees, conifers or broad-leaved should be chosen is a matter of judgement in individual circumstances. Trees should harmonise with their surroundings and with each other. Deciduous trees have the advantage of looking different at each season of the year and the native species usually look better in the churchyard setting. Evergreens give shade, shelter and colour all the year round. If there is room for both, so much the better.

It considers the yew, so often background to a church war memorial:

The traditional churchyard tree is the yew, and many churchyards contain ancient yews. Their value and significance cannot be over-estimated. Many are important historically, and they are often of considerable, even exceptional antiquity. The churchyard yew at Fortingale in Perthshire is said to be 1,500 years old, and there are countless trees in England and Wales whose age can be reckoned in hundreds of years.

What better accompaniment to a cherished churchyard war memorial than preserving beside it yew-trees that grew there in the early 1900s, trees which those commemorated there would have known in their youth.

Almost by definition, war memorials in churchyards, or in enclosures beside the parish church, are guaranteed their greenery. This is generally denied the memorials that are monuments in their own right in the middle of towns – the Blackpool (Lancs.) obelisk or the memorial at Jedburgh, even though this is alongside Jedburgh Abbey.

It is hard to decide which is the most 'common' placing for a war memorial. Probably it is the village memorial at a road junction or on the green, or in a town's market-place. There is no doubt, however, in my mind that the most pleasant are the ones that are surrounded by greenery, by flowers or trees, or situated on the edge of parks or open country, or those on the magnificent Scottish hillsides.

Kenilworth, Warwicks., and Keswick, Cumberland, benefit from their siting, as does the memorial at Oxshott, Surrey, out on the common. The war memorial at Alnwick, Northumberland, though at an ordinary road-junction of Broadgate Without, is somehow landscaped into the park behind it, on which stands the eighty-foot Percy Tenantry Column. This was put up in 1816 by grateful tenants who had been given a rent-reduction by the then Duke of Northumberland; and atop the monument is a Percy lion, with its tail ramrod-stiff behind it. The sad link between the two monuments is one of those among the 1939–45 dead, listed simply as: 'Northumberland, the 9th Duke of'.

But, above all, the ones which look most at peace with their surroundings are the war memorials on village greens which have been used, or are still used, for that very English game of cricket – at Meopham, Kent; Dunsfold, Surrey; The Lee, Bucks; Holtye Common, Sussex, and many more, too numerous to mention. Even where village greens are little more than small open spaces in front of a pub, a war memorial can often sit with dignity as part of village life – as at Abbots Bromley, Staffs (floodlit at night), and at Horton, Bucks.

Some memorials are better kept than others, and the object of real village endeavour and pride. Several counties run, or used to run, Best Kept Village War Memorial competitions. To stop the same villages winning time and time again, special Winners' Class categories were established – and again, quite often, the same villages featured here too.

Drayton St Leonard, in the south-east of Oxfordshire, has been the winner of many of its county's Best Kept Village War Memorial awards.

**Best Kept Village War Memorial (Oxfordshire)**
**1962 1963 1964 1965 1974**

**Best Kept Village War Memorial (Winner's Class) (Oxfordshire)**
**1967 1975 1976**

Woodstock, whose war memorial is seen by many overseas and other visitors to Blenheim Palace, is another Oxfordshire winner:

Winner of the Best Kept Village War Memorial – 1978
Winner's class – 1979, 1980, 1981
Best Kept War Memorial 1983

The village gardeners of Oxfordshire do at least still 'Remember'.

# 17   Still More Kinds of Memorial

Forget not how they fought, and how they died.

Ufton, Warwicks.

Those killed in the two world wars are commemorated in many ways. In the previous two chapters, we looked at just some of the wide range of memorial buildings, gardens and playing-fields. Here I suggest a few more lines of enquiry open to the social and military researcher into 1914–18 and 1939–45.

Among the most interesting, because not so well known and because of the vast amount of detail they supply, are the memorial books that were published in the early years of the First World War. Most of these deal with officers, but to a lesser extent the non-commissioned did get a look in, at least in the first two years of that war. It seems that later the task of compiling such registers became just too great, too appalling, to be pursued. Most of the projected later volumes seem never to have been printed. Some of their function was taken on in the 1920s by the publication of school, university and company rolls of honour. Only then could the numbers be kept to manageable proportions.

There were also local newspaper commemorations, such as the one produced by the *Craven Herald* in 1920. It deals with 1,562 men and one woman from the then Skipton parliamentary division who died. *Craven's Part in the Great War* is a hardback of 400 pages, with an average of four entries per page for the 1,563 who died. Inscribed copies were presented to each of the families of the commemorated.

In this book we have a unique document about those who served and died from one area.

'Craven' corresponds to the Skipton parliamentary division, then the largest (435,450 acres) in England. Its 71,000 electors lived in hundreds of towns, villages, hamlets and farming communities in the valleys of the Rivers Wharfe, Aire and Ribble. Its main town is Skipton (13,000), centre of a largely farming area, which also includes limestone-quarrying and lead-mining; and south, on the Lancashire borders, some cotton-weaving. Places with sizeable populations include Settle and Sedbergh, Barnoldswick and Earby.

This publishing venture was basically the work of four men: Colonel John Birkbeck JP, CO of the local Territorial Force battalion, the 1/6th Duke of Wellington's (West Riding) Regiment; Thomas Brayshaw, a Settle solicitor; J.T. Clayton, Editor of the *Craven Herald*; and, one of the richest men in the area, who financed it all, Walter Morrison JP, owner of 14,000 acres, and a former MP.

1,562 men and one VAD nurse from the Craven area died in the First World War: they are all listed, and there are 1,500 photographs. In the case of the 112 officers, there are generally full details of their civilian and military careers; for the rank and file we are given rank, name, regiment or ship, home address, the cause and date of death, and generally where this occurred. In seventy per cent of cases the age of the serviceman is given.

In a sense it is a tribute to the men of Colonel Birkbeck's battalion, the 1/6th Duke of Wellington's, and there is a history of its service in France and Flanders from April 1915 to June 1919. There is a full nominal roll of the men who embarked at Folkestone for France on 14 April 1915, and group photographs of the officers of both the 1/6th and 2/6th battalions. There is also an account of the wreck of the hospital ship *Rohilla* (sunk on 30 October 1914) off the east coast of Britain, near Whitby, which had fifty men from Barnoldswick serving in the Royal Navy Sick Berth Reserve. Twelve of them were drowned, leaving twenty dependants – widows and orphans.

Most of the early books dealt only with officers. One of these was *The Bond of Sacrifice: A Biographical Record Of All British Officers Who Fell In The Great War*, published by the Anglo-African Publishing Contractors of High Holborn, London. Volume I covers only August-December 1914 and is a handsome book, with photographs of all those whose obituaries appear. The majority of them are regulars, though a number of Yeomanry and Territorial officers also appear. They also include naval officers, and officers of the Indian Army, who are not always available for consideration together in this way.

As an example of the kind of details revealed, let me quote from my notes on Lieutenant C.L. Mackenzie of the Highland Light Infantry:

Lieutenant Colin Landseer MACKENZIE 2 HLI
Born Malvern, 4 May 1892. Grandson of Sir Edwin Landseer.
Educated Cheltenham. 3 Bn (Reserve) Seaforths on probation.
Gazetted 2/Lt in HLI May 1913

'The young officer had a family right to his position in the Clan Connaich regiments, in both of which he served, uniformed in his own clan tartan, in the Seaforths wearing on his bonnet the "Caber-Feidh", this being also the cognisance of Redcastle, of which house he was a cadet.'

Buried with Lt. J.A.H. Fergusson and Lt. O'Connel RAMC on a ridge above the village of Verneuil.

Less patently designed for purchase by the upper classes – at least from its chosen title – was *The All Ranks ROLL OF HONOUR, being A Biographical Record of All Members of His Majesty's Naval and Military Forces Who have Fallen in the War.* Compiled by the Marquis of Ruvigny, the first volume contained 8,000 names and 2,500 portraits, listing mainly those killed in the first year of the war. A few names are added from later periods, so that their obituaries could be placed with those of relatives. This first volume was published in December 1916, and later volumes were promised.

Taking as an example a few of the officers called Stewart, my notes still suggest a certain class-consciousness in the details given:

Lt-Colonel Douglas Everard Macbean STEWART
1 Canterbury Regt. NZEF
Born Ashburton 25 May 1877. Son of Francis Macbean Stewart of Canterbury, NZ; formerly of Inverness, Scotland.
Killed at Dardanelles landing 25 April 1915 (aged 37)

Captain Geoffrey STEWART              1st Bn. Coldstream Guards
Killed in action 22 Dec 1914.
Born Berkshire 28 Oct 1878; mother related to Earls of Galloway.
Eton. 2/Lt 13 July 1898. Served in South African War. Retires 1910.
Joins Leicester Yeomanry (TF) as Captain, then Major.
Rejoins Coldstreams. Killed Givenchy (aged 35)

Lieutenant James Alexander Logan STEWART    1st Bn. Rifle Brigade
Killed in action 13 May 1915 (Ypres) (aged 22).
Father a Lt-Colonel 7th Hussars; Mother a sister of Baron Dormer.
Born Bombay 7 March 1893. Winchester and Trinity College, Cambridge.

*The British Roll Of Honour* – or, as it was described on the inside title-page, *The Roll of Honour of The Empire's Heroes* – was published in several editions. They generally list about 150 officers, but many of the obituaries are common to several editions. The portraits alone are invaluable to the military historian for the details of uniform given, a great majority of them pre-war. The biographies (based on what the next-of-kin or the editor of the book thought important) make almost incredible reading today.

Many of our larger churches, cathedrals and abbeys, especially those with direct links to a Regiment or Corps, have another kind of memorial book, a '**Book of Remembrance**'. These are generally housed in a memorial chapel or a corner of the church dedicated to those killed in the wars, with in many cases regimental colours, the Union flag or British Legion flags flying over a glass case, in which the book or books are displayed.

In the memorial chapel to the Durham Light Infantry in Durham Cathedral, several Books of Remembrance are kept – with the pages turned daily or every few days as required, so as always to be open at the correct date. They list the men of the DLI killed on that same day in the war years. Generally the pages of each Book of Remembrance cover several days.

## ROLL OF HONOUR 1914–1918

### 17th January 1916
| | |
|---|---|
| 1/6th Bn | Private C. CRANNEY |

### 1917
| | |
|---|---|
| 2nd Bn | Private W. CHEETHAM |
| 1/6th Bn | Private C.L. COLLIN |
| 20th Bn | Private J.S. TANSEY |
| 2nd Bn | Private T.S. WHELAN |

### 1918
| | |
|---|---|
| 1/6th Bn | Private J.L. HAMMOND MM |

(killed 1919)

### 18th January 1916
| | |
|---|---|
| 10th Bn | Private F. ATKINSON |
| 10th Bn | Private T. DAVIDSON |

### 1917
| | |
|---|---|
| 2nd Bn | Corporal J.P. REGAN |
| 1/9th Bn | L/Corporal B. THOMAS |
| 1/9th Bn | Private F. COOPER |
| 2nd Bn | Private A. CRANSTON |
| 1/9th Bn | Private J.W. LOCKEY |

### 19th January 1915
| | |
|---|---|
| 4th Bn | L/Corporal J.S. HOWSON |
| 4th Bn | Private J.K. FOX |

### 1916

| | |
|---|---|
| 10th Bn | 2/Lieut. C.F. BATTY |
| 2nd Bn | Private J.K. BELL |
| 10th Bn | Private W. COOK |
| 13th Bn | Private J. CLARKE |
| 2nd Bn | Private C. FRANCIS |
| 14th Bn | Private A.W. ROBINSON |
| 1/6th Bn | Private W. STEPHENSON |

### 1917

| | |
|---|---|
| | L/Corporal L. PATERSON |
| 1/7th Bn | Private J. DUNN |

### 1918

| | |
|---|---|
| 3rd Bn | Private A. JAKEMAN |

The layout of the Second World War book is slightly different, reflecting the far smaller numbers of DLI men killed in the second conflict: 12,606 for 1914–18 versus 3,011 for 1939–45.

#### *17th January*

| 1944 | Private A. BAILEY | 8th Bn |
|---|---|---|
| 1944 | Private J. THOMAS | 16th Bn |
| 1945 | L/Corporal R. BERRIE | 9th Bn |
| 1945 | Private P.G. CLEMENTS | 10th Bn |
| 1945 | Private H. HALL | 9th Bn |
| 1945 | Private C. HARGREAVES | 9th Bn |
| 1945 | Private E. KING | 10th Bn |
| 1945 | Private K. LEE | 10th Bn |
| 1945 | Private A. LEIGHTON | att.10 DWR |
| 1945 | Private M.M. PEDDELTY | att.10 DWR |
| 1945 | Private J.W. WILSON | 16th Bn. |
| 1945 | Private R.H. WINTERINGHAM | att.10 DWR |
| 1945 | Private A. YATES | att.10 DWR |

#### *18th January*

| 1941 | Private A. CURTIS | 2nd Bn |
|---|---|---|
| 1944 | L/Corporal S. BERVIDGE | 9th Bn |
| 1945 | Corporal W.J. CHEESE | 9th Bn |
| 1945 | Private E.S.C. HESTER | 9th Bn |
| 1945 | Private L. JOBLING | 9th Bn |
| 1945 | Private G.N. PATERSON | 9th Bn |
| 1945 | Private D. TOMLINSON | 9th Bn |
| 1945 | Private H.G. WILES | 9th Bn |
| 1945 | Private R. WILLS | 9th Bn |

*19th January*

| 1945 | Corporal H. JORDENS | 9th Bn |
| 1945 | L/Corporal W. BRITTAIN | 9th Bn |

'Colours' – flags – were presented to every new battalion of the British Army which served overseas in the 1914–18 War. Existing battalions already had their own regimental colours.

Many of these wartime-only colours are now laid up as memorials to the men who served and died with the Territorial or Service battalions involved – as also are the colours of regular or militia units which have since been disbanded or amalgamated, making the issue of new colours necessary. These flags are to be found throughout the country, again generally in the regimental chapels of cathedrals or minsters of garrison towns, but in the case of Territorial units, often laid up in parish churches from which a large proportion of their volunteers had come.

An example is the King's Colour of the 2/5th Battalion (Prince Albert's) Somerset Light Infantry which was consecrated on 9 September 1920 and laid up in St Mary's, Ilminster. A brass plaque on the flagpole reads:

The King's Colour
of the
2/5th Battalion
The Prince Albert's Somerset Light Infantry
Formed 1914 Disbanded 1920

Served overseas throughout the Great War.

Regimental histories are also a form of memorial and often print a full roll of honour as an appendix. A very readable example is the story of the 2/5 SLI, *A Strange War: Burma, India & Afghanistan 1914–1919* by C.P. Mills, which prints a full roll of honour.

One of the more esoteric rolls from World War I, republished in facsimile recently, is that previously mentioned *List of British Officers taken prisoner in the various Theatres of War between August, 1914 and November, 1918.* It was compiled by the Army bankers, Messrs Cox & Co, and was first published for private circulation in 1919. It qualifies as a kind of war memorial because it not only lists when officers went 'Missing' and the date of their repatriation but shows which ones died of wounds or other causes in captivity.

Its interest to the military historian lies in the patterns which can be traced for specific actions, such as that sad surrender at Kut-al-Amara in the Mesopotamian campaign, and the heavy losses suffered in the German spring offensive of March/April 1918. In the latter case, whole infantry battalions were overrun, and the great bulk of their officers, including several colonels, were put in the bag. Thus the Sherwood Foresters lost seven officers from their 2nd Battalion, twenty-one from the 2/5th, seventeen from the 2/6th, and fourteen from the 7th Battalion – at a time when most battalions had at most about thirty officers each. Of these captured Forester officers, three died in German hands.

The South Africans similarly lost heavily in the fighting on 23/24 March 1918, with many officers from their 1st, 2nd and 4th Infantry regiments taken prisoner: sixteen officers from the 1st, twelve from the 2nd, and twenty-one from the 4th, plus a doctor and a chaplain.

One of war's little ironies was that this list was compiled not by the Army itself but by the bankers Cox & Co, who were often the first to hear that an officer was a prisoner of war, either when he cashed a cheque with his German captors or when his wife, who had heard by postcard where he was, called in to arrange to draw on his pay.

Cox & Co would later merge with Henry S. King & Co to become Cox & King's, bankers and agents to thousands of officers whose pay was paid directly to their accounts. 6 Pall Mall was a first port of call for many an officer returning from abroad. The company is now merged anonymously into one of the Big Four (Lloyds).

This might be an appropriate place to mention a kind of war memorial it is so easy to overlook: plaques on the wall in a bank or department store. Each is a minor footnote to history: of war, banking and trade.

On the wall inside the lobby of the National Westminster Bank at 208 Piccadilly, W1 branch:

### N.P.U.B.E.

A tribute to the 2681 members
of the staff of this Bank
who served in The Great War 1914–1918
and in honoured memory of the
415 who gave their lives for their country.

On the main staircase at Lloyds Bank, 6 Pall Mall, SW1

(Cox's Bank)
**1914–1919**
In Proud and Grateful Memory
of the Members of our Permanent Staff
Killed in the Great War.

| | |
|---|---|
| ALLIES A.E. | KIRKPATRICK A. |
| BARNETT W.M.C. | LONG G.S. |
| BOWLBY G.E.L. | McCONNELL H.J. |

| | |
|---|---|
| CHESHIRE E.M. | MARRIOTT O.D. |
| COGGIN A.B.C. | MATTHEWS F.R. |
| CURLING F.T. | NOSS A.R. |
| FELL G.F. | PAULL C.W.T. |
| FISHER C.H. | PORTER A.W. |
| GILL H.G. | SALTER R.C.F. |
| HUMPHREYS L.P. | THOMAS L.J. |
| JONES R.H. | |

**1914–1919**
In Proud and Grateful Memory
of the Members of the Permanent Staff
of Henry S. King & Company
Killed in the Great War.

COCKERTON E.A.
CARSON R.S.
GRETTON H.E., Captain
GREEN C.
HALE F.T.
JEFFREYS H.L., Lieutenant
SHERRING F.W.
SIMONDS M.C.
VENNING E.C.
WELLS D.

**1939–1945**
In Proud and Grateful Memory
of the Members of our Permanent Staff
Killed in the War
Cox & King's Branch, 6 Pall Mall, SW1

| | | |
|---|---|---|
| BELL E.W. | CREED F.C. | RODGERS G.W. |
| BINNINGTON G.L. | DAVIES K.W. | WEBBER B.C. |
| CHAPMAN D.J.S. | FIELD K.C. | WILLIAMS E.J. |
| COX I.H.G. | HARDING W.R. | WOOD L. |
| | MARSHALL J.W. | |
| | PARSONS H.C. | |
| | PATTERSON B.H. | |

Many other companies and institutions carry such wall-plaques. Almost all are well preserved and make interesting reading.

The memorial to the staff of Harrod's who fell in the First World War has been studied in Chapter 3. A similar one is on the stairway at Liberty's of Regent Street in London. Here there are two decorated wooden wall-plaques designed to blend with the wooden panelling. That for the First World War includes the regimental badges of those commemorated. There is perhaps a significant change of wording from the 'Gave Their Lives' of World War I to that 'Lost Their Lives' of World War II, who include civilian staff killed by bombing.

### In Memory Of
### Those Members of the Staff of LIBERTY & Co. who Gave
### Their Lives For Their Country During the War 1914–1918

| | | |
|---|---|---|
| ASTELL E.D. | HENNESSY T. | PAVEY P.E. |
| BEAKHOUSE H. | HIGGINS P.T. | POWERS W. |
| BEAUMONT C.E. | HIGHAM C. | PRANCE W. |
| BIRD F.J. | HONEY W.J. | REECE W.J. |
| BROWN A. | HONEY G. | SALTER J.E. |
| BRYCE A. | HOOPER T.W. | SELWOOD A.C. |
| CLARIDGE A.H. | HUNT E.W. | SEWELL H.C. |
| DORE A.W. | KALISCH E. | SNAITH W.E. |
| DOWNS M.S. | LEETE F.E. | STRAW L.H. |
| EDWARDS C.H. | MAY C.H. | THORNING S. |
| GARDNER T. | MEYERS T.F. | TOMBLESON H. |
| GOODE W.G. | NILSON C.E. | UNDERWOOD W. |
| GRIFFIN N. | PAGE G.W. | WAIGH L.E. |
| HASTINGS FL.T.DCM | PATTEN C.W. | WARWICK F.W.F. |
| HAWKINS H.C. | | WHENMAN J.C. |

### In Memory Of
### Those Members of the Staff of LIBERTY & Co.
### Who Lost Their Lives during the War 1939–1945

| | |
|---|---|
| BRAUND J.P. | GILES R.H. |
| CARPENTER S. | HEAVENS R. |
| CORSIE E.W. | LLOYD J.W. |
| ELLINGWORTH A.B. | PAYNE R. |
| FIGGINS R.J. | PROTO J. |

SPEED J.

| | |
|---|---|
| Miss E.S. BRANE | Mrs F. McDONNELL |
| Mr A.W. GWILT | Miss A. MITCHELL |

Miss V. ROFFERSMAN

Another excellent source of day-to-day local knowledge can generally be found in regimental museums. These are often a repository for medals, uniforms, swords and other military accoutrements, their display being a memorial to the serviceman whose effects they were.

In the museum of the Royal Highland Fusiliers in Sauchiehall Street,

Glasgow, are displayed the belongings of a First World War officer of one of the regiments amalgamated in 1959 to become the RHF. He was Lieutenant Hubert R. Kerr, belonging to the 1st Battalion of the Highland Light Infantry, killed in action near the village of Gorre, a little way north-east from Béthune, France, just twenty-two days after his battalion landed in France after its voyage from India. A regular soldier, he died on 19 December 1914, aged twenty-two.

The next-of-kin of those killed received a memorial scroll or card, and examples of these from the two world wars are on display in the regimental museum of the Royal Hampshire Regiment in Winchester.

> He whom this scroll commemorates was numbered among those who, at the call of King and Country, left all that was dear to them, endured hardness, faced danger, and finally passed out of the sight of men by the path of Duty and Self-Sacrifice, giving up their own lives that others might live in Freedom. Let those who come after see to it that his name be not forgotten.

Private Thomas Frederick DAY,
Hampshire Regiment

21190 Private T. DAY MM

> This scroll commemorates Private C.H. KEW, Royal Hampshire Regiment, held in honour as one who served King and Country in the World War of 1939–1945 and gave his life to save mankind from tyranny. May his sacrifice help to bring the Peace and Freedom for which he died.
>
> George VI R.I.

Regimental museums, regimental journals, regimental histories. All pay tribute to those who died fighting for the general cause, and for their particular part of England, Ireland, Scotland or Wales. The territorial bases for so much of the British Army's structure and strength must never be forgotten.

*A Bibliography of Regimental Histories of the British Army*, a labour of love undertaken by Arthur S. White, lately librarian of the War Office, is an invaluable starting-point for those whose approach to social and military history is through the printed word. This is surely a *must* for all reference libraries.

The 'In Memoriam' columns of *The Times* and other newspapers, down to the most local weekly, still sometimes carry notices relating to 1914–18 casualties, seventy and more years after the death. They too are thus a war memorial, to be read together with the church rolls of honour, and the books in regimental chapels or published by schools, universities and even employers.

*The Times* of 21 March 1988 carried an 'In Memoriam–War' notice: 'DIMMER – Lt-Colonel John Henry Stephen, VC MC KRRC, killed in action at Marteville, 21 March 1918. Job 19, verses 26–27.' Dimmer won his VC as a 31-year-old lieutenant, in the regular 2nd Battalion KRRC at Zillebeke in Belgium on 12 November 1914. He was killed, after nearly four years war service, as a 35-year-old Lt-Colonel commanding the 2/4th (TF) Battalion Royal Berkshires. The verses from Job chosen for his notice read:

> And though after my skin worms destroy this body; yet in my flesh shall I see God:
>
> Whom I shall see for myself, and mine eyes shall behold, and not another; though my reins be consumed within me.

Another 'In Memoriam–War' notice in *The Times* in 1988 records the death of Corporal George Albert Pledger, Bucks Hussars, killed in action with the Camel Corps CO/2 on the banks of the River Jordan, 1 May 1918. Another was for Second Lieutenant Reginald Lambert Lack, Royal Irish Rifles, mortally wounded on the Somme 2 July 1916 whilst rescuing a friend, which said:

> All you had hoped for, all you had you gave,
> to save mankind, yourself you scorned to save.

# 18   Who Provided the War Memorial?

'Their Fellow Parishioners'

Most of the village war memorials of Britain were provided by those who lived in the villages and towns themselves. They probably organized the effort at parish level, through the work of the parish or borough council or through a special local war memorial committee. In the main, these memorials represent genuine community effort and thus have historical value in illustrating the viewpoints and activities of those living there at the time.

As in most such endeavours, there was almost certainly a driving force of some kind: be it squire or vicar, chairman of the council or a parent of one of The Fallen. A good example is described by Caroline Dakers in her book, *The Countryside At War 1914–1918*, in which she reports on what went on in the village of Great Leighs, near Chelmsford, in Essex: 'The Great Leighs Memorial was first discussed at a meeting of the Parish Council in September 1919. A public meeting was held; then the War Memorial Committee met at the Church and agreed to the suggestion of J. Herbert Tritton, lord of the manor, that a tablet should be erected in the churchyard wall facing the road.'

The memorial tablet was presented by J. Herbert Tritton Esq., of Lyons Hall, in effect the squire of Great Leighs. Set in a flint and mortar wall between the churchyard and Boreham Road, it was unveiled in December 1920 by Major-General Sir George Scott Moncrieff. An inscription reads:

> This tablet was placed here by the parishioners of Great Leighs,
> in honoured memory of fellow parishioners who gave their lives
> for our country in the Great War 1914–1919.
> They whom this tablet commemorates were numbered among those
> who at the call of King and Country left all that was dear to them,
> endured hardness, faced danger and finally passed
> out of the sight of men by the path of duty and self-sacrifice,
> giving up their own lives that others might live in freedom.
> Let those who come after see to it that their names be not forgotten.

| | | | |
|---|---|---|---|
| Charles | CLOUGHTON | Frederick | MANSFIELD |
| Ernest George | CLOUGHTON | Charles Jonathan | RAYNER |
| Charles | COOK | Harry | SARGEANT |
| Charles Joseph | DIGBY | Alan George | TRITTON |
| Ernest | DIGBY | Alfred Reginald | WARD |
| William | DUKE | Charles Henry | WARD |
| Archie | FITCH | Ernest | WRIGHT |
| Arthur | FITCH | Herbert George | WRIGHT |
| Dick | FITCH | Louis Walter | WRIGHT |
| George Bennett | FITCH | | |

Captain Alan George Tritton was the youngest son of J. Herbert Tritton.
He was a regular soldier and was killed in action with the 3rd Battalion of
the Coldstream Guards on 26 December 1914. Educated at Winchester
and the RMC, he was commissioned in the Coldstream Guards in 1900
and served in the Boer War. Captain Tritton was adjutant of his
battalion from 1907 to 1910. He was 'Mentioned in Despatches' on 8
October 1914 and was thirty-two when he died.

   Lyn Macdonald, in *1914* (p.266), quotes Drummer E.L. Slaytor of the
3rd Battalion Coldstream Guards (4 Brigade, 2 Division): 'Captain
Tritton was wounded, badly wounded in the hand and probably in the
leg as well, because I remember seeing him on his horse, deathly pale,
and the whole of his trouser leg saturated in blood. The Germans were
treading on our heels! And they must have got round us. Bullets were
flying about in all directions – ricocheting off the trees – smack, smack,
smack, smack. It was terrible confusion.'

There are many variations on the phrase 'Their Fellow Parishioners',
ranging from the simple 'The Villagers' to 'Fellow Townsmen and
Friends', but the local involvement is often recorded:

| | |
|---|---|
| 'The Inhabitants' | (Middleton-in-Teesdale, Durham) |
| 'Relatives and Friends' | (Great Torrington, Devon) |
| 'Relatives and Fellow Parishioners' | (Theale, Berks.) |
| 'Heritors, Members and Adherents' | (Kirkurd, Peebles.) |
| 'Erected by the People of ....' | (Long Sutton, Som.) |

– and a phrase is often inscribed to make it clear that the cost was borne
locally, even if the site was provided by church or landowner:

| | |
|---|---|
| 'By General Subscription' | (Tadmarton, Oxon.) |
| 'By Public Subscription' | |
| (Wiveliscombe, Som.; Chipping Norton, Oxon.; Kirton-in-Lindsey, Lincs.) | |

Others were straightforward presentations, as at Westwell, named for the most western well in Oxfordshire, whose war memorial consists of a large granite boulder. Inset in it is a brass numeral from a clock, and the memorial is inscribed:

To the brave who gave their lives
for England in the Great War.

Erected by Stretta Aimee Holland
in memory of her brothers

Lieutenant Harold S. Price   Royal Fusiliers
Lieutenant Edward John Price   Royal Navy

This brass numeral formed
part of the Clock
of the Cloth Hall, Ypres.

There is a whole book to be written about war memorials as monuments of architectural style. Derek Boorman's excellently illustrated book *At the Going Down of the Sun* is by far the best introduction to British First World War memorials published to date. Another book, to be published by Dr Alan Borg, Director of the Imperial War Museum, examines the work of artists and architects responsible for war memorials. Dr Borg argues that many British war memorials are unjustly neglected works of art.

Any discussion of the architecture and design of war memorials must include reference to the Cenotaph in Whitehall by Sir Edwin Lutyens. In the New Year's Honour List of 1918 he was made a Knight of the Most Eminent Order of the Indian Empire. This was one of four British orders later discontinued for political reasons – in this case the Independence of India and Pakistan in 1947. At the same time, it was announced that Lutyens was to be chief architect to the War Graves' Commission. Even then, it was probably not till the end of June or the beginning of July 1919 that Prime Minister Lloyd George told him the government wanted a 'catafalque' erected in Whitehall. It was to be the saluting-point for the march-past of Allied troops on Saturday 19 July 1919 during the peace celebrations in London, at which Marshal Foch and General Pershing of the USA would be present.

Lutyens' daughter wrote:

Father said that it should not be a catafalque, which bears a coffin, but a cenotaph, which is an empty tomb. He remembered a massive stone seat he had designed ... being once compared to some celebrated cenotaph. Thus the hitherto obscure word became associated with the best-known of all modern funerary monuments. Since it had to be ready in 10 days' time it could only be a temporary structure of wood and plaster.

The simplicity of The Cenotaph, its non-denominational character, its universality and timelessness, caught the imagination of the hundreds of thousands of people who passed it during the Peace Celebrations. It was so perfectly right for its setting, and for the England of the time, that within a week it had become a national monument.

The only inscription on it – THE GLORIOUS DEAD – was suggested by Lloyd George. It is the best-known and best-loved of all Lutyens's work. In his own words 'the plain fact emerged and grew stronger every hour that The Cenotaph was what the people wanted, and they wanted to have the wood-and-plaster original replaced by an identical memorial in lasting stone'.


Lutyens was adamant in not having a cross on the Cenotaph, as Indian troops, among others, would have to salute it, and this Christian symbol was therefore inappropriate. He also wanted coloured marble flags on the permanent structure, instead of real silk ones. He knew silk flags would get bedraggled and need frequent changing. But he was disappointed here, as the Cabinet overruled him. He did have stone flags, however, though not in colour, on his great war memorial at Etaples in France. Lutyens also designed the All India War Memorial, and a Victory Column for Colombo, Ceylon.

The permanent Cenotaph in Whitehall was unveiled 11 November 1920.

However, a good deal has already been written about this fine memorial, and equally famous statues, such as the Artillery Memorial and the Machine Gun Corps Memorial at Hyde Park Corner, so perhaps the true war memorial hobbyist should concentrate instead on the design and construction of war memorials at town and village level.

Many of the major town memorials follow the Cenotaph in general style, without being exact copies. Many of them incorporate a cross. There are also triumphal arches and gates, clock-towers and catafalques, pillars and columns and obelisks, and a host of statues of every kind. In some a mounted St George destroys a dragon, in others Victory spreads her wings or offers a comforting wreath to a serviceman, and there are numerous memorials which simply show a soldier in uniform.

Among the more symbolical ones is that at Shaw's Corner, between Reigate and Redhill, Surrey. It shows a man carrying a child in one arm and a torch aloft in another, making his way through a tangled thicket. The bronze, by Captain Richard Goulden who served as a Royal

Engineer, is meant to show man triumphing over the difficulties that lie in his path.

But pride of place at grassroots level must go to all the war memorials which consist of the British soldier, the primordial Tommy Atkins, shown with head bowed in mourning over a reversed rifle. There are infinite variations, each of interest to the student of military history – for many faithfully reproduce the uniform and accoutrements worn by 'The Parishioners of This Village' who went to war in their local regiment – and did not return.

In addition to the mourning figure, other soldiers are seen waving their arms and rifle in victory, as engaged in attack with the bayonet, or falling backwards in death, or simply standing on guard or at ease. Some of these soldier-memorials are extremely moving, particularly those which capture the extreme youth of so many soldiers of that time. I think of the Scottish soldier at Lochmaben, Dumfriesshire. Others show mature men in the prime of life (Canonbie, Dumfries; Royal Tunbridge Wells, Kent; and those on the Artillery Memorial, London).

Collecting photographs of all the soldier-memorials and studying the uniforms portrayed would be a lifetime's work in itself. Nonetheless the military hobbyist can learn a lot from the way the soldiers are dressed and the weapons and equipment they carry or wear.

Is the soldier properly dressed, for war or parade, with well-arranged puttees, or does he show signs of the fighting he has endured? Many war memorials show wounded figures, helped by a comrade or stretcher-bearer, or bandaging their wounds themselves.

Do the men belong to the county regiment and wear an actual cap-badge, or is the unit deliberately non-identifiable? An expert should be able to recognize the weapons and accessories displayed: is the bayonet fixed or sheathed, and what vintage is it? Is he wearing a service cap or tin helmet or is he bare-headed, and in Scotland does he wear a tam o'shanter or glengarry or officer's balmoral?

There are many things to notice about war memorial soldier-statues. A realistic point, not always made, is that, when the man's rifle is reversed in mourning, is it resting on his boot – as it would be to stop dirt getting inside it.

When there is more than one figure on the memorial, one should ask oneself why the others, in addition to the ordinary Tommy Atkins, are there. Is there a seaman to represent a significant number of naval dead, or if there is an airman or a machine-gunner shown, for what reason? If there are several soldiers, one is likely to be an officer, with a revolver. If a solitary figure, is it always a private soldier or is the man wearing the stripes of a corporal or sergeant?

Only when we come to the public school war memorials are we more likely to find an officer alone: beckoning his men into attack, as at Nottingham High School, or doing the same while falling, like the Highland officer featured at Fettes School in Edinburgh, (designed by Birnie Rhind RSA), which has the words 'Carry On' inscribed boldly on the plinth below him.

Some of the sculptors deserve special mention for the quality of their work on these soldier-memorials. Kellock Brown was responsible for the soldier standing on a granite block at Penpont, against a background of the Dumfriesshire hills; and his beautifully sited statue of a Highlander is on the greensward at Inveraray, by Loch Fyne. Henry Price, a Londoner, did the KOSB figures at Annan and Maxwelltown, Dumfries – the former stocky, resolute, with upright rifle; the latter without a rifle but with arms outstretched as though appealing against the slaughter, or perhaps at the moment he became a victim of it.

The more elaborate regimental memorials which also include sculpted figures are almost all worth studying. Pre-eminent among them – and I apologize for what may seem to be a Scottish or northern bias – are the Cameronians' memorial in Glasgow and the York & Lancaster Regiment's figures at Sheffield. To balance this, I offer the Duke of Cornwall's Light Infantryman at Bodmin, Cornwall, and the rifleman (Rifle Brigade) at Grosvenor Gardens, near Victoria in London.

Looking at all war memorials from an architectural angle is most rewarding. There was a 'pause' in building at the start of the 1920s as the nation recovered from war, and many of the great names of architecture (or those who would become great names) were only too glad to work on memorial buildings or even humble crosses. Many of these architects suffered personal losses in the war, and some acknowledged their indebtedness by working without reward.

Once again it was the public schools and universities which could afford to commission major memorial buildings. Sir Giles Gilbert Scott RA was responsible for the magnificent large memorial chapel at Charterhouse (686 Carthusians died out of some 3,000 who served). Sir Giles was also responsible for memorials at many of the leading Roman Catholic public schools (Ampleforth, Beaumont, Downside).

In many cases, however, schools chose as architects and designers of their war memorials Old Boys, and in particular those who had returned to the architectural profession after themselves serving in the war. At Edinburgh Academy (298 Old Boys killed) the architect of the War Memorial Building was R.S. Reid, an Old Boy; and at Campbell College, Belfast, the memorial was designed by Captain James R. Young, an old Campbellian who had served in the war. 610 old boys from this Belfast college served, 125 were killed.

One figure the war memorialist must be aware of is Sir Reginald

Blomfield RA, who designed 'The Cross of Sacrifice' for the Imperial War Graves Commission – the cross put up on several hundred overseas battlefields and at official British and Commonwealth cemeteries established abroad. This Battlefield Memorial Cross or Great War Cross, as it is also sometimes called, is seen in many cemeteries in Britain in which wartime dead are buried. It is also used at many schools (Highgate School, London, and Haileybury College, Herts.), as well as in towns (such as Sir Reginald's home town of Rye, Sussex, and in Chelsea's Sloane Square) and even in small villages throughout the country.

Sir Reginald was determined to keep the design of his cross simple and not let it reflect any specific style or period of architecture. It is on a hexagonal base, topped by three plinths, and its only adornment is an unsheathed warrior's sword in bronze.

Blomfield went on to design one of the most impressive of the overseas war memorials – the Menin Gate at Ypres (1927). That memorial, whose decorative carving alone took four years to complete, is dedicated to 56,000 British soldiers who died in battles around Ypres and 'who have no known grave'. (Sir Edwin Lutyens' Somme memorial at Thièpval commemorates another 73,000 British dead whose bodies were not recovered.)

Most of the 'Crosses of Sacrifice' in Britain carry the words:

THIS CROSS OF SACRIFICE
IS ONE IN DESIGN AND INTENTION
WITH THOSE WHICH HAVE BEEN SET UP IN FRANCE AND BELGIUM
AND OTHER PLACES THROUGHOUT THE WORLD
WHERE OUR DEAD OF THE GREAT WAR
ARE LAID TO REST.

In most cemeteries where 400 or more dead are buried, or near Memorials to the Missing, a Stone of Remembrance is also placed. It is generally a granite monolith, acceptable to those of any faith (or none) and thus used as the focal point for ceremonies and wreath-laying rather than the Cross of Sacrifice, with its Christian symbolism. The Stone of Remembrance also carries the words from the Book of Ecclesiasticus THEIR NAME LIVETH FOR EVERMORE, which were chosen by Rudyard Kipling, who lost his only son in the war.

Whole books could be written about the inaugural parades which accompanied the unveiling of each town and village's war memorial. These are generally well documented in the local press of the time, with accompanying pictures of the official party and the crowd, and are often reprinted in regimental magazines and local guide-books. It is interesting to see that, while the accounts are full of details about the Great and the Good present, few carry the kind of 'human interest' stories which equivalent papers would print today.

Earl Haig must have attended scores of such parades in the early 1920s, and his presence is sometimes mentioned on the memorial.

At St Andrew's in Scotland, the memorial is a massive granite Celtic cross, with a wall and panels of the names behind it, standing at the east end of North Street, near the cathedral ruins. Designed by Sir Robert Lorimer, the great Scottish architect of numerous memorials overseas, it was unveiled by Earl Haig on 23 September 1922. On a wild night in January 1968, the cross on the memorial was blown down in a gale and broken. It was restored in 1985.

Other unveilings were performed by members of the Establishment whose sons or close relatives were named there. The Beaconsfield (Bucks.) war memorial was unveiled in 1921 by Field Marshal Lord Grenfell, two of whose nephews (as described in the Introduction) are to be found there. Prayers were said by the Right Reverend Bishop Shaw, Archdeacon of Oxford, three of whose four sons' names appear on the same memorial.

War memorial sculptures did not end with those erected by a grateful nation within a few years of the ending of the wars. They are still being produced even today to mark special anniversaries or to commemorate relationships stemming from wartime days.

A 1989 introduction was a memorial to the men of the midget submarines and 'chariots' of the Second World War. This was to go at the submarine museum at HMS *Dolphin* at Gosport, Portsmouth, Hants. Incidentally, the present chairman of the Victoria Cross & George Cross Association is a former midget-submariner, Rear-Admiral (then Lieutenant) Godfrey Place VC, CB, DSC, who won the supreme award in an attack on the battleship *Tirpitz* in a Norwegian fiord in 1943.

Another VC, Group Captain Leonard Cheshire VC,OM,DSO,DFC, has proposed the 1914–18 and 1939–45 World War Memorial Fund. He sees it as 'a living memorial to the victims of World War' and as 'their gift to future victims of natural disaster', such as had occurred in Ethiopia, Mozambique, Jamaica, Sudan and Bangladesh. He proposed a donation by those who had survived the two world wars of £5, as a memory for each person who had lost their lives – estimated at 80 million people. The United Nations Secretary-General would use the income from the fund for immediate emergency relief. A huge vision, but is the world ready for such supra-nationalism?

# 19   Remembrance: 'We Will Remember Them'

The Armistice which ended the Great War came into effect at the eleventh hour of the eleventh day of the eleventh month of 1918. Later, 11 November was decreed to be Remembrance Day with a two minutes' silence to be observed at exactly that moment in succeeding years. And so it was until the Second World War.

In my schooldays, 11 November was a full holiday, and the two minutes' silence was observed meticulously, with traffic coming to a stop and quiet reigning until the last post and reveille was played at the Cenotaph, and the nation once again came to life.

The village-church parades, now held on the nearest Sunday to 11 November, and the annual ceremony at the Cenotaph, still remain the most meaningful celebrations of the spirit of Remembrance Day. And there are other commemorations. Each year, in the grounds of Westminster Abbey, by permission of the Abbey's Dean and Chapter and the Rector of St Margaret's, small crosses are planted by regimental associations. These range from the Household Cavalry – Life Guards and Blues and Royals – down to the humblest supporting arms and services.

The military historian will find among the infantry many regiments no longer extant under their old proud county titles, or which like the Cameronians (Scottish Rifles) and the York & Lancaster Regiment, chose disbandment in preference to enforced merger.

The London Regiment, a unique Great War amalgamation of the Territorial Force units of the capital into one giant regiment, is still well represented by a few surviving old comrades or by their Territorial Army successors.

The battalions are often celebrated under their subsidiary titles or nicknames: the Shiny Seventh (7th Bn.), the Post Office Rifles (8th); Princess Louise's Kensington Regiment (13th); and the London Scottish (14th).

There too, perhaps somewhat incongruously beside the busy traffic circling Parliament Square, are crosses to those who represent a part of the history of rural Britain, the men of the Yeomanry.

Queen's Own Warwickshire and Worcestershire Yeomanry
Nottinghamshire and Sherwood Rangers Yeomanry
Shropshire Yeomanry
Derbyshire Yeomanry
Fife & Forfar Yeomanry
City of London Yeomanry
Westminster Dragoons
3rd/4th County of London Yeomanry
Northamptonshire Yeomanry
East Riding of Yorkshire Yeomanry
Royal East Kent Yeomanry
Middlesex Yeomanry
Norfolk Yeomanry
Essex Yeomanry

Another manifestation of Remembrance are commemorative plaques marking royal visits to war memorials. At Greengates, near Bradford, West Yorks., which has a fine 'winged victory' war memorial in a plaza by a busy road-junction, there are plaques in the flower-beds marking a visit in 1923 by the Prince of Wales and another by the Duke and Duchess of York, five years later.

Remembrance is only one step towards acknowledging the sacrifice made by so many in both world wars and afterwards. I suggest we owe them a continuing duty to preserve these unique monuments of war as a permanent record of their part in our heritage and history.

It is a sad fact that many war memorials have been allowed to deteriorate, while many more could do with cleaning and repainting. It is ironic to find the inscription 'Their Name Liveth For Evermore' or 'Their Glory Shall Not Be Blotted Out' and find that this is exactly what has happened: the names on the memorial are illegible.

Other war memorials have had to be moved, because of redevelopment or road-widening. Local authorities are officially responsible for the war memorials on public ground. Some authorities fulfil their obligations, especially when prompted by local ex-servicemen and women, others do not.

Most war memorials and official cemeteries overseas are the responsibility of what is now the Commonwealth War Graves Commission, which does an excellent job of caring for them. An account of the work of the War Graves Commission is to be found in *Courage Remembered* by T.A. Edwin Gibbon and G. Kingsley Ward (HMSO, 1989) and makes good complementary reading.

Many war memorials are, however, on private property (in schools and churches, in company courtyards and on buildings), and are at the mercy of developers and simple forgetfulness and neglect. The Imperial War Museum (Lambeth Road, London SE1 6HZ), thanks to a generous grant from the Leverhulme Foundation, has now embarked on a five-year plan to compile a national register of war memorials in Britain, both public and private. Members of the Royal British Legion and the Western Front Association 1914–1918 (47, Smith Street, London SW3 4EP) have volunteered to help compile this register of war memorials. The idea is to list them all on a computer database, record who is responsible for their maintenance, and thus give them a better chance of being kept in good repair and safe from the bulldozers.

Many communities took the opportunity when adding the 1939–45 dead to their Great War memorials, to tidy and renew the originals; in a few cases even to build a brand new memorial devoted to both wars. The war memorial cross at Bicester, Oxon., is one of many memorials updated and restored after the Second World War. It is an ornate cross, with Gothic writing, a Christ crucified, Mary and child, and a knight in shining armour. It stands in the churchyard of St Edburg, and in the porch two plaques list the names of the dead – 102 for 1914–18, twenty-six for 1939–45. At the Church of England Parish Church of St Augustine of Canterbury, in Queen's Gate, Kensington, the 1914–18 memorial

(THIS CALVARY WAS ERECTED BY THEIR FRIENDS 1919/1920)

was restored in 1982 in memory of those killed in the Falklands.

The numbers lost in British campaigns after 1945 are, of course, very small compared with the numbers killed in the Great War and World War II: a few hundred in the 'emergencies' such as Palestine, Malaya and Cyprus; less than a thousand in Korea and at Suez; 400 or so in Ireland; and 255 in the Falklands in 1982.

In the crypt of St Paul's there are memorials to those who died in the two major post-war conflicts, Korea and the Falklands.

The Korean plaque, only unveiled in 1987, is inscribed thus:

Remembering the British Servicemen who died in the first war
fought in the name of the United Nations.
Thank God for their courage and endurance and pray for Peace and
Reconciliation among the peoples and nations of the world.

**KOREA 1950–1953**

'Not one of them is forgotten before God.'

None of the dead are named, and over thirty years elapsed before their sacrifice was marked.

The Falklands War memorial is a very elaborate one inscribed:

IN HONOUR OF THE SOUTH ATLANTIC TASK FORCE
AND THE ABIDING MEMORY OF ALL THOSE WHO GAVE THEIR LIVES.

Then follow the names of 255 men from the Royal Navy, Royal Marines and from the Royal Fleet Auxiliary service; and from the Army, including the two parachute regiment VCs (Lt-Colonel H. Jones and Sergeant Ian McKAY). There is one RAF name and six from the Merchant Navy.

The value of war memorials, as this book suggests, lies in the details they provide for the social or military historian, the genealogist or family historian. Starting with a name, and if lucky with a regiment and service-number, a great deal of other information can be found, from published works, reference books and local newspaper files.

For the Army, you need access to a copy of *Officers Died in the Great War 1914–1919*, if dealing with an officer, or the relevant regimental volume of *Soldiers Died in the Great War 1914–1919*, if not. The next best source is always a Regimental History. A *Bibliography of Regimental Histories of the British Army* compiled by Arthur S. White, former Librarian at the War Office, is a very full record of what has been written over the past seventy years.

If you are the immediate next of kin, i.e. the senior and most direct descendant, you can write to the appropriate Service Records Department, and ask for a copy of your relative's record of service. You must provide as many identifying details as possible: full names, rank and regiment, and rough dates of service. An enquiry about a John Smith who you think once served in the Guards (or was it the Fusiliers?) may not succeed.

If your interest is more general – in a unit, or a regiment – the place to start is the regimental museum. A list of regimental museums across the country, with days and times of openings, is provided in *A Guide to Military Museums* by Terence Wise (Athena Books). Local librarians are also often extremely useful sources of information about units from their area. They too may be able to give advice on further reading, and order the books for you.

It is best to begin with a regimental history and a visit to the appropriate local museum, before aiming higher, such as the Public Record Office at Kew; or the reading-rooms at the Imperial War Museum or the National Army Museum in London. These organizations welcome serious researchers, but expect a letter or telephone call explaining the interest and line of enquiry before any visit is made. Their experienced staff can soon tell if their resources are the right ones, or suggest better places to try first. There is a necessary procedure for acquiring a reader's ticket in order to use their facilities.

But the real pleasure of 'war-memorialing' is seeing them as social and historical monuments in their proper setting: in village street or market-square, in churchyard or on a Scottish hillside. And perhaps in attending a Remembrance Day service held beside the memorial. Everyone is welcome, for almost everyone in Britain must have had some relative who died or served in their country's cause.

Each 11 November there is generally a parade at most village memorials. They are all different. The one at Beaconsfield, where this story began, is well attended. This is because the town has grown considerably since the 1914–18 War, but also because the home of the Grenfells at Wilton Park is now an Army Educational Centre.

## 'We Will Remember Them'

# Appendix: A Note on Abbreviations and Style

In setting out the details on the war memorials in this book I take a few liberties with what I record. The overriding reason for any change being to help a non-military reader grasp a point quickly. Where long lists of abbreviations for regiments might irritate, these are spelled out. I sometimes correct obvious errors, where they do not provide us with an insight into views held at the time.

In some cases the abbreviations used are significant, as are some of the errors. Abbreviations which can mislead include those where the same initials represent different units. Thus ACC after a name on a 1914–18 war memorial refers to the Army Cyclists Corps; while the same abbreviation in a 1939–45 list stands for the Army Catering Corps. There are cases where an area or district chooses to use one part of a regiment's title only, or where a regiment's title was changed during the war years, or shortly afterwards. There are generally differences between the 1914 titles of regiments and their 1939 ones. The Black Watch (Royal Highlanders) appears abbreviated as BW, or RH or even R.Hdrs. in World War I, and is The Black Watch (Royal Highland Regiment), or in abbreviation as BW or RHR, in the 1939–45 conflict. There is no unanimity of style even in the regimental heartland of Perthshire.

Light Infantry regiments are generally abbreviated to their initials.

| | |
|---|---|
| SLI | Prince Albert's (Somerset Light Infantry) |
| DCLI | The Duke of Cornwall's Light Infantry |
| OBLI | The Oxfordshire and Buckinghamshire Light Infantry |
| HLI | The Highland Light Infantry |
| KOYLI | The King's Own (Yorkshire Light Infantry) |
| KSLI | The King's (Shropshire Light Infantry) |
| DLI | The Durham Light Infantry |

Sometimes with full-stops between the letters, often not.

Few of those preparing the inscriptions for war memorials tried to follow the exacting rules of the army's *Field Guide* or that latter-day bible, *Staff Duties In The Field*. Even the writers of regimental war diaries did not always use the official abbreviations.

At the risk of irritating the methodical, I have rung the changes on describing the Great War as the First World War, World War I (WWI) or the 1914–18 War; and the Second World War as World War II (WWII) or 1939–45. This is done to vary the reading rhythm – but *also* to reflect the wide range of titles on the war memorials themselves.

The style for describing warrant officers and senior NCOs varies considerably. A few of the more common abbreviations include:

| | |
|---|---|
| RSM | Regimental Sergeant Major |
| RQMS | Regimental Quartermaster Sergeant |
| CSM | Company Sergeant Major |
| SSM | Squadron Sergeant Major |
| CQMS | Company Quartermaster Sergeant |
| SQMS | Squadron Quartermaster Sergeant |
| S/Sgt | Staff Sergeant |
| Sgt | Sergeant |
| L/Sgt | Lance-Sergeant |

Corporals and Lance-Corporals become shortened as Cpl. or L/Cpl. but there are other variants too, such as Lce-Cpl. The abbreviated artillery equivalent ranks of Bdr. (Bombardier) or L/Bdr. (Lance-Bombardier) can generally be identified by a following set of initials for the Royal Field Artillery or the Royal Garrison Artillery. On several memorials I have met, a bombardier appears among the private soldiers, the war memorial designer not recognizing that the soldier was an NCO and not a member of a bombing section.

But all sorts of shortened versions of army ranks can be found, often obviously chosen from the point of view of design. WO for Warrant Officer and NCO for Non-Commissioned Officer are fairly usual, but a WO is sometimes a Wireless Officer in the Merchant Marine, or in World War II a Wireless Operator/Air Gunner (WO/AG) in the RAF. In the official War Graves Commission cemeteries and the service headstones of World War I, a sergeant is spelt 'Serjeant'. This carries over to many Second World War memorials, and looks strangely archaic. Most civilian war memorials seem to prefer 'Sergeant'.

Private soldiers appear as Pte., Pvt. or Priv. Keep an eye out for ditto marks, which are not always obviously there and tend to be worn away. When no rank is given it may mean that it was not known, or that the memorial designer decided only to record rank when it was higher than Private, Gunner, Sapper, or equivalent.

Army specialists are sometimes identified, such as the Farrier Sergeant or Shoeing Smith. Men of the Royal Engineers may appear as Sapper, Pioneer or Private; artillerymen as Gunner or Driver. Bandsmen may be listed as Trumpeter or Bugler or Private. In Scottish regiments, a piper may take precedence over all other private soldiers, and even without a stripe may be included among the NCOs.

Appreciating the equivalent ranks to the Army in the Royal Navy and Royal Air Force is a study in itself. The layman should remember that a naval lieutenant is the equivalent of an army captain, and a sub-lieutenant equal to a full lieutenant in the army, and not as one might assume an army 2/lieutenant. A Gunner in the Royal Navy has been commissioned from the ranks and dines in the Officer's Mess, a gunner in the Royal Marine Artillery is a humble private soldier. Officers of the Royal Naval Division generally held naval rank, except for those in the Royal Marines, or those on loan from the Army. Reservists serving in the RND jealously retained their naval ranks, as did, of course, the Royal Marines who were sergeants, corporals – and marines. Abbreviations for naval petty officers (Chief Petty Officer, Petty Officer 1st and 2nd Class) are generally easy to understand; as are the usual abbreviations for seamen: Ldg.Smn. (Leading Seaman), AB (for Able Seaman, technically Able-Bodied Seaman) and OS or O/S (Ordinary Seaman).

Military historians will note interesting changes in nomenclature and style which came in *after* the soldier was killed in the Great War, but before the war memorial was erected in the 1920s. Do private soldiers in the Guards Regiments appear as privates or as guardsmen? What about troopers, fusiliers and riflemen?

On some Great War memorials, quite correctly, a casualty is listed as Army Service Corps, with another from the same arm of the service designated as belonging to the Royal Army Service Corps – the 'Royal' being awarded during the course of the war.

The Royal Welch Fusiliers insisted on their favoured spelling of Welch with a 'c' instead of an 's'. This was finally accepted by a 1919 Army Council instruction. Some memorials use 'c', others 's'. I mostly follow the style of *The Official History of the Great War.* Thus, Third Army or Fifth Army, spelled out; with Roman numerals for IV Corps or VIII Corps; and Arabic numbers for battalions, brigades and divisions. Where I break the rules, it is to help the reader. When in doubt myself, I generally follow the unit designations used by Brigadier E.A. James OBE, TD, in his book *British Regiments.*

Most of the abbreviations found on war memorials can be traced in publications such as *Who's Who, Whitaker's Almanack,* the *Oxford Dictionary, Soldiers Died* or *The Army List.*

One aspect of war memorials that *is* really worth thinking about, if we are to use them as a primary source, is their *accuracy.* They may be excellent value for researchers into British social and military history, but they are quite often plain wrong in what they say. As in all research work one must check facts against other sources.

It is worth remembering again that the person providing details for inscription might have no military knowledge or awareness at all. Ranks and regiments, and the finer points of military etiquette might mean nothing to the local newspaper, the compiler of the village records or the war memorial designer.

Even the true facts might be hard to check a few years after a soldier's death. Well-meaning relatives providing details about a soldier often contributed their own misinformation. Would you know, for instance, whether your late great-uncle was Arthur Edward or Edward Arthur, especially when he was always known in the family as Ted? And what exactly had he meant when he wrote saying he had been transferred to the 2/5th Battalion from the 2nd?

War memorials do not settle the vexed question of 'Mc' or 'Mac'. They simply emphasize that the spelling-out in English of what is no more than a transliteration from the Gaelic for 'son', is almost entirely a matter of local habit. Even the listing of the Mcs (or Macs) alphabetically is seldom consistent, either on war memorials or in *Soldiers Died*. Sometimes they are even separated: with the Macs coming first and the Mcs not appearing until after Macey, Madden and Masefield. On some memorials the abbreviation M' is used instead of Mc, as at St Andrew's in Fife, where you have either M' or Mac.

The use of Roman numerals and Latin phrases on 1914–18 war memorials shows how better understood these were in days gone by. In CHELSEA, the memorial is a typical 'cross of sacrifice' with sword.

'INVICITIS PAX'

and the war years are:

MDCCCCXIV
MDCCCCXVIII
MCMXXXIX
MCMXXXXV

At Muncaster, a village on the River Esk, in West Cumberland, the years of war are described differently: MCMXIV–MCMXIX for the 1914–19 war, and MCMXXXIX–MCMXLV for the 1939–45 war, representing a change in the style for using Roman numerals.

War memorials, and particularly those of the public schools and universities, do presume a knowledge and awareness of classical languages. Luckily, Latin tags and Greek inscriptions are still easily traced; perhaps more easily, say, than the Gaelic. One of the most common is a quote from Horace's *Odes* (III.ii.13)

DULCE ET DECORUM EST PRO PATRIA MORI
(Lovely and honourable it is to die for one's country)

This Horace quote is often abbreviated: *Dulce et Decorum Est*, or *Pro Patria*. The reader is expected to know the full quote.

An impressive war memorial in St Stephen's entry at the House of Commons lists all members and officers of both Houses of Parliament who fell in the Great War, as well as the sons of Members. It includes among the twenty peers, the venerable Earls Kitchener and Roberts, but also young aristocrats killed in their twenties with their Yeomanry regiments: Captain Lord Kesteven of the Lincolnshire Yeomanry and Captain Lord Vernon of the Derbyshire Yeomanry. Perhaps the most sadly impressive part of this memorial are four panels listing 86 sons of Members of Parliament who were killed, including several brothers. Nobody can say that Parliament was not aware of all the costs of war.

The House of Commons memorial ends with a passage from Cicero.

O FORTUNATA MORES, QUAE NATURAE DEBITA PRO PATRIA
EST POTISSIMUM REDDITA. EST ERGO EXTRUCTA MOLES
INCISAEQUE LITTERAE, VIRTUTIS TESTES SEMPITERNAE NUNQUAM
DE VOBIS EORUM QUI VESTRUM VIDEBUNT MOMENTUM
GRATISSIMUS SERMO CONTICESCET. ITA PRO MORTALI
CONDITIONE VITAE IMMORTALITATEM ESTIS CONSECUTI

CICERO, XIV PHILIPPIC

'Happy was your death. You paid for your Fatherland the common debt that all men owe to Nature. So this fabric is reared, and the letters inscribed upon it, as eternal testimonies of your valour. Those who look upon your monument will never cease to tell of your deeds in words of gratitude. And so instead of the Mortality of human life you have obtained Immortality.'

# Bibliography

## 1 Social History

Beckett, Ian F.W., and Simpson, Keith, *A Nation In Arms: A Social Study of The British Army in the First World War* (Manchester University Press, 1985)

Burman, Peter, and Stapleton, Henry (eds.) *The Churchyards Handbook* (Church House Publishing for The Council for the Care of Churches, third edition, 1988)

Coombs MBE, Rose E.B., *Before Endeavours Fade: A Guide to the Battlefields of the First World War* (Battle of Britain Prints International Ltd., 1983)

Kernot, C.F., *British Public Schools War Memorials* (Roberts & Newton Ltd., 1927)

*List of Etonians Who Fought in the Great War 1914–1919* (Privately printed for Eton College by Philip Lee Warner, Publishers to the Medici Society Ltd., 1921)

*Officers Died in The Great War, 1914–1919*, Part 1: Old and New Armies; Part 2: Territorial Force (HMSO, 1919; facsimile reprint by Samson Books, 1975). Compiled in the Officers' Casualties Branch of the War Office from reports coming to the notice of the Military Secretary

McKernan, Michael, *Padre – Australian Chaplains in Gallipoli and France* (Allen & Unwin, 1986)

Wilson, Trevor, *The Myriad Faces of War: Britain and the Great War* (Polity Press, 1986)

## 2 Military History

Bryant, Arthur, *Jackets of Green* (William Collins, 1972)

Cheyne, G.Y., *The Last Great Battle of The Somme: Beaumont Hamel 1916* (John Donald, 1988)

Hay, Ian, *The First Hundred Thousand* (William Blackwood & Sons, 1915; paperback edition by Richard Drew, 1985)

James, OBE TD, E.A., *British Regiments 1914–1918* (Samson Books Ltd., 1978 edition)

Middlebrook, Martin, *The First Day on The Somme – 1 July 1916* (Penguin Books, 1971)

*Soldiers Died in the Great War 1914–1918* (80 volumes) (HMSO, 1921; facsimile reprint by J.B. Hayward & Son, 1988)

Terraine, John, *The Western Front 1914–1918* (Hutchinson, 1964) *The Road to Passchendaele: The Flanders Offensive of 1917* (Leo Cooper, 1977)

Turner, William, *A History of the battalion raised from Accrington, Blackburn, Burnley and Chorley in World War One* (Graphics & Features Department, *Barnsley Chronicle*; Wharncliffe Publishing Ltd, 1988)

### 3   The Ideal War Memorial

Boorman, Derek, *At The Going Down of the Sun: British First World War Memorials (Derek Boorman, Dunnington Hall, York, 1988)*
Cheyne, G.Y., *The Last Great Battle of The Somme: Beaumont Hamel 1916* (John Donald, 1988)
Fuller, J.F.C., *The Conduct of War 1789–1961* (Eyre Methuen, 1972)
White, Arthur S. *A Bibliography of Regimental Histories of the British Army* (The London Stamp Exchange, 1988 edition)

### 4   Names

Cottle, Basil, *The Penguin Dictionary of Surnames* (Penguin Books, 1967)
Dunkling, Leslie, *The Guinness Book of Names* (Guinness Superlatives, Ltd, 1974; updated, 1986)
Ekwall, Eilert, *The Oxford Dictionary of English Place-Names* (Oxford University Press, 1951 reprint)
Hanks, Patrick, and Hodges, Flavia, *A Dictionary of Surnames* (Oxford University Press, 1988)
Muir, Richard, *Shell Guide to Reading the Landscape* (Michael Joseph, 1981)
Reaney, R.H., *The Origin of English Surnames* (Routledge & Kegan Paul, 1967)
Veerstappen, Peter, *The Book of Surnames: Origins and Oddities of Popular Names* (Pelham Books, 1980)
Withycombe, E.G., *The Oxford Dictionary of English Christian Names* (Oxford University Press, 1977 edition)

### 5   Age and   6   Rank and Number

Adams, R.J.Q., and Poirier, Philip P., *The Conscription Controversy in Great Britain 1900–1918* (Macmillan, 1987)
Edmonds, J.E., *The Official History of the Great War* (Shearer Publications, August/October 1914)
Graves, Robert, *Goodbye To All That* (Cassell, 1929; revised 1957; fourth edition, 2nd impression, 1977)
*Kelly's Handbook – 1929*
Terraine, John (ed.), *General Jack's Diary, 1914–1918: The Trench Diary of Brigadier-General J.L. Jack, DSO* (Eyre & Spottiswoode, 1964)
*Whitaker's Almanack* (1914, 1938, 1942, 1984, 1988 Complete Edition)
*Who's Who* (Adam & Charles Black, 1984)

### 7   Awards and Medals

Ascoli, David, *The Mons Star: The British Expeditionary Force 1914* (Harrap, 1981)
Colville, J.R., *Man Of Valour: Field-Marshal Lord Gort VC* (Collins, 1972)
Creagh, Sir O'Moore, VC GCB GCSI and Humphris, E.M. (eds.), *The VC and the DSO: A Complete Record* ... Volume 1: VCs; Volume 2: DSOs from 1886

to 31 December 1915; Volume 3: DSOs from 1 January 1916 to 12 June 1923 (Standard Art Book Company Ltd, 1924.)

Hogben, Arthur, *Designed to Kill: Bomb Disposal from World War I to the Falklands* (Patrick Stephens, 1987)

Joslin, Edward C., *The Observer's Book of British Awards & Medals* (Frederick Warne & Co Ltd, 1974)

*The Register of the George Cross* (This England Books, 1985)

*The Register of the Victoria Cross* (This England Books, 1981)

Smyth VC MC, Sir John, *Great Stories of the Victoria Cross* (Arthur Barker, Ltd. 1977)

## 8   The Battles and the Places

*Atlas for the Great War* (The West Point Military History Series; Avery Publishing Group Inc. USA, 1986)

Coombs MBE, Rose E.B., *Before Endeavours Fade: A Guide to the Battlefields of the First World War* (Battle of Britain Prints International Ltd, 1983)

Gilbert, Martin, *First World War Atlas* (Weidenfeld & Nicolson, 1985)

Gliddon, Gerald, *When the Barrage Lifts: Topographical History and Commentary on the Battle of the Somme 1916* (Gliddon Books, 1987)

Lindsay, J.H. (ed.), *The London Scottish in the Great War* (Published by Regimental HQ, 1925)

*List of British Officers taken prisoner in the Various Theatres of War between August 1914 and November 1918* (published for private circulation by Cox & Co, 1919; facsimile reprint by London Stamp Exchange, 1988)

*The Official Names of the Battles and Other Engagements fought by the Military Forces of the British Empire during the Great War 1914–1919 and the Third Afghan War 1919* (Report of the Battles Nomenclature Committee as approved by The Army Council. Presented to Parliament by Command of His Majesty; HMSO 1921)

Tuchman, Barbara, *August 1914* (Constable, 1962; Macmillan Papermac, 1980)

## 9   The Causes They Fought For and How They Died

Cross, Tim, *The Lost Voices of World War I: An International Anthology* (Bloomsbury Publishing, 1988)

Keegan, John, *The Face of Battle* (Jonathan Cape, 1976)

Lloyd George, *War Memoirs of David*, 2 volumes (Odhams Press Ltd., 1938 edition)

Marks, Thomas Penrose, *The Laughter Goes from Life: In the Trenches of the First World War* (William Kimber, 1977)

Mills, C.P., *A Strange War: Burma, India & Afghanistan 1914–1919* (Alan Sutton, 1988)

*The Oxfordshire & Buckinghamshire Light Infantry Chronicle*: Volumes XXIV (1914–1915), XXV (1915–1916), XXVI (1916–1918) (Eyre & Spottiswoode)

## 10   Religion

*The Holy Bible*, Authorized King James Version (Oxford University Press)

*The Apocrypha*, Revised Version, 1894 (Oxford University Press – The World's Classics)

*The Book of Commom Prayer* (Eyre & Spottiswoode Ltd)

*Hymns Ancient and Modern* (William Clowes & Sons Ltd)

Burman, Peter, and Stapleton, Henry (eds.) *The Churchyards Handbook* (Church House Publishing for the Council for the Care of Churches, third edition, 1988)

Foster, Richard, *Discovering English Churches* (BBC, 1981)

Muir, Richard, *Shell Guide to Reading the Landscape* (Michael Joseph, 1981)


**11   Local Affiliations**

*Bartholomew Gazetteer of Places in Britain* (Guild Publishing, 1986)

*Gazetteer of the British Isles* (John Bartholomew & Son Ltd., 9th edition, 1943; reprinted, 1966)

Gelling, Margaret, *Signposts to the Past: Place-names and the History of England* (J.M. Dent & Sons Ltd, 1978)

Melville, Ian Leslie, *The Story of The Lovat Scouts 1900–1980* (The Saint Andrew Press, 1981)


**12   Empire and Commonwealth**

Cooke, O.A., *The Canadian Military Experience 1867–1983: A Bibliography* (Monograph Series No.2, Department of National Defence, Directorate of History, second edition, 1984)

Gammage, Bill, *The Broken Years: Australian Soldiers in the Great War* (Australian National University Press, Canberra, 1974; Penguin Books, Australia, 1975)

Perry, F.W., *The Commonwealth Armies: Manpower and Organisation in Two World Wars* (Manchester University Press, 1988)

Walker, R.W., *To What End Did They Die?: Officers Died at Gallipoli* (R.W. Walker Publishing, 1985)


**13   Civilians**

*Register of One-Name Studies 1987* (The Guild of One-Name Studies, fifth edition, 1987)

Byron, Arthur, *London statues: a guide to London's outdoor statues and sculpture* (Constable, 1981)

Denholm, Decie (ed.), *Behind the Lines: One Woman's War 1914–1918 – The Letters of Caroline Ethel Cooper* (Jill Norman & Hobhouse, 1982)

Steel, Don, *Discovering Your Family History* (BBC, 1980)


**14   The Royal Navy and the Merchant Marine**

Beesly, Patrick, *Very Special Admiral: The Life of Admiral J.H. Godfrey CB* (Hamish Hamilton, 1980)

Bennett, Geoffrey, *Naval Battles of the First World War* (B.T. Batsford, 1968; Pan, 1983)

Boyle, Andrew, *The Riddle of Erskine Childers: A Biography* (Hutchinson, 1977)

*British Vessels Lost At Sea: 1914–1918 and 1939–1945*, 4 volumes (HMSO, 1919 and 1947; facsimile reprint by Patrick Stephens, third edition 1988)

Coles, Alan, *Three Before Breakfast: How a German U-boat Sank three British* cruisers in *One Desperate Hour* (Kenneth Mason, 1979)

Hough, Richard, *The Great War at Sea: 1914–1918* (Oxford University Press, 1983)

Jerrold, Douglas, *The Royal Naval Division*, with an introduction by the Rt.Hon. Winston S. Churchill (Hutchinson, 1923)

Laffin, John, *Damn the Dardanelles: The Story of Gallipoli* (Osprey, 1980)

## 15   Other Kinds of War Memorial and 16 More Kinds

Barker, G.F. Russell, and Stenning, Alan H., *The Record of Old Westminsters (From the Earliest Times to 1927)*, 2 volumes (Chiswick Press, 1928)

Kernot, C.F., *British Public Schools War Memorials* (Roberts & Newton, Ltd, 1927)

King, Norman C. (ed.) *Haileybury Register 1862–1946* (Haileybury & ISC, Hertford, seventh edition, 1947)

St. *Peter's College, Radley: Register 1847–1933* (Oxford University Press, fifth edition, 1933)

## 17 Still More Kinds of Memorial

*The Bond of Sacrifice: A Biographical Record of All British Officers who Fell in the Great War* (Anglo-African Publishing Contractors, 1915) Volume I, August–December 1914

Mills, C.P., *A Strange War: Burma, India & Afghanistan 1914–1919* (Alan Sutton, 1988)

*The Roll of Honour of the Empire's Heroes* (Published for private circulation): Various editions, some obituaries common to all.

Ruvigny, Marquis of, *The All Ranks Roll of Honour: A Biographical Record of All Members of His Majesty's Naval and Military Forces Who have Fallen in the War* – 8,000 names and 2,500 portraits (Standard Art Book Company, 1916)

Turner, William, 'Craven's Part in the Great War' in *Stand To! – The Journal of the Western Front Association*, no. 17, summer 1986

White, A.S., *A Bibliography of Regimental Histories of the British Army* (The London Stamp Exchange, 1988 edition)

*W.D. & H.O. Wills: Roll of Honour and War Service Roll 1914–1918* (Picton Publishing (Chippenham) Ltd. 1987)

Wise, Terence, *A Guide to Military Museums* (Athena Books, 1986)

## 18   Who Provided the War Memorials?

Boorman, Derek, *At the Going Down of the Sun: British First World War Memorials* (Derek Boorman, 1988)

Dakers, Caroline, *The Countryside at War 1914–1918* (Constable, 1987)

Ewart, Peter and Lynne, *Monuments to Memory: Rye's War Memorials* (Ewart Publications, 1988)

Kernot, C.F., *British Public Schools War Memorials* (Roberts & Newton, 1927)

Lutyens, Mary, *Edwin Lutyens* (John Murray, 1980)

Macdonald, Lyn, *1914* (Michael Joseph, 1987)

**19 Remembrance**

Aries, Philippe, *The Hour of Our Death* (Penguin, 1983)

Burgess, Frederick, *English Churchyard Memorials* (SPCK, 1969)

Enright, D.J. (ed.), *The Oxford Book of Death* (Oxford University Press, 1987)

Gibson, T.A. Edwin, and Ward, G. Kingsley, *Courage Remembered* (HMSO, 1989)

Grasby, Richard, *An Introduction to the Study and Classification of Lettering on Memorials* (NADFAS, 1983)

Meller, Hugh, *London Cemeteries: An Illustrated Guide and Gazetteer* (Gregg International, second edition, 1985)

# Index

All numbers in bold refer to the plates (see p. 7).
The symbol † indicates those who died in the world wars.